CONTRASTING ARGUMENTS

An Edition of the *Dissoi Logoi*

T.M. Robinson

CONTRASTING ARGUMENTS

An Edition of the *Dissoi Logoi*

T.M. Robinson

ARNO PRESS
A New York Times Company
New York • 1979

First publication 1979 by Arno Press Inc.

Copyright © 1979 by T. M. Robinson

GREEK TEXTS AND COMMENTARIES
ISBN for complete set: 0-405-11412-5
See last pages of this volume for titles.

Manufactured in the United States of America

———•———

Library of Congress Cataloging in Publication Data
Main entry under title:

Contrasting arguments.

  (Greek texts and commentaries)
  Text in English and Greek.
  1. Ethics, Greek. I. Robinson, T. M. II. Series.
BJ182.D5713   170   78-18598
ISBN 0-405-11439-7

CONTRASTING ARGUMENTS

An Edition of the <u>Dissoi Logoi</u>

CONTRASTING ARGUMENTS

An Edition of the Dissoi Logoi

by

T. M. Robinson

Professor of Philosophy, University of Toronto

FOR CECELIA DUNLEAVY

<u>quel</u> <u>savio</u> <u>gentil</u>, <u>che</u> <u>tutto</u> <u>seppe</u>

TABLE OF CONTENTS

PREFACE

Before beginning this book, I had often wondered why a full-length edition of the _Dissoi Logoi_ had never yet appeared. After embarking on the project, I came to know the reasons why. The imponderables are so many and so wide-ranging that scholars more cautious than I have understandably given up in the face of such a disheartening string of negatives: authorship--uncertain, date--uncertain, state of completion--uncertain, purpose--uncertain, dialect--uncertain, and much more. The fact that I persevered will serve as evidence that any discouragement I may initially have felt I finally overcame, though the amount of conjecture that (necessarily, it would seem, given the problems) underpins my conclusions I still find disconcertingly large, and would cheerfully wish away. But that is a pipe-dream. The _Dissoi Logoi_ is the intractable animal that it is, and I considered it important at the outset and still consider it important that--whatever the problems of interpretation--it should by some means or other be made accessible to a wider audience than at present. Few who claim acquaintance with the sophists know more about them than Plato, in his own way and with his own particular bias, was prepared to tell us; to such people, scholars and students alike, I hope that an edition of an _opusculum_ apparently from the pen of a sophist of Socrates' generation will prove enlightening. I also hope that, in stressing the importance of such _ipsissima verba_, and in suggesting that their author is not the philosophical dunce many have taken him to be, I have not gone to the opposite

extreme and over-emphasized the philosophical importance
of what he wrote.

As far as the text is concerned (for MSS. consulted see p. 86, n. 45), I have been less drastic in
my emendations, additions, and deletions than was Diels,
on the grounds that the Δ. Λ. is in my estimation simply
an unpolished set of lecture-notes; I have also left it
in quasi-Doric, on the grounds that the author, for
whom Doric was not his native dialect, almost certainly
wrote it in imperfect Doric in the first place. (An
arguable alternative view, of course, would be that the
original dialect of the Δ. Λ. was unadulterated Doric--
or perhaps even, if Thesleff is right, Ionic--and the
present state of the text to be accounted for in terms
of the standard, unconscious atticization performed on
all 'peculiar' texts by librarii. While I myself am not
persuaded of this, I do not think the matter a substantive one; at no point, to my knowledge, does our understanding of the argument turn on it.)

Readers of the book will quickly see how much
I am indebted to predecessors in the field, notably
Weber, Mutschmann, Trieber, Wilamowitz, Diels, Taylor,
and Kranz. The same can be said for Untersteiner, in
spite of my many disagreements on points of detail. I
should also like to express my gratitude to the Editor
of Illinois Classical Studies for permission to reprint
material from volume 2 of that series; to Professors
†G. Ryle, R. K. Sprague, J. M. Rist, F. Solmsen, W. R.
Connor, G. W. Bowersock and L. E. Woodbury for criticism
of the book at various stages in its composition; and to
Professors N. E. Collinge and W. E. McLeod for advice on
particular problems of dialect. They are, of course, in
no way committed to my conclusions, which are necessarily

so speculative on so many (and such substantive) points that even partial assent is grounds for satisfaction. The book is in my eyes at best a beginning; should some of its argumentation win general acceptance as firm ground on which to build further, I shall consider the labour expended on it not entirely in vain.

I dedicate the work, with gratitude, affection and respect, to a noble woman and great teacher. May her years of retirement be many and happy.

T. M. Robinson
Toronto
September, 1977

INTRODUCTION

1. Transmission of the Text

The Dissoi Logoi was first published by H.
Stephanus in 1570, as an appendix to his edition of
Diogenes Laertius (1. 470-482). The text, printed
without commentary or translation, was prefaced with
the words:
ʾΑΝΩΝΎΜΟΥ ΤΙΝῸΣ διαλέξεις Δωρικῇ διαλέκτῳ, Περὶ τοῦ
ἀγαθοῦ καὶ τοῦ κακοῦ, Περὶ τοῦ καλοῦ καὶ τοῦ αἰσχροῦ,
Περὶ τοῦ δικαιοῦ καὶ τοῦ ἀδίκου, Περὶ τοῦ ψεύδους
καὶ τῆς ἀληθείας, Περὶ τῆς σοφίας καὶ τῆς ἀρετῆς, εἰ
διδακτόν.
It falls into five parts, corresponding to the five
divisions of the title. The titles heading each part
are found at the same place in the text as the corresponding five titles in the Diels-Kranz edition.[1] He
offers no indication of what MS. or MSS. he is following, or of what emendations he has introduced into his
text.

A century was to pass before the first translation and critical commentary appeared. In 1671 a book
entitled Opuscula Mythologica Physica et Ethica was
published in Cambridge by Thomas Gale, and in the
middle of the section entitled Πυθαγορείων ἀποσπασμάτια
(dated Cantabr. 1670) appears the Dissoi Logoi (47-76).
The general title (ʾΑΝΩΝΎΜΟΥ ΤΙΝῸΣ etc.) is repeated
from Stephanus, with a Latin title "Incerti cujusdam
dissertationes quinque Dorico sermone conscriptae", and
a subscript "Versione & Notis Jo. North". The Greek

1

text is that of Stephanus, but a number of (frequently
important) suggestions for textual emendation are made
in individual footnotes. A Latin translation (which
at difficult points almost invariably construes North's
own suggested textual emendations rather than the Greek
text in front of him) is placed side by side with
Stephanus' text. The Greek titles to individual sections are omitted, and in their place we have just the
Latin translations (e.g., De bono et malo).

A second edition of Gale's work appeared in
Amsterdam in 1688, and North's version and notes are
included. This time, however, a number of important
changes have been made in the Greek text by M. Meibom,
and the same scholar has added the occasional note of
his own (usually suggesting a textual emendation) to
those of North. Gale only mentions the "notae elegantes"
(xxi), but in fact the former point is much more important; large numbers of the (nearly always un-annotated)
textual changes show a great deal of philological
acumen, and have been accepted with gratitude by all
subsequent editors.

From the evidence of his reading ἀν ἀν χ' at
7.3, it seems likely that he had before him the Codex
Leidensis.

His general opinion of the contents is evinced
by his changing of the title of the treatise from "Dissertationes Quinque" to "Dissertationes Morales".

The next editor was J. A. Fabricius, in his
Bibliotheca Graeca 12 (Hamburg 1724) 617-635. He
entitles the work "Sexti Disputationes Antiscepticae".
The Sextus in question, however, is not Sextus Empiricus;
on that point Fabricius is in agreement with Stephanus.

He is in fact the <u>anti</u>-sceptical Sextus of Chaeronea,
thinks Fabricius; it was simply the accident of posses-
sing a <u>praenomen</u> in common with the renowned sceptic
that led to the inclusion of his work in the major
Sextus Empiricus MSS.[2]

The Greek text that he prints is basically that
of Meibom, but his access to two new MSS., the Codex
Cizensis[3] and the Codex Savilianus,[4] provides him with
information not available to his editorial predecessors.
Most of this is of little importance, such as the constant use of Doric spelling (e.g., -έν for -εῖν, α for
η, etc.) or a variation in punctuation. One crucial
change, however, is the reading μύστας at 4.4. This
corrects an important error (the reading Μίμας) found
in all three previous editions, and effectively scotches
the notion that the treatise might not, after all, be
anonymous. Apart from this major change, Fabricius
uses his codices with exemplary caution. On several
occasions the Meibom text is favoured, and the Cizensis
reading simply noted.[5] Twice he tacitly corrects what
look like typographical errors that had escaped North's
(5.9) and Meibom's (2.19, 5.9) attention.[6] Once, in a
footnote, he offers an alternative to a translation by
North,[7] and on a few occasions he makes small changes
in both the translation of North and the text of North/
Meibom.[8] However, he is himself not immune from carelessness. At 8.12 Meibom's ὃς κα is changed to ὃς γάρ,
yet the North/Meibom translation "et qui" is retained.
At 5.12 σάκκος and σάκος get confused in the text and
translation. There are two major misprints (3.5,
κατεστασιασμένα, and 2.28, retulerint), and at 5.2 two
words, καὶ πίνοντι, are accidentally omitted, though

North's rendering "bibunt" is retained. All in all, the progress made in the edition is small. Its claim to fame is the fact that it takes account of two codices not apparently used by Stephanus, North, or Meibom.

Almost a century was to pass before Orelli next edited the Dissoi Logoi in his Opuscula Graecorum Veterum Sententiosa et Moralia 2 (Leipzig 1821) 210-233 [Text, with facing Latin translation] and 632-654 [Notes]. The text and translation are basically those of the North/Meibom edition of 1688, though he occasionally accepts a textual variant and/or new translation of Fabricius, and sometimes a conjecture by Koen, Valckenaer, or Heringa (the one Porson conjecture cited --at 2.18--is rejected). Orthographically speaking, he sides with Fabricius; when offered a choice between an Atticism and a Doricism, he takes the Doricism.[9] In matters of grammar, syntax, and general interpretation he is more eclectic, sometimes siding with North and/or Meibom,[10] sometimes with Fabricius,[11] and sometimes with Koen,[12] Valckenaer,[13] or Heringa.[14] Apart from a few punctuation changes (1.13, 6.11, 9.2-3), and the occasional correction of an obvious slip in previous translations (e.g., "qualia" for "quae", translating οἷάπερ, at 2.26), the only changes in the text that appear to be entirely his own work are found at 2.26 (λέγοντι) and 2.28 (οἱ). The footnotes are replete with his own suggestions for textual emendation,[15] but none except the two mentioned above are incorporated into the text.

The North translation is retained when (presumably) changes in the Greek text are judged to affect the sense negligibly, if at all.[16] In a few instances,

where North and Fabricius are in disagreement (over
text, or translation, or both), the Fabricius translation is accepted,[17] or the Fabricius translation with
minor changes.[18] On one occasion a new translation of
his own is based upon a Fabricius suggestion,[19] and
several of the emendations taken over from Koen,
Valckenaer, and Heringa carry with them appropriate
new translations.[20] All in all, greater care seems to
have been exercised over the translation than over the
original. At 2.28, for example, he notices that
"retulerint" in Fabricius is a misprint, and tacitly
returns to the "retulerunt" of North, and at 5.15
North's "ergo" (translating οὐκοῦν) is tacitly (and
rightly) preferred to the "enim" of Fabricius. Similarly, a feeling for stylistic purity leads him to
convert "poterat" to "posset" at 6.3 (against both
North and Fabricius) and "evasit" (Fabricius) to
"evaserit" at 6.11.

The notes are taken bodily from North and
Fabricius, with the occasional additional comment of
Orelli's own. Such comments (with the notable exception of an introductory comment on authorship) are
nearly always to do with textual conjectures. When the
author of the conjecture is Koen, Valckenaer, or
Heringa, the conjecture is on almost every occasion
incorporated into the text; when Orelli is himself the
author, the conjecture (in all but the two instances
mentioned) stays modestly in the footnote. The modesty
is commendable, but it unfortunately goes with an
editorial carelessness, as Schanz's damning scrutiny
makes clear (370-371), that renders the edition little
or no advance over any of its predecessors. A few
examples will suffice. At 8.3-4 the North/Fabricius

text reads:

ἔτι δὴ ὁ τὰς τέχνας τῶν λόγων εἰδὼς ἐπιστασεῖται καὶ
περὶ πάντων ὀρθῶς λέγεν. δεῖ γὰρ τὸν μέλλοντα ὀρθῶς
λέγεν περὶ ὧν ἐπίσταται, περὶ τούτων λέγεν.

Orelli's eye unfortunately skips a line, and he reads:

. . . περὶ πάντων ὀρθῶς λέγεν, περὶ ὧν ἐπίσταται, περὶ
τούτων λέγεν. δεῖ γὰρ κτλ.

But the translation he prints is that of the North
version, not of his own. Similarly, at 8.8, the phrase
αἱ δυνασεῖται αὐλὲν is inadvertently omitted--but
North's translation (which includes it) retained. At
2.17 the adjective καλόν is accidentally omitted after
ἐργάζεσθαι, and the result is an unintelligible sentence;
North's translation "honestum", however (which makes
perfect sense of his own, but not Orelli's, text), is
retained. At 5.9 he reads ἅτερος λόγος, but his note
ad loc. is a defense of ἅτερος ὁ λόγος. Similarly, at
5.12, his (Greek) text reads σᾶκος καὶ σᾶκος; but in the
translation directly opposite he reads σᾶπος (sic) et
σᾶκος. At 3.11 he attributes the reading βιαίως to
Heringa; but in fact Fabricius had suggested it a
quarter of a century earlier (the same mistake is made
over the phrase καὶ τἆλλα καττωϋτό at 3.16 and 5.14;
Fabricius ante-dates both Heringa [3.16] and Koen [5.14]).
On some occasions he has undoubtedly consulted the
Stephanus edition (as a note on 8.12 makes clear), but
at 2.26 he can hardly have done so, since the reading
λέγονται is said to have "[irrepsisse] (ut videtur
operarum vitio) in editionem Galei", when in fact it is
found in the Stephanus text as well.[21]

   Examples of such carelessness could be multi-
plied; suffice it to refer the reader to Schanz. If,
to this, one adds the fact that Orelli appears to have

consulted no new manuscripts, the edition can be summed
up as very largely an exercise in academic parasitism.
And even at that low level of life it is disconcertingly
unreliable. Its entire contribution to knowledge, in
fact, consists of a handful of worthwhile conjectures by
Koen, Valckenaer, and Heringa, two by Orelli himself,
and a sensible comment on the work's authorship. Partu-
rient montes; nascetur ridiculus mus.

Fifty years later F. W. Mullach produced a text
and translation of the Dissoi Logoi in his Fragmenta
Philosophorum Graecorum 1 (Paris 1875) 544-552, with
supplementary comments on its authorship and style and
the nature of his own commentary and translation in Vol.
2, xxxiii-xxxiv. This edition has been strongly
criticized by Schanz (370-371) on the grounds that it
"hängt ganz von Orelli ab." As evidence Schanz points
out that the transcriptional errors made by Orelli at
8.3-4, and 8.8 and 2.17 are repeated ad litteram by
Mullach. In the latter two instances Mullach is apparently unaware that there is anything wrong; in the
former instance he at least feels an oddity in the
Greek, but compounds the mischief by suggesting the
insertion of καί, thereby offering a pseudo-answer to a
non-problem. (For additional evidence of a similar
sort see Schanz, ibid.)

Writing eight years later, Trieber, too, says
(212, n.2) that Mullach reprints all of Orelli's errors,
though his next comment--"doch bietet auch er einige
Verbesserungen"--suggests that he has examined the
Mullach version with more precision and less spleen
than had Schanz. For, while the particular criticisms
of Schanz are justified, his charge of total dependence
on Orelli is demonstrably false, as can easily be shown.

While, for example, Mullach undoubtedly does draw (usually without acknowledgement!) on Orelli's notes or text, or both, to a large extent,[22] and on occasion prints a version of his own which is technically new but clearly inspired by Orelli,[23] on several other notable occasions he emends the text, and sometimes with a great deal of flair and acumen, on what would seem to be entirely his own initiative.[24] As for the translation, the one that Orelli had largely taken over from North and Fabricius is completely overhauled. Apart from the material changes in it necessitated by textual changes in the original, every second or third sentence has some stylistic change or other of Mullach's own fashioning.[25]

However, while it is true that Schanz has not given Mullach credit for his many positive achievements, it also appears lamentably true that, in preparing his edition, Mullach confines himself entirely to the Orelli text, notes, and translation; he does not appear to have looked at any earlier edition, or to have consulted a single manuscript. The evidence for this is overwhelming. Some of it has been put forward by Schanz; two further examples will suffice here. At 3.11 the reading βιαίως is attributed to Heringa; but Mullach has simply followed Orelli in making this attribution, and clearly has not bothered to look at the Fabricius edition. Had he done so, he would have discovered that it was Fabricius (who antedates Heringa) who had in fact first made the suggestion (at any rate in print). And at 7.4 Mullach prints τυχόν as an emendation of his own, when in fact it is to be found in the editions of Stephanus, North, and Fabricius--i.e., in every edition antecedent to his own apart from Orelli's! Having thus

in a single damning sentence effectively demonstrated
that he is confining himself, for information, to the
Orelli edition, he goes on, in the same passage, to
make the assertion that the Orelli reading τυχών is
that of "the manuscripts" ("Codd."). But the reading,
alas, is not to be found in a single manuscript; all
read τυχόν. And worse is to come. Having demonstrated
that he is not consulting any manuscripts (while--what
is unpardonable--trying to give the impression that he
is[26]), and that he is reading (at any rate systematic-
ally and critically--see n.27) no earlier editor except
Orelli, he finally demonstrates that even his reading
of _Orelli_ is inaccurate. Had he looked more carefully
at the Orelli _translation_ of 7.4 he would have noticed
that Orelli was clearly translating τυχόν, not τυχών
(his translation is in fact identical to that of North
and Fabricius, both of whom read τυχόν); τυχών is merely
a misprint that has crept into Orelli's text. In one,
suicidal phrase Mullach has shown himself to be commit-
ting almost every possible sin that an editor can commit.

It should be pointed out that Mullach is convinced that the text was originally pure Doric, and
many of his emendations are consequently simply
restorations of Attic forms to what he thinks might be
the original Doric forms. On two occasions such emendations turn out to be identical to the text printed by
Fabricius (which was based largely, it will be remem-
bered, on the doricizing Codex Cizensis); but this
seems to be a coincidence. At any rate Mullach makes
no reference to Fabricius as a possible precursor for
the changes. As for the conversion of ἐστί to ἐντι at
6.12, Mullach achieves perhaps the most ignominious

"low" of all by demonstrating that in this instance he has not read with care either the Orelli text or the relevant Orelli note (let alone Fabricius). He prints ἐντι as his own emendation when in fact Orelli had printed (and defended) the very same word; the error is no more pardonable for the fact that Orelli had himself relied on Koen for the emendation, without apparently noticing that Fabricius had printed it before him![27] Quis custodiet ipsos custodes?

In 1878 Adolf Matthaei published a number of minor textual emendations to the text (17-18), all of them to do with instances of the particle κα, which he wished to insert wherever the MSS. read ἄν. Like so many of his predecessors, he, too, assumed that the original was in Doric Greek, and that textual corruptions (like that of κα to ἄν) were the responsibility of "librarii". In spite of this belief, he is clearly puzzled by one particular phrase--πονηρὸν ἄν ἐξείποιεν at 3.2--and in this instance makes no attempt to change ἄν to κα. One might legitimately ask why.

A new wave of activity on the text began in Germany in 1881. In that year Friedrich Blass sent a small sketch of an edition to Ernst Weber which, in addition to later personal correspondence between the two, played a significant part in Weber's own edition of 1897. In a short article published in the same year Blass suggested (739) that the reading μύστας (4.4) of the Codex Cizensis was a corruption, and that the original reading must have been Σιμμίας. Blass clearly sensed that more manuscript information was important to his case, and promised a larger study of the topic, with more "handschriftlicher Hilfsmittel" (740), but

this never appeared. Presumably, if it was ever completed, it was incorporated in the sketch of an edition
sent to Weber,[28] or communicated to him at some later
date.[29] Certainly Blass was working on fresh manuscripts in or not long after 1881, since he sent to
Weber some time between 1881 and 1897 not only the sketch
of an edition previously mentioned (a sketch dating from
1881) but his own collation of the four Paris MSS. (Pl.
2.3.4) which he thought useful (P5.6 he felt added
nothing, so all he supplied Weber with of these two
were "charakteristische Notizen"), a copy of the Codex
Leidensis, some comments by Bywater on the Codex
Savilianus, and a study of the dialectal forms of the
treatise.[30] As it happened, all except the Codex Leidensis (which read μύμας) read μύστας at 4.4; we have
no knowledge of how Blass reacted to this information.
However, more important for our purposes is the fact
that new MSS. were now starting to come to light, and
the first serious work on the text since Stephanus could
begin.

The first major article based on new MSS.
information was by Martin Schanz in 1884. Like Blass,
he, too, apparently planned to produce an edition,[31]
but the project never materialized. In his article he
refers to twelve MSS., of which he possesses either
collations or "charakteristische Notizen": they are R
(first used by Bekker in his edition of Sextus in 1842,
and mentioned by Bergk [122] as containing a text of the
Dissoi Logoi) and Z, Fl.2, Vl.2, Pl.2.3.4.5.6, C. He
is particularly impressed by the Königsberg Codex, which
he thinks has the undoubtedly correct reading on a
number of occasions (376-377). The rest of the article

is important (377-end) for a very large number of
conjectures and emendations of his own.

In the same year G. Teichmüller published a
lengthy chapter on the authorship of the Dissoi Logoi,
to which he added the first German translation (205-224).
Of some importance is the fact that he divides the text
into eight sections, rather than five. This is not the
result of any new manuscript-information (he tells us
he is merely translating the Mullach text, though he
rejects Mullach emendations when the traditional reading
seems intelligible to him [203]); it stems from his
assumption that the author is Simon (the shoe-maker
mentioned in Plato's Theaetetus), whose Σκυτικοί
Διάλογοι, of which he says the Dissoi Logoi are part,
have been lost (DL 2. 122). The fifth, sixth, and
seventh of these divisions are identical to those published in Weber and DK$^{3ff.}$; (the eighth is sub-divided
in DK$^{3ff.}$ into two parts, 8 and 9). In keeping with
his contention that the eight parts of the treatise
are fragments of the 33-section Σκυτικοί Διάλογοι, he
uses the section-titles supplied by Diogenes Laertius
to summarize the contents of his own newly-made divisions:
(5) περί τοῦ ὄντος, (6) περί ἀρετῆς, ὅτι οὐ διδακτόν
(111), (7) περί δημαγωγίας, (8) περί ἐπιστήμης. The
Diogenes titles for the first four sections, he thinks,
are (1) περί τοῦ ἀγαθοῦ (110), (2) περί τοῦ καλοῦ (110),
(3) περί δικαίου, <πρῶτος> (110), (4) περί δικαίου,
<δεύτερος> or περί κρίσεως (111, 214n.).

A further set of emendations and conjectures--
though without reference to new MS. readings--was put
forward by Wilamowitz in 1889, and in subsequent years
he seems to have made a number of other conjectures

(some supplanting those of 1889), which were communicated to Diels, and found a place in the latter's own
apparatus criticus (DK[3ff.]).

If one passes over two conjectures offered by
H. Gomperz in 1890,[32] the next significant contributor
to the establishment of a text was Conrad Trieber. In
a major article, which touches on almost every aspect
of the treatise, he puts forward a number of important
conjectures and emendations, many of them based on
Matthaei's earlier assumption that the text was originally Doric (ἄν, for example, is ruthlessly expunged or
converted to κα). All his work, however, stems from a
study of earlier editions and printed scholarship; there
is no evidence to suggest that he has personally consulted any MSS. at this stage. Yet he must certainly
have done so later, if not then, since the stemma and
other manuscript information found in his Nachlass
proved invaluable to Diels in his own edition of 1912.[33]
Like Blass and Schanz before him, he seems to have
planned to produce an edition,[34] but this never materialized, and his unpublished papers passed at his death
into the possession of Wilamowitz. While they were
still in Wilamowitz' possession, Mutschmann and Diels
were fortunately allowed access to them;[35] since then
they have been lost.[36]

The first edition of the text to incorporate
significant new manuscript-information, and to come
complete with an imposing apparatus criticus, was that
of Ernst Weber in 1897. The influence of Blass, his
teacher, is evident throughout; indeed, it might almost
be called Blass's edition. The number of MSS. known to
Weber is 18: Pl.2.3.4.5.6, B, Fl.2, Z, T, Vl.2, C, R,

M, S, and L. Following Schanz (372) he suggests that there is a single archetype (now lost), from which stem two "families": the first consists of Pl.2.3 and the second of three groups:

    (a) R, Fl.2 (R being outstanding and the best MS. in the family)

    (b) C, V2, P4

    (c) B, M, S (B being outstanding, and second only to R in the family)

Vl is called "useless", and L Z and T "very bad"; P5.6, he says, according to Blass "add nothing" (34-35). In his apparatus criticus R B Z L Pl.2.3.4 and the Stephanus text are treated with respect; the rest are seldom considered (P5.6 never at all).[36] His text is ruthlessly "Doric"; all Attic and Ionic readings in the MSS. have been converted (along lines suggested by Heiberg in his edition of the fragments of Archimedes).[37] It is also remarkable for the number of textual reconstructions, and the filling-in of (real or imagined) textual lacunae that it contains, usually without an iota of manuscript-support; in this respect, as in so many others, the over-riding influence of Blass is admitted (see app. crit., passim).

    Unlike Mullach, Weber clearly took great care to consult the editions of all his predecessors, and to inform himself about the manuscripts, as well as to take into consideration the work of the German and Austrian scholars that had been printed in the previous two decades. All this emerges from his painstakingly constructed apparatus criticus. His ordering of the known MSS. into degrees of worth and reliability (34-35) is a major step in the right direction, and his

Whether Y is a misprint by Mutschmann, or a mistake on Trieber's part, is not clear; but this MS. (Paris. 2128) does not in fact contain the Dissoi Logoi at all.

In 1911 A. Kochalsky produced a book on Sextus, in which he clearly inclines more to Mutschmann's understanding of the manuscript tradition than to Weber's. P3, for example, is thought to derive from the latest hyparchetype; and F1 is dubbed an apograph of F2.

The now-standard edition of the Dissoi Logoi was first published by Hermann Diels in 1903 in the first edition of his Fragmente der Vorsokratiker. For his apparatus criticus (which first appeared in the second edition of 1907) he relies on those of Weber and Trieber (like Mutschmann, he had been allowed by Wilamo-witz to consult Trieber's Nachlass); for what he calls the "main manuscripts" he relies (in the same second edition) on Trieber alone, and finds three "main classes":

  (1) H, V1
  (2) R, F2
  (3) P4.6, V2

As will be seen from a glance at the Trieber stemma printed by Mutschmann, there are obviously doubts in Diels' mind about the status of P1, P3, and Y, though whether this is due to unclarity on the part of Trieber or to inaccuracy on the part of Mutschmann and/or Diels cannot now be known. It seems clear, however, that if Y was printed by Trieber, V2 is a conscious correction of it by Diels.

By the time of the third edition (1912), however, Diels had changed his mind, no doubt under the stimulus

of the recent publications of Mutschmann and Kochalsky.
The MSS. he now divides into two main classes--

    (1) Pl

    (2) P3, H, Vl, R, F2, P6, P4, V2.

To these, he says, he "would add B." (Presumably he
means as a further member of class [2], rather than as
the sole member of a putative class [3]).

        As will be seen at a glance, this list of MSS.
is identical to the list of the main MSS. of Trieber as
printed in Mutschmann, with the substitution of V2 for
Y; the only other difference is the class-division
drawn between γ and δ. But one is again left in doubt
about the exact content of Trieber's own Nachlass. Did
he himself suggest a double or triple class-division?
Was he dealing with all the MSS. he had consulted, or
merely with the "major" MSS. as he saw them? To what
degree--if any--was his own Nachlass unclear, and to
what degree--if any--has he been misrepresented by
Mutschmann and/or Diels? Till the Nachlass is redis-
covered it would seem impossible to give a precise
answer to these questions.

        The Diels edition differs significantly from
that of Weber in the number of conjectures of Diels
himself that are incorporated into the text, the number
of suggestions of Wilamowitz[40] that are accepted, or,
if not, treated with suitable respect, and a general
move away from the "doricizing" trend of Weber. Four
conjectures by de Varis (from Yl.2) are incorporated
into the text, but an unfortunate reliance on Trieber's
notes and/or a selective and/or careless misreading of
the same notes leads Diels to fail to mention that de
Varis is the original proponent of nine other conjec-

tures that he accepts(!).[41] The text is quite the most
grammatically and syntactically respectable, and quite
the most philosophically coherent, of all editions so
far, but this is frequently achieved at the cost of
large-scale textual reconstruction, and the filling-in
of hypothetical lacunae, even though manuscript-support
for such moves is often negligible or non-existent. In
this respect the edition has many affinities with that
of Weber.

Since 1912 the Diels text has been revised by
Walther Kranz. Textual changes are few, and are discussed by Kranz in his study, "Vorsokratisches IV, Die
sogennanten Δισσοί Λόγοι", Hermes 72 (1937) 223-224.
This text (hereafter DK) is adopted by Untersteiner[42]
and Dumont,[43] and used as the basis of their translations into Italian and French respectively, and is also
used as the basis for the first-ever English translation,
by Rosamond Kent Sprague.[44]

In preparing the present edition I have, it will
soon become clear, been more impressed by Weber's assess-
ment of the worth and inter-relationship of the main MSS.
than I have been by those of Trieber, Mutschmann, and
Kochalsky. In the matter of the less important MSS., I
find myself in agreement with Trieber that Y2 is an
apograph of Y1; with Trieber, Mutschmann, and Kochalsky
that C is an apograph of V2; with Trieber and Mutschmann
that P5 is an apograph of R; with Mutschmann that Q is
an apograph of P1; and with Weber that F1 is independent
of F2.[45]

To begin at the beginning: no archetype of the
Δ.Λ. has been found; what we have is simply three main
families, the third of which falls into three groups.

In the first family, we have two major MSS., both very
valuable (P1 P2; Q, an apograph of P1, can be discounted); in the second family we have P3, again very
valuable; in the third family (group a) we have R, F1
and F2, and the apograph of R, P5 (of these R and F2,
and especially R, are of some value); in group b we
have C, P6, V2, Y1 (and its apograph Y2), E, and P4, of
which P4, P6, and V2 are of some small value; and in
group c we have V1, B, S, M, H, Z (with its apograph T),
L, and the manuscript read by Stephanus, all of which
(except in some small measure B and V1) are near totally
worthless.

1. Archetype

A version of it, δ, with the last pages missing,
I hypothesize as the source of the extant MSS. of the
first family. Another version of it, β, containing the
complete volume of material known as the Dissoi Logoi
(including the lacunae at 8.5, 8.6, and 8.9), I hypothesize as parent to the sole surviving member of the
second family, P3, and ancestor to the third family.

2. First Family

P1 and P2 are not copied from any extant MS.,
since from some now-lost source they fill out (at 1.3
and 2.13) unwitting lacunae in all other MSS. That they
are doing this (and not just inventing) is demonstrable,
since P1 and P2 are themselves independent of each
other. P1 is not an apograph of P2, since P2 has
lacunae of its own at five places (1.11, 1.16, 1.17,
2.8, 2.28) which are not found in P1. Nor is P2 the
apograph of P1: at 1.16 P1 has the sound reading τῶ
(with R F1.2 St), P2 the inferior reading τῶν (with all
other MSS.); at 2.14 P1 has the sound reading τᾷ (with

P3 Y2 St), P2 the (nonsensical) reading τῶ (with R V2
E Yl); at 2.26 Pl has the unique and sound reading
νομίζοι, P2 the less good reading νομίζει (with St).
And the converse is occasionally the case, clinching
the point: at 2.2 P2 preserves the sound reading
ἐξαγεύμενος, Pl (uniquely) the poorer reading ἐξαγούμενος; at 2.14 P2 writes ποιήσας (with η over the α),
offering a hint of the correct reading ποιήσαι, Pl
ποιήση (=ποιήσῃ), with all other MSS. It should be
added that Pl offers more Doric forms than P2, and is
freer of careless transcriptional errors. The two
MSS. are, however, still sufficiently close for one to
conclude with confidence that they stem from one and
the same source. This source would appear to have
written ἀπο for ἀποστατεῖ at 3.12, uniquely in the
tradition; it is picked up as ἀπο by Pl and P2, and
stops there. Given that ἀπο in Pl comes at the end of
a column, it might under normal circumstances be argued
that P2 (in which it does not) is an apograph of Pl;
but the other evidence just cited suggests the ἀπο
must in fact have been a characteristic of δ.

Pl and P2 are a major source of sound readings;
on 17 occasions I accept their combined reading over
all or most other MSS., on three occasions the reading
of Pl alone (see above), on one occasion P2 alone (see
above). In addition to this, the reading of Pl at 3.13
(ὁμολογοσοῦντι) seems to me a valuable pointer to the
correct ὁμολογησοῦντι, and the reading of P2 ποιήσας at
2.14 a valuable pointer to the correct ποιήσαι.

3. Second Family
Pl and P2, as it happens, contain only the first
three chapters of the Δ. Λ., and it is a matter of great

good fortune that an excellent MS., P3, containing the
present nine chapters, is extant.[46] Like P1, it is
full of Doric forms, many of them found only in this one
MS., and two of them suggesting even a specific dialect
of Doric (πειρασεῦμαι 2.2, ποιεῦντι 2.28; cf. ἐξαγεύμενος [P2], 2.2). It is also unique in containing the
remarkable Ionic forms σοφίη (5.7, 6.1) and σοφίην
(6.7) (cf. the claim of P1 and P2 that the treatise is
in 'Ιωνική διάλεκτος). It is clearly not the apograph
of any extant MS., and I hypothesize as its source a
manuscript β, containing lacunae at 1.3 and 2.13 (as do
P3 and all MSS. of Family 3), but also reading σοφίη
at 5.7, 6.1, and πειρασεῦμαι and ποιεῦντι at 2.2, 2.28.
In this edition I have adopted from it 28 readings that
are in the vast majority of cases unique to it, of
which the important ones are those just mentioned above
and ἐπόμενα (cf. also P4, F1.2) at 5.6. Two other
valuable pointers to correct readings are ποιεν (=ποιέν,
6.8) and ἄμε (=ἀμέ, 6.12). As in the case of its peer,
P1, there are a few minor orthographical errors and
general lapsus calami (e.g., οἰκέται for οἰκέταις, 7.2),
but these do not detract from the central value and
importance of the MS. as a whole.

4. Third Family

          This family has an unknown fountain-head, Υ,
characterized (almost certainly; cf. P3) by the reading
ὁ αὐτός at 4.6 and (very possibly) the reading καί
ἀγαθὸν ἤμεν at 7.5. The family then subdivides into
three groups. Group a has as its immediate source a
descendant of γ (which I call ε) characterized by the
omission of both ὁ and καί; groups b and c differ in
that group b retains (or adds?) καί at 7.5 and ὁ at

4.6, while group <u>c</u> retains ὁ but <u>omits</u> καί.

Group a

The three main members of this group are C (the MS. used by Fabricius), V2, and P4. Of these C and V2 are almost twins, diverging only 20 times in their readings and agreeing on everything else, including several features unique to the two of them (among many examples, one might mention the readings ἐν γάρ ἐν at 8.11 and τὴν πέρσαν at 1.8; for the complete list see Weber [II] 97). It seems therefore more than likely that they stem from a common source, which I have called ε, which will have contained the vast majority of the features they have in common. Whether they are themselves independent of each other is uncertain. On the one hand the remarkable similarity of the two MSS. might suggest that one is the apograph of the other; on the other hand pieces of internal evidence suggest that they are independent. V2 certainly cannot stem directly from C, since C omits the sentence καί . . . αἰσχρόν at 2.3 (it is also dated 1556, while V2 is fifteenth-century); but C can hardly stem directly from V2 either, claims Weber, citing as evidence 3.14 ἄ.ρα V2 αἷρα C, 1.8 νεότατι V2 νεότητι C, 2.4 τοίχοις V2 τοίχους corrected to τοίχοις C (exactly as in Z), 2.15 ἕλλανες V2 ἕλληνες C, 2.19 νομίζοντι V2 νομίζοντες C (as in F1), 2.26 νομίζεν V2 νομίζειν C. Weber's evidence, however, seems to me thin. What happens at 1.8, 2.15, and 2.26, for example, is surely just a standard case of the unconscious tendency to atticize which is found to a greater or lesser degree in many transcribers of non-Attic Greek texts. As for 2.4 and 2.19, these appear to be standard cases of homoeoteleuton, frequently

found in inferior texts (and Fl and Z are inferior, as will be seen later). In view of this, I am myself inclined to think that C is simply an apograph of V2. Whatever the truth, C can for purposes of this edition safely be ignored, since its twin is a more carefully written piece of work and on the two occasions when C preserves what seems to me correct readings its twin preserves them also. These are: 2.14 τὼς C V2 St τοὺς rel.; 8.1 ἐγένετο C V2 P4.6 (E M S Yl.2) ἐγίνετο rel. To these might be added, as pointers to a correct read- ing, 2.27 ἀπάγον C V2 P4.6 (E Yl.2) and (if the Weber or DK text is correct here, rather than my own) 3.14 ἀποθανέτω ἀποθανέτω C V2 P6. But both could simply be standard transcriptional errors, of haplography and duplication respectively, the first going back as far as ε.

The other useful MS. in this group is P4, which corroborates the sound reading of P3 at 5.6, ἐπόμενα (along with E, Yl.2, Fl.2); one can conjecture that γ and ε offered a choice between ἐπόμενα and ἐπόμνα/ἐπόμνα in similar fashion.

The other MSS. in the group, P6, E, and Yl.2 are of little value. The peculiar features of P6 are shared in the great majority of cases by both P4 and C V2, but in three cases it has features shared only by C V2 (αὐτὸν αὐτὸν 1.12; τὰ κατ᾽ αὐτὸν 3.14; ἀποθανέτω ἀποθανέτω 3.14) and in three other cases features shared only by P4 (αἴ τι 6.2; τοῦτο αὐτὸν 6.2; om. καὶ 7.3). I accordingly hypothesize that it stems from both these MSS.

Yl.2 and E constitute the near-valueless items of the stock; on the handful of occasions where they

preserve the sounder reading (or a pointer thereto)
such a reading is preserved in all three better MSS.
in the group P4.6 V2 (ἀπάγον 2.27; ἐγένετο 8.1) or in
P4 alone (ἐπόμενα 5.6). Y1.2 have the further merit,
however, of preserving the interesting pointer λέγοι
μέν at 4.4, suggesting a choice between λέγοιμεν and
λέγοιμι in ε (picked up by P4), and a couple of less
good readings that they share only with P3 (οὐκῶν 5.8)
or only with P2 E (ἕτερα 5.12) are valuable in that
they preserve readings that take us back to very early
divergences from the archetype; a further reading they
share with P3 (and E)--διαφέρει at 5.7--I have in fact
accepted, though ἄν (=ἐάν) διαφέρῃ could well be
correct. They also have several astute marginal emendations by Matthew de Varis. Y2 seems to be fairly
clearly an apograph of Y1: at 5.4 κουφώτερον (Y1) is
copied, but changed to κουφότερον, and at 3.13 τούς
(Y1) is copied, but changed to τώς (see also 2.15,
where the same thing appears to have been done, suggesting that the copyist has felt the force of the opening
phrase of his exemplar, δωρικῆς ὂν διαλέκτου). The
reading τώνύματα at 6.11 (ex τ' ὀνύματα) stems clearly
from a reading τὰ ὀνύματα in Y1, where the α in τὰ is
written in such a way that it appears to have been at
once deleted with a diagonal stroke; the scribe of Y2
has simply assumed ignorance (on the earlier scribe's
part) of the laws of crasis and corrects accordingly.
The point is worth mentioning because DK appear to
have adopted this reading (without acknowledgement)
either directly from Y2 or from some source of information (Trieber?) who had scanned Y2; but its similarity
with the τὰ ὠνύματα of P3 is wholly accidental, and the

reading τά όνύματα, with all other MSS. here and at
6.12 (bis), should be retained. E is an atticizing
MS., full of errors and misspellings, and is the least
valuable item in its group.

Group b

The members of this group are R, Fl.2, and P5
(the apograph of R); of these R and F2 are of some value.
R's specific claim to fame is the excellent (and unique)
reading καινός at 6.1; an ε over the αι suggests
strongly that it is the scribe's own emendation. This
could also be true of the equally sound reading αὐτός
(found also in Pl.2 B) at 1.11. And useful pointers to
correct readings are found at 2.7 and 2.8, where
φε᾽ῦγεν and φονεῦ᾽εν (φεῦγεν rel., φονεῦεν rel., pr.
Pl.2 φονεύεν) indicate the correct readings φεύγεν (St)
and φονεύεν. Apart from this, other sound readings
found in R are also to be found in Fl.2: τῶ 1.16 (with
Pl St); αἴσχιστον 2.5 (with E H Pl.3 Vl); ὁ αὐτός 4.6;
πότερον 5.9; καί ἀγαθόν 7.5; from the evidence of 1.16
and 5.9 in particular I infer the existence of a common
source ζ. Of the two MSS. Fl and F2 the latter is much
the more reliably written, and the better readings it
preserves in a number of places make it clear that it is
not the apograph of Fl: 5.1 πρᾶτον F2 πρῶτον Fl; 1.11
καί αὐτό τοῦτον F2 καὐτό τοῦτο Fl; 1.12 όφείλεις F2
όφείλοις Fl; 1.16 ποιέν F2 πϊεῦν Fl (ποιεῦν rel.); 2.13
ποιήσαντι F2 ποιήσαντα Fl; 5.13 τι F2 δέ Fl.

We must therefore conclude either that Fl is
in fact the apograph of F2 or that they are independent
of each other. Weber ([II] 93) has argued for the latter
case, and is, it seems to me, convincing, though his
evidence is not all equally strong. The readings άλλά

(6.3), τῷ δικαίῳ καὶ τῷ ἀδίκῳ (3.1), τῷ ἀλαθείας (4.1), δὲ ὄντα (8.7) (corrected by a later hand to δέοντα) and διαλάξας (2.19) (corrected by a later hand to διαλλάξας), for example, are simply the common or garden errors that mark out the second-rate MS., and nothing can be inferred from the fact that they crop up in equally poor MSS. like C, M, and S. At 1.1 a reading λέγονται seems to have been corrected by a later hand to λέγοντι (C offers a choice), but this too seems to be simply an error on the part of the would-be corrector, stemming perhaps from the fact that λέγοντι is used in the subsequent sentence, and at 2.17 an original reading τοῖδε τοι (corrected by a later hand to τῆδε τοι) seems readily accountable for in terms either of the identity of pronunciation of οι and η or the (not unnatural) assumption that we are dealing here with a pronominal adjective, not an adverb. Significantly, all the MSS. divide just about evenly over whether τοῖδε or τῆδε (=τῆδε) should be read, and Y2 also, as it happens (like F1 here) corrects its exemplar's reading τοῖδε to τῆδε.

On the other hand, I find it impossible to believe that F1 could have written πϊεῦν at 1.16 after reading ποιέν in F2. (There is no indication that it has been 'corrected' to πϊεῦν by a later hand in the way that διαλλάξας [2.9] and δέοντα [8.7] have been corrected.) And the genitives in -ῶ (οῦ erased) at 1.1, shared by B R Vl.2, suggest a choice -ῶ/-οῦ going back at least as far as γ, and probably as far as β (it was probably also there in δ: cf. the reading of Pl). In view of this it seems to me more than likely that F1.2 are independent of each other, and I accordingly place them on different links of the ζ branch. If my

understanding of the matter is correct, given the
choice of -οῦ and -ῶ at 1.1 F2 will have opted for
-οῦ, R for -ῶ, and F1 for -ῶ after a certain hesitation
over whether the -οῦ alternative should not be at least
noted; and at 1.16 R will have copied down the ζ (γβ)
reading correctly, F1 will have copied down the same
reading but this time <u>incorrectly</u> (an error due to
identity of pronunciation; see also 1.2 ὀφείλεις F2
ὀφείλοις F1), and F2, suspecting (correctly) that the
-εῦν form was in fact erroneous, and probably the
result of a transcriptional slip (cf. the immediately
preceding word ἀσθενεῦντι), will in fact have <u>conjec-</u>
<u>tured</u> ποιέν. Of the two MSS. F2 is clearly the best
written, as was noted above, and is cited in the <u>app.</u>
<u>crit</u>. in preference to F1 except for the one instance
τῶ at 1.1. R is similarly cited in preference to P5,
its poorly written apograph.

   Group c

     This group consists of B, H, Z, L, T, Vl, S,
M, and the MS. apparently used by Stephanus. In
addition to the characteristic mentioned above (25),
it is differentiated from groups <u>a</u> and <u>b</u> by the reading
ἄν (for δ' ἄν) at 2.28. With the exception of B, which
has two pointers to correct readings, they have nothing
to offer. To take them in turn: B reads τοῖς at 1.1,
suggesting the correct τοί (P1.2, <u>rel</u>. οἱ), and ἄμε at
6.12 (with P3.4.6 R Vl), suggesting the correct ἀμέ.
The first could no doubt simply be an error, but the
existence of the alternative λέγουσι (for λέγοντι) in
P1 suggests as an alternate possibility that B has a
pedigree going back some distance beyond γ. That it has
a healthy pedigree stretching back at least as <u>far</u> as γ

seems clear from the reading ἄμε. Vl has similarities
with R, but does not have the valuable readings and
pointers found in R and B respectively. Its link with
B is the peculiar reading ῥύξαι at 3.11, suggesting a
common ancestor to group c which I have called η. M
and S, which inter alia transmit ῥύξαι, are the worthless, shoddily written apographs either of Vl (as DK
hold; see ad 410.2) or of a MS. of the third group that
has much in common with Vl. If the latter is the case,
we can be fairly sure from the evidence of M and S that
it was characterized (uniquely) by the omission of γάρ
before ἀλαθές at 4.8. But a simpler explanation seems
possible: M is the apograph of Vl, and as part of a
generally muddled performance makes the omissions above
mentioned, and S is in turn a slavish apograph of M.
(See, for example, the repetition of voces nihili such
as [1.14] ἔγε (for ἄγε), [7.11] κράρω (for κλάρω), and
several more.) Weber, overlooking the fact that Vl as
well as B reads ῥύξαι, takes S and M to be independent
MSS. in the B tradition, but the readings they share are
in fact basically those of Vl. Nor, it seems to me, are
they independent of each other. For while Weber is no
doubt correct in claiming that M does not derive
directly from S, on the grounds that S omits τάς at
8.3 (and M is much too slavish a MS. to attempt grammatical corrections), the readings πολόκλειτος M and
πολύκλειτος S at 6.8 seem to me less good evidence that
S is not the direct apograph of M, since while the
scribe of S may well have feared (like M) to tamper
with the grammatical and syntactical state of the text,
given the general obscurity (if not incomprehensibility)
with which it must have presented itself to him, he had

the backing of a famous parallel passage in Plato's
Protagoras to encourage him to read Πολύκλειτος rather
than Πολόκλειτος as the proper name in question at 6.8.
I accordingly take S as the direct apograph of M, and
M of Vl, though from the point of view of establishing
a text of the Δ. Λ. the matter is of negligible
importance.

The other branch within group c consists of H,
Z (with its apograph T), L, and the MS. used by Stephanus, and none is of textual importance. Z L St all
clearly go back to the same MS.: at 3.13 all uniquely
read ἄδικοι (for ἄδικον); at 3.16 καὶ τωὖτό; at 4.2
λόγω (for λέγω), and several more (see Weber [II] 90).
Yet all seem themselves independent. St cannot stem
directly from L, since L has several gaps not found in
St (or Z): ἐλὼν has dropped out at 3.5; καὶ μέγαν . . .
τωὐτόν at 3.14; τὸν αὐτόν at 4.6; etc. Yet they are
clearly very close, and share a number of readings not
found in Z: at 5.3 they omit τὸ and at 5.6 καὶ after
τὼς σοφὼς; at 5.3 they read μεῖζον and μεῖον, Z μίζον
and μῆον (rel. μέζον and μῆον); at 6.13 διδακτός, Z
(correctly) διδακτόν; and perhaps most interestingly of
all at 4.6 L reads πόλα, St πολλά and Z (correctly)
πόκα, but corrected from πόλα. I accordingly hypothesize a MS. ϑ that (inter alia; see above) read πόλα or
πόλα/πόκα, from which were copied both Z and a further
MS. ι which inter alia read μεῖζον and μεῖον at 5.3 and
διδακτός at 6.13. From this latter MS. L and the
Stephanus text were copied.

H is a MS. of group c sharing some of the
characteristics of the η group and some of the ϑ/ι
group; it reads, e.g., αἴσχιστον at 2.5 (with Vl Z St)

33

and πρασσεῖται. χρή at 8.7 (with B Z L St). It has
nothing of textual value, and can with T, the apograph
of Z, be passed over.

I conclude with the following <u>stemma</u>:

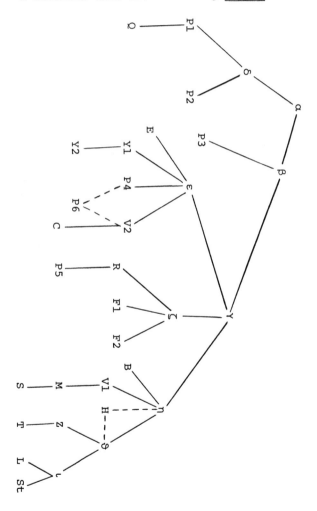

2. Date

The <u>Dissoi Logoi</u> was first published in 1570, and since that date there has been dispute concerning its authorship, its local provenance, its dialect, and the nature of its philosophical content. Only one thing has been universally accepted--its date, or at any rate the <u>terminus a quo</u>. What looks like a clear reference to the end of the Peloponnesian War occurs at section 1.8, and not a single editor or critic till Mazzarino (286 ff.) saw fit to doubt that the document could possibly have been written prior to the year 404 B. C. His arguments (for a date of about 450) must be examined.

We might begin with the curious question of the number of sons of the sculptor Polyclitus. At section 6.8 the author tells us, in a passage concerning the teachability of ἀρετή, that Polyclitus taught his <u>son</u> (singular) how to be a sculptor. In Plato's <u>Protagoras</u>, however, where the same topic is being discussed, Protagoras has the following to say--". . . even the sons (plural) of Polyclitus, who are contemporaries of Paralus and Xanthippus here, cannot hold a candle to their father, nor can the sons of many other craftsmen. But it is too early to bring a charge against these two; they are young, and there is still promise in them." (328c) Following Burnet and others in assuming that the dramatic dates of Plato's dialogues are chosen with an eye for historical accuracy, in spite of the occasional anachronism,[47] Mazzarino dates the events dramatized in the <u>Protagoras</u> at around either 429 or 423/2 B. C. This means, he concludes, that the <u>Dissoi Logoi</u> must have been written some time <u>before</u> one or other of those dates, since the phrase "his son" is the natural locution for referring to a single son. So the terminal possibility for the writing of the Dissoi Logoi is somewhere near the beginning, not after the end, of the Peloponnesian War.

In the light of this Mazzarino is now in a position to offer an alternative explanation of the supposed reference at section 1.8 to the end of the Peloponnesian War. The passage in question, which serves as one of a number of illustrations of the supposed relativity of good and evil, runs as follows--

"In the case of war (and I shall speak of the most recent events first) the victory of the Spartans which they won over the Athenians and their allies was good for the Spartans but bad for the Athenians and their allies. And the victory which the Greeks won over the Mede was good for the Greeks but bad for the barbarians." It is question-begging, thinks Mazzarino, to assume that the first reference is necessarily to the events of 404, particularly when in his estimation we have some sort of evidence for thinking that the terminal date of the Δ. Λ. may be the beginning, not the end, of the Peloponnesian War. He suggests as an alternative that the reference is to the battle of Tanagra in 457, where the Spartans defeated a combined force of Athenians and Argives. His contention, he feels, is corroborated by the fact that the author's account would in fact be a very accurate one of the battle of 457, and a singularly inaccurate one of the events of 404.

If Mazzarino happens to be right, the implications for our understanding of the development of Greek

philosophical thought are startling indeed, so it comes
as a surprise to find that only one scholar, to my
present knowledge, Mario Untersteiner, has commented in
print on the attempted redating.[48] To take the question of the number of Polyclitus' sons first: perhaps
the most significant thing in Untersteiner's reply
([II] 168-169) is his implicit acceptance of Mazzarino's all-important point that the reference to τὸν
υἱὸν in the Dissoi Logoi is most naturally interpreted
as a reference to a time when Polyclitus only had one
son. The difficulties this might have caused, however,
are circumvented, he thinks, if we take the Protagoras
reference to two sons as anachronistic; Plato's attention has faltered momentarily, and the time when Polyclitus had two sons (plural) is really the year 395 or
394, when the Protagoras (he says) was itself written;
so appearances are saved, and we can continue to date
the Dissoi Logoi at about the year 400.

As for the second argument, Untersteiner argues
(ibid.) that the Dissoi Logoi is clearly referring to
two wars, the one involving the Persians and the Greeks,
the other Sparta and Athens. Since the first did not
end officially till about 448, with the Peace of Callias,
the dating of victory (νίκα) in the second at 457 is
clearly out of the question.

There is a certain pleasing simplicity about
Untersteiner's rebuttal, but it is at a price that few
will be prepared to pay. We know, for example, that
Polyclitus' teacher was the elder Hageladas, one of
whose statues can be dated 520 B. C. Even if, for the
sake of argument, we say that Hageladas was a mere 20
years of age at that time, this would make him 80 in the

year 460, when Polyclitus was beginning his career.
And if, again opting for the most cautious estimate
possible, Polyclitus was himself a mere twenty years
of age in 460, this would still make him in turn 80
years old in the year 400 when, according to the Dissoi
Logoi on the old dating, and according to Untersteiner
now, he had still not produced his second son!

Again, Plato points out in the Protagoras that
the sons of Polyclitus are ἡλικιῶται of two men present
at the discussion, namely Paralus and Xanthippus.
Since the latter are in fact the two sons of Pericles
by the unnamed woman whom he had married after Hipponi-
cus had divorced her, they were therefore presumably
born some time before 450 or thereabouts, when Pericles
abandoned the said woman for Aspasia, and they would be
in their twenties or early thirties in 429, when they
both died as a result of the Great Plague (cf. Protagoras A 11 DK[6]). This presents Untersteiner with a singular problem that he does not appear to have noticed.
For, even if we grant that the reference to Paralus and
Xanthippus is anachronistic, the careful reference to
the sons of Polyclitus as their ἡλικιῶται would compel
us, on Untersteiner's grounds, to believe that the said
sons of Polyclitus were in their twenties or early
thirties in 395/4, when the Protagoras was written.
What Untersteiner is left to explain is how one of them
can be born in or after 400 and reach the age of, say,
25 by the year 395.

As for Untersteiner's suggestion that the war
with the Persians did not end till the Peace of Callias,
this may be correct, but it is irrelevant to the discussion. The author of the Dissoi Logoi is not committed

to the view that there were two <u>successive</u> wars, one
between Greeks and Persians, and one between Athens and
Sparta. He is merely talking about <u>instances</u> of war.
As Professor Sprague, the most recent translator of the
<u>Dissoi Logoi</u>, sees clearly (cf. Renehan 71), the phrase
ἐν τῷ πολέμῳ means simply "when it comes to war", "in
the matter of war", or the like: this translation is
guaranteed by the context, where similar generic
instances are in question. What the author is discussing is not necessarily two <u>consecutive</u> wars, but rather
two instances of <u>victory</u> (νίκα) <u>in</u> war. There is no
suggestion that two states of war cannot be concomitant;
indeed what little evidence we have suggests that <u>some</u>
Greeks at any rate felt that a state of war between
Athens and Sparta did exist long before the Peace of
Callias. Pausanias, for example (5.10), has saved for
us the text of an inscription on a golden shield at
Olympia, which tells of the Spartan victory at Tanagra.
This shield had been offered, it states, as "our tithe
for victory in the war" (τὰν δεκάταν / νίκας τοῦ
πολέμου). <u>This</u> Greek, at any rate, did not feel tied
to the curious notion that one war must stop before
another begins. So there is no need for Untersteiner
to feel tied to it either, as far as I can see.

If Untersteiner's attempted rebuttal introduces
more problems than it solves, this hardly means that
Mazzarino's case is unassailable. I list a number of
alternatives, for brief examination:

1. The fact of Polyclitus' ability (or inability)
to teach his son (or sons) his own particular craft
seems to have been a <u>topos</u> at this time. The author of
the <u>Dissoi Logoi</u> was more interested in this general

topos than in particular details, and simply made an
error of fact.

2. The same as (1), except that it was Plato/
Socrates who made the error of fact.

3. Neither author has made a factual error. Assume
merely (with most scholars) that the dramatic date of
the Protagoras is about 433 and that only one of Polyclitus' sons was still living in 400, and the supposed
discrepancy disappears at once.

4. Again assume that neither author has made a mistake. The appearances are saved by the hypothesis that
the 'dramatic' date of the Protagoras is about 433 and
that about 450 Polyclitus did in fact have more than
one son, but that only one had reached an age where it
made sense to talk of his being taught a trade by his
father.

5. The Dissoi Logoi, written c.400, refers simply
to that son of Polyclitus (otherwise unknown) who did
in fact become a sculptor; the question of the remain-
ing son is passed over, as being irrelevant to the point
at issue. And the 'dramatic' date of the Protagoras is
more or less correct.

The first and second objections are difficult
to assess, relying as they do on assertions that are
impregnable merely because they are totally uncheckable.
Which author, if either, might have made the supposed
mistake seems at the moment a question impossible to
answer for lack of evidence. At most one might assert
that, apart from this particular passage, there is no
evidence to suggest that the author of the Dissoi Logoi
has made any other errors of fact in the rest of his
work, whereas there is plenty of evidence, as Zeller

has pointed out, to suggest that Plato is not particularly worried about anachronisms in the dramatic dates
of his dialogues. Some might see this as a minor argument in favour of Mazzarino's thesis, but it seems to
me to veer dangerously close to the argumentum ad
ignorantiam, and should probably be discounted as
evidence one way or the other.

The third and fourth arguments, both of which
base themselves on the assumption that the respective
authors got their facts right, seem to me to have the
merit of methodological respectability as well as making
fair sense. Each assumes, however, that the dramatic
date of the Protagoras is around 433, and each adds a
subsidiary hypothesis concerning a matter of fact for
which there is no corroborative evidence. The one
argument, if true, clearly undercuts Mazzarino's contention; the other, if true, would both support it and
strengthen it. However, given that each position involves the introduction of two hypotheses of what seem
to be equal plausibility, the safest policy for the
moment would again appear to be to adhere firmly to
neither, as in the case of the first and second arguments.

The fifth argument appears to account for the
discrepancies without undue strain on our credulity, and
should probably be accepted.

What can be said for Mazzarino's contention that
the reference to the Spartan victory over the Athenians
and their allies is really a reference to the battle of
Tanagra? Its merit, it seems to me, lies in the fact
that it would credit the author of the Dissoi Logoi with
a simple statement of the truth; the alternative hypothesis would involve us in talk about the supposed "Doric

prejudices" of the author. In favour of the latter
hypothesis, however, is the apparent fact that the
author is addressing a Doric-speaking audience, and a
somewhat coloured account of the ending of a war
which Dorians had won is not in the context inappropriate. This seems to me a clear equipossibility, and
in view of it Mazzarino's case cannot be said to have
been demonstrated.

  I conclude that the Δ. Λ. was written some time
around 403-395 (the date accepted by most scholars).[49]
This seems to me a date which both withstands the
arguments of Mazzarino and accounts most simply for the
treatise's philosophical contents.

3. Authorship and Dialect

  The MSS. unequivocally announce the Dissoi
Logoi as ἀνωνύμου τινος, but editors and commentators
since Stephanus have consistently refused to give up
so easily. Stephanus read Μίμας at 4.4, and was
followed in this by North and Meibom. Whether Stephanus was reading a manuscript (now lost) which read
Μίμας is unknown; the nearest to it is the reading
μύμας found in L and Z. This Μίμας Stephanus took to
be a Pythagorean, one can assume, since the Dissoi
Logoi is placed by him among a series of documents
globally labelled "Pythagorean" (no doubt on account
of their Doric dialect; see Rostagni 174), and in this
he was followed by North and Meibom (704, n.1). North
(ibid.) makes the further suggestion that the author
probably came from Sicily or Italy, and he offers as
reasons the Doric dialect and the way in which the
author "tam solenni more ac particulari, ἐν τῇ ῾Ελλάδι

ὑπὸ τῶν φιλοσοφούντων, opiniones istas praevalere
dixit, quod non facturum puto, si istam patriam suam
agnoverat."

Fabricius (617), basing himself on the reading
found in the Codex Cizensis and the Codex Savilensis,
read μύστας at 4.4. Like his immediate predecessors,
however, he was not content to leave the author anonymous, and suggested as the author the Stoic philosopher Sextus of Chaeronea, the nephew of Plutarch and
friend and teacher of Marcus Aurelius. In this way he
no doubt felt he could account for the fact that the
treatise is invariably found as an appendix to the
works of Sextus Empiricus: scribes had simply been misled by a common praenomen.[50] The textual evidence
suggesting that the author was writing about the year
400-390 B. C. (1.8) is not discussed.

For Orelli (2.633) the author was clearly a
sophist (unnamed)--but a sophist of "more recent" date
than the fourth century. The supposed references in
the text to events like the end of the Peloponnesian
War (1.8) are simply "lies" and "fiction". He hints
(ibid.) that the author lived either at the time of
the author of the "Letters of Aristippus" or at some
time later than that, on the grounds that his Doric is
very similar to the Doric of that author (and of other
authors after him) and very dissimilar to the Doric of
Archytas and other "genuine" Pythagoreans. (It might
be pointed out that Valckenaer[51] and Koen[52] had already
made the suggestion that the author was a sophist, not
a Pythagorean; Orelli makes no mention of them, though
he is normally careful to acknowledge particular debts
to them in his commentary.)

Mullach (xxiii-xxiv) followed Orelli in thinking that the author was a sophist "more recent" than the fourth century B. C., who "antiquitatis minime ignarus Pythagoreorum exemplo dorica dialecto usus est." He adds the comment that in his judgment the author must also have preceded Pyrrho and the sceptical school. The view of Fabricius is discussed, and categorically rejected.

The most eccentric of all suggestions on authorship appeared in 1840, when O. F. Gruppe put forward the view that the author was the same man as forged the (supposed) "Fragments of Archytas."[53] He was, said Gruppe (144 f.), an Alexandrian Jew living at the time of Caligula, and put together his treatise at the time of, or a little later than, the persecution of Flaccus (who is seen as the κλέπτων mentioned in the riddle at 3.11). The entire thesis turns upon a gratuitous assumption that the lines attributed to Cleobuline at 3.11 are a fabrication of the author's, and refer obliquely to a historical figure, Flavius Flaccus; it died (mercifully) with Gruppe.[54]

The search for an author, however, continued apace. In 1872 Theodor Bergk ([I] 86) suggested that the author was the Sophist Μίλτας, "ein Schüler Platos." No defence of the move was offered, and by 1883 it had been relegated to an auto-prosopographical footnote ([II] 134, n.1). Forestalling an obvious objection, Bergk suggested in the same note that Miltas perhaps forswore his sophistic profession to join Plato's circle, as Helikon was said to have done (Pl. Epist. 13, 360c). Wilamowitz, however ([I] 295), had already in 1876 rejected the whole idea that it might be Miltas,

arguing simply that the author was a man "e sophistica
Protagorae et Gorgiae disciplina pendentem."

In 1881 Friedrich Blass suggested (739) that
the reading at 4.4 should be Σιμμίας, not μύστας or
Μίμας (he makes no reference to Bergk's suggestion).
The author, he argued, was no Pythagorean, but one of
the Socratic circle--Simmias the Theban, who figures
prominently in Plato's Phaedo. Simmias and Cebes had
associated with the Pythagorean Philolaus (Phaedo 61d)
--whence Simmias could have picked up the quasi-Doric
dialect of the Dissoi Logoi (740). Simmias and Cebes
are also, says Blass, portrayed in the Phaedo as
sceptics--and scepticism is the mood of the Dissoi
Logoi (ibid.). Diogenes Laertius (2.124) also attributes to Simmias a total of twenty-three διάλογοι. Of
these Blass equates περί φιλοσοφίας with Δ. Λ. 1-3,
περί άληθείας with Δ. Λ. 4, περί γραμμάτων with Δ. Λ.
5 (DK), περί διδασκαλίας with Δ. Λ. 6 (DK), περί τοῦ
έπιστατεῖν with Δ. Λ. 7 (DK), περί τέχνης with Δ. Λ.
8-9 (DK) (ibid.).

In 1884 Schanz (following Mullach) conjectured
(374) that the name of the author was Μύστας, and Teichmüller (105 ff.) that the author was Σίμων the
philosopher-shoemaker. Schanz states his belief without
further argument, but Teichmüller defends his view with
a lengthy series of arguments, combined with a precise
criticism of the views of his predecessors Blass and
Bergk (105 ff.; 97 ff.). Like Blass, he looks to
Diogenes Laertius for enlightenment. According to
Diogenes (2.122) Simon had put together thirty-three
διάλογοι (thereinafter called the σκυτικοί λόγοι,
because of his profession) within the compass of a single

book. Though the διάλογοι have been lost, the titles
have been preserved by Diogenes, and Teichmüller
attempts to equate particular ones with sections of the
Dissoi Logoi. περὶ τοῦ ἀγαθοῦ he equates with Δ. Λ. 1,
περὶ τοῦ καλοῦ with Δ. Λ. 2, περὶ δικαίου πρῶτος with
Δ. Λ. 3, περὶ δικαίου δεύτερος or περὶ κρίσεως with Δ.
Λ. 4, περὶ ἀρετῆς, ὅτι οὐ διδακτόν with Δ. Λ. 6 (DK)
[Δ. Λ. 5 Stephanus], περὶ τοῦ ὄντος with Δ. Λ. 5 (DK),
περὶ δημαγωγίας with Δ. Λ. 7 (DK), and περὶ ἐπιστήμης
or π. τ. διαλέγεσθαι with Δ. Λ. 8 (DK). He is unper-
turbed by the use of the term διάλογος (rather than
διάλεξις, the term used by Stephanus), arguing that
διάλογος and διάλεξις amount to the same thing: in
either instance "es dreht sich um eine Erörterung der
Begriffe durch Dialektik" (113-114). Corroborative
evidence that the author was Simon he finds in "der
banausische Charakter der Schrift", a phrase he eluci-
dates in a sentence so superb in its disregard for
elementary logic as to be worth quoting in full: "Das
Schusterhafte (sic) dieser Dialoge liegt also vor Allem
in dem augenfälligen Mangel an dialektischem Talent, in
der Unbehilflichkeit der Rede und der Unverdaulichkeit
der Gedanken." (116) [55]

From 1889 onward scholars have stressed the
relationship between some of the things said in the
Dissoi Logoi and what we know of the writings of particular sophists, especially Protagoras, Hippias, and
Gorgias. (The move had been adumbrated by Wilamowitz
in 1876.) In that year F. Dümmler suggested (259), from
the evidence of the final section of the treatise, that
the author was dependent on Hippias, and in 1892 Trieber
suggested (236, 245) that the author was either Hippias

himself or one of his followers.[56] The thesis was
extended considerably by H. Gomperz ([II] 179 ff.), who
offered reasons for thinking that the author had drawn
upon Protagoras, Hippias, and Gorgias--and also upon
the Socratic circle![57] In the following year Pohlenz
(77) put forward a view basically in agreement with
that of Dümmler and Trieber, and criticized Gomperz's
contention that the treatise had links with the Socratic
circle. On Gomperz's side, however, was A. E. Taylor,
who claimed (128) to be able to find "unmistakable
traces of Socratic influence" in the treatise. The
author, he argued, showed "clear indications of belonging to the class of semi-Eleatic thinkers represented
for us in the Socratic circle by Euclides and his
Megarian associates."[58] Since that date Dupréel and
Untersteiner have gone on to argue independently that
the work is an attack on a number of characteristically
Gorgian ideas (specifically the concept of καιρός) by a
man using the ideas of Hippias.[59] Among other opinions
one might mention those of Zeller and Nestlé, who saw
the author as a sophist-compiler, drawing on other
sophists,[60] and that of W. Kranz (232), who felt that
the author was a man under the influence of Socrates
and the sophists to about the same extent.[61] By
contrast with this, Rostagni's view (175 ff., see
above, 41) of the author as a sophistic maestro di
scuola of Pythagorean provenance marks a return to the
status quo ante. The move won the support of Luria,
who went even further and suggested (447, n.2) that the
author draws on two distinct sources, one sophistic and
one Pythagorean, and Luria's view has in turn been
accepted in recent times by Mario Untersteiner ([II]

162). In spite of Untersteiner's authority, however, the move has not won universal acceptance. For M. Timpanaro Cardini (213, n.1) the author is someone who has transcribed the lectures of a sophist who was a follower of Protagoras; for K. Freeman ([I] 417) (like Gomperz) he is some superficial compiler of ideas and arguments to be found in Herodotus, Heraclitus, Protagoras, Hippias, and Plato. J. L. Fischer (33, 36), following the path of Gomperz, considers the author to be a "weak imitator" of models of reasoning to be found, in all probability, in Protagoras' Antilogies, Hippias, the circle of Socrates, and Gorgias (the model for whose paradoxes was in turn one or a number of Eleatic eristics).

As the massive disagreement indicates, we are dealing with 'evidence' of more than usual unreliability, and any conclusions can be at best tentative. To begin with 4.4: is the author of the treatise named? The MS. evidence suggests that he was not (see app. crit. ad loc.), and the conjectures are all fairly flimsy. Fabricius' solution of the problem firmly grasps one horn of the dilemma, in that it offers a specific reason why the treatise is always found in Sextus Empiricus MSS. However, it fails to offer reasons why a Stoic nephew of Plutarch should be writing in quasi-Doric, in a manner so far removed from, and on a topic so alien to, basic Stoic belief. Given the internal evidence for dating, one must assume that Fabricius thought the whole thing a piece of elaborate historical fiction. But he offers no reason why a teacher of Marcus Aurelius should have felt the need to engage in such an exercise.

However, Fabricius did adopt what seems to be

beyond all reasonable doubt the correct reading--
μύστας--at 4.4, and in this was followed by Orelli.
The latter made even further progress--following the
earlier suggestions of Valckenaer and Koen--in his
suggestion that the (anonymous) author was a sophist,
not a Pythagorean. But it is difficult to believe his
further suggestion that the author lived at a later
date than the fourth century, and that the supposed
references to historical events are "lies" and "fiction". To say, as Orelli does, that the Doric of the
Δ. Λ. differs from the Doric of Archytas and other
bona fide 'Pythagoreans' is beside the point, since he
has already claimed that the author is a sophist, not
a Pythagorean. This leaves him with only one remain-
ing piece of evidence, the affinity between the Doric
of the Δ. Λ. and that of the "Letters of Aristippus"
and even later Doric writings (where the Doric is
similarly interlarded with a good deal of Attic), but
this, as will be seen below (51), can be accounted for
by a hypothesis much less extreme than the one he
himself propounds.

One can pass quickly over Mullach's view, as
being largely a paraphrase of Orelli's, and Gruppe's
view, as being an exercise in eccentricity. Bergk's
suggestion Μίλτας was seen to be a weak one, even by
Bergk himself, and turns upon the gratuitous invention
of an item of biography. Schanz' conjecture (following
Mullach) that Μύστας is a proper name is weakened by
the fact there is no other extant instance of the name
in the language.

Of greater interest are the views of Blass and
Teichmüller. For Blass the author is the Simmias of

the Phaedo (for the reasoning behind the attribution
see above, 44 f.). But his arguments overstate the
plausibility of the attribution. Simmias and Cebes can
indeed be said to be 'sceptics' in the Phaedo; but
about life after death, not about everything. And in
any case it is far from clear that the author of the
Δ. Λ. is a sceptic; to propound (apparently) antithetical views is not to suggest that each is equally
acceptable. Again, if a man writes twenty-three
διάλογοι on philosophical problems, it is almost inevitable that some will coincide with problems touched on
in the Δ. Λ. (e.g., problems περὶ ἀληθείας and περὶ
τοῦ ἐπιστατεῖν). It is also far from clear that the
nine sections (or even the first four sections) of the
Δ. Λ. can be classified as διάλογοι; there may be two
views expressed, along with a number of rebuttals of
particular theses, but the atmosphere of a dialogue is
almost totally absent. Blass's final suggestion, however, that the author may have picked up his quasi-
Doric dialect by association with Pythagoreans, remains
an interesting and not implausible one.

Like Blass, Teichmüller is impressed by the
coincidence in subject-matter of a number of the
διάλογοι of Simon and the subject-matter of particular
sections of the Δ. Λ. But the same objection can be
made here as was made against the thesis of Blass: a
coincidence would be natural, and indeed something to
be expected. And the wholly different atmosphere
between the Δ. Λ. and our best examples for comparison,
the Platonic dialogues, suggests that the grounds for
equating the terms διάλογος and διάλεξις are (in this
instance at any rate) flimsy ones. As for the supposed

'evidence' presented by "der banausische Charakter der
Schrift", the less said the better.

The evidence for 'compilation' theories, and
the general or particular influence on the author of
Gorgias, Hippias, Protagoras and the Socratic circle
is discussed below, 54-73. Something should be said,
however, about the hypothesis of Untersteiner. Combin-
ing the views of Luria (447, n.2) and Rostagni (174-
178), he has suggested ([II] 161-162, 165) that the
author's own views stem from two sources, the one
sophistic, the other Pythagorean, and that he is in
fact "un pitagorica della corrente etica" ([II] 165).
The evidence for the first source seems to me clear,
the evidence for the second less so, and the conclusion
very unlikely. Nothing in Δ. Λ. 7, for example, suggests that the author is attacking democracy as such;
he is rather attacking the lot-system as being not in
the least democratic, and goes on to say that it is
necessary that the people (ὁ δᾶμος) elect its public
officials, etc. This if anything suggests to me a
respect for democracy--if it be of the thinking and
responsible sort. As for the evidence from Diogenes
Laertius (see Rostagni 176)[62] suggesting that the
Pythagoreans despised the lot-system, it can hardly be
claimed--even if the evidence were firmly based--that
the Pythagoreans were unique in this. (For Socrates'
apparent objection to the lot-system see Xen. Mem.
1.2.9, Ar. Rhet. 1393b 4-5.) And the phrase μύστας
εἰμι (4.4) could refer to membership in the Eleusinian
mysteries, or could be simply metaphorical; there is
nothing in the context to suggest a specifically
Pythagorean allusion. The only piece of evidence in

favour of the thesis seems to be the view attributed
to Pythagoras at Iamblichus V.P. 130 (Rostagni 177):
μηδὲν εἰλικρινὲς εἶναι τῶν ὄντων πραγμάτων, ἀλλὰ
μετέχειν καλὸν αἰσχροῦ καὶ δίκαιον ἀδίκου καὶ τἄλλα
. . . ἐκ δὲ ταύτης τῆς ὑποθέσεως λαβεῖν τὸν λόγον τὴν
εἰς ἐκάτερον μέρος ὁρμήν.
But even this at best suggests that Pythagoreanism is
one of a number of sources for the different instances
of the 'identity' thesis in the Δ. Λ.; it does not
suggest that the author is himself some sort of Pythagorean.

In a situation like this, where incontrovertible
evidence is a near-impossibility to come by, I state my
own opinion only with the greatest diffidence. Drawing
particularly upon Pohlenz (75) and Thesleff (93-94), I
incline to the view that the Δ. Λ. was written for a
Doric-speaking audience by a sophist of Ionian provenance, speaking an Ionian or Ionian-cum-Attic dialect,
who had been largely influenced by Protagoras and in
some smaller measure by Hippias, Gorgias, perhaps
Socrates himself, and a number of the ethnographers
(see below, 54-73). The dialect in which he writes is
basically West Doric, though no exact locality can be
pin-pointed with certainty. I hypothesize as the reason
for the latter fact the possibility that the author
himself translated what he had to say into Doric (a
Doric of a generally functional 'Western' form to suit
a number of different audiences, from Megara to Magna
Graecia, and also one which is happily fairly close to
his own brand of Ionic in its readiness to convert εο
to ευ; see below), with large-scale but not total
success; several ionicisms[63] remain, and perhaps even

a number of atticisms[64] (though it is always possible
that the latter are to be attributed to an atticizing
MS. tradition). Obvious places for a Doric-speaking,
philosophically alert audience at this time would be
Megara (Taylor 128, Kneale 16) and Sicily or Southern
Italy (North, 704, n.1) (we know that Protagoras himself
either visited or planned to visit Magna Graecia--
Protagoras A1, 3 DK[6]), specifically Tarentum, the city
of Archytas. It is true, as Høeg (111) has pointed
out, that the idiosyncratic dative plural participial
forms πωλεῦντι and ἀσθενεῦντι, though belonging to no
known location, are nearest to those found in Cos, but
this does not seem to me clinching evidence that the
intended audience was specifically Coan; it is at least
possible that such forms are simply an error on the
author's part. Having noticed that εο>ευ is common to
several Doric dialects, and assuming--falsely--that,
because the third person plural present in Doric ends
in -οντι, the dative masculine plural of the present
participle will (as in Attic and Ionic) have an identical ending, he offers us (interchangeably?) endings
in -ευντι (1.3, 1.16) and -εοντι (e.g., 1.3 μισθαρνέοντι), rather than -εουσι, for *-εονσι.[65] However,
analogous -οντι forms have been discovered in Crete
(see Thesleff, 94, n.1) and perhaps Messenia (Thesleff,
ibid., though DK ad init. feel that this may be a
stonemason's mistake), and such evidence, small though
it is, suggests that the author may be correctly trans-
mitting a rare dialectal feature, though of what
geographical area we cannot be sure. Megara seems
prima facie a more reasonable possibility than Cos,
given the active philosophical community there (see

Taylor 128, Kneale 16). And we know (from Theophrastus, ap. D.L. 2.108) that it was a disciple of Euclides of Megara who first formulated the Liar Paradox--which has strong affinities with Δ. Λ. 4.6. If specific linguistic forms are to count as evidence (but see above), it might also be pointed out that ἐσεῖται (2.26) is Megarian (see Bechtel 2.194, Untersteiner [I] ad loc.). (The 'Eleaticism', however, which Taylor finds in the Δ. Λ.--particularly in chapter 4--and which he associates with Euclides of Megara, I must confess I fail to find.)

Tarentum, which still had a significant Pythagorean community at this time, would also be a natural place for the author to put forward his views (Rostagni 174, Mazzarino 293). A Pythagorean audience would, one can assume, be intrigued by the antithetical nature of the thesis, given the importance of the Table of Opposites. Tarentum in particular would also, even though Dorian, prove sympathetic to the author's stance as a "thinking democrat" (7.5-6; Wilamowitz [II] 626, Maier 250, n.1), since in 467 the city had adopted a quasi-democratic political system, after the expulsion of the tyrant Micythos (Ar. Pol. 1303a; Diod.9.66). They could also be expected to feel the force of his criticism of the lot-system[66] as being ultimately anti-democratic in the sense of "to the detriment of the demos" (7.5)--particularly in the aftermath of a war that Athens lost; cf. the probable date of the Δ. Λ.-- for we know that their constitution was composed of elements drawn from both Athenian and Spartan models; some official posts were drawn by lot, some on an elective basis (Ar. Pol. 1230b; cf. Wuilleumier 177;

Sartori 85-86).[67]

Whether the text as we have it was part of something meant to be delivered in that state (as a Schulvortrag perhaps; see DK ad init.), is doubtful. I am myself inclined to agree with those scholars (Gaiser 56, n.40; Mazzarino 290) who see it rather as a sophist's fairly full but unpolished 'lecture-notes' (not really planned for publication) round which he would compose his more formal address. This accounts for its imperfect Doric dialect in a way which other hypotheses--such as the hypothesis that the Δ. Λ. is part of a set of student-notes taken down from a sophist's lecture or lectures (Zeller [II] 1. 1333, n.1; Pohlenz 72-74; Guthrie 3. 316)[68]--do not; there is no reason, for example, to think that a student would, if he were Doric-speaking, do other than take down his notes in unadulterated Doric.[69]

4. Influences on the author

The question of influences on the author of the Δ. Λ. is a much-disputed one.[70] There are four main figures involved, and each will be discussed in turn.

1. Protagoras

We have it on the evidence of Diogenes Laertius (9.50 ff. = Protagoras A 1, B 6a DK[6]) that Protagoras

1. πρῶτος ἔφη δύο λόγους εἶναι περὶ παντὸς πράγματος ἀντικειμένους ἀλλήλοις,

2. [αὐτοῖς] καὶ συνηρώτα, πρῶτος τοῦτο πράξας

3. πρῶτος . . . καιροῦ δύναμιν ἐξέθετο

4. πρῶτος . . . λόγων ἀγῶνας ἐποιήσατο

5. πρῶτος . . . σοφίσματα τοῖς πραγματολογοῦσι

55

προσήγαγε

6. τὸ Σωκρατικὸν εἶδος τῶν λόγων πρῶτος ἐκίνησε

7. ὡς οὐκ ἔστιν ἀντιλέγειν . . . πρῶτος διείλεκται

8. πρῶτος κατέδειξε τὰς πρὸς τὰς θέσεις ἐπιχειρήσεις.

We also know (ibid.) that he wrote a Τέχνη ἐριστικῶν and two books of Antilogies, and Aristotle (Rhet. 1402a 23 = Protagoras B 6b DK[6]; cf. Aristoph. Clouds 882-884) claimed that [Πρωταγόραν] τὸν ἥττω . . . λόγον κρείττω ποιεῖν.

This has led to a number of claims concerning the 'Protagorean' nature of much of the Δ. Λ., either in structure, or content, or both. To take structure first: the 'antilogical' form of the opening chapters in particular, with their repeated assertions that there are δισσοὶ λόγοι on a number of (if not all) moral questions, has been thought by many to be clearly Protagorean in tone, and perhaps even to indicate the way in which his own books Τέχνη ἐριστικῶν and Ἀντιλογίαι were structured.[71] As for content, much has been made of Δ. Λ. 6 and Plato's Protagoras, where the teachability (or otherwise) of ἀρετή is again a central question. Individual scholars have made further claims, such as the 'Protagorean relativism' of the theses of the opening chapters (e.g., Versényi 11, 18 ff.), the 'Protagorean' nature of the 'doctrine of καιρός' (e.g., Gomperz [II] 167) and the Protagorean basis of much of chapter 8 (cf. phrases such as ὀρθῶς λέγεν, κατὰ βραχὺ διαλέγεσθαι, etc.). For Trieber the evidence for the influence of Protagoras on the treatise is so compelling that he concludes (236): "So zeigen sich die Διαλέξεις fast in allen Punkten . . . von Protagoras vollkommen abhängig."

If Diogenes Laertius is right, the argument from
structure has a fair cogency (see above, especially
statements [1], [2], and [8]). In chapters 1-4 in particular we have a clear instance of δύο λόγοι . . .
ἀντικείμενοι ἀλλήλοις and an author who sees it as his
job to συνερωτᾶν, rather than overtly side with either.
While it is perhaps true that he himself veers in the
direction of realism, he still appears to be doing his
best to state the counter-case in each instance, though
more often than not the supposed counter-case is no
genuine counter-case at all. His commitment to a philosophical approach that involves the (hopefully dispassionate) examination of arguments for particular positions is nowhere better evidenced than at the end of
chapter 6:

καὶ οὐ λέγω ὡς διδακτόν ἐστιν, ἀλλ' οὐκ ἀποχρῶνταί μοι
τῆναι ταὶ ἀποδείξιες.

Whether these opening chapters copy structurally the
specific works Τέχνη ἐριστικῶν and/or Ἀντιλογίαι we
cannot know for certain, but the evidence of (2) above
(καὶ συνηρώτα) and (8) suggests that it is at least a
fair possibility. Aristotle (De Soph. El. 183b 37)
tells us of "Manuals of Eristic" put together by fee-
taking sophists, in which specimen pro and contra
arguments are set out for memorization, and the four
opening chapters at any rate of the Δ. Λ. appear to
fit the description well. If Protagoras is included
(and we must assume he is; cf. Pl. Meno 91de, Hipp.
Mai. 282e) among Aristotle's fee-taking sophists, then
Protagoras' Τέχνη ἐριστικῶν and Ἀντιλογίαι could well
be included among the Manuals that Aristotle has in

mind. Be this as it may, the evidence of chapters 1-4 and 6 suggests strongly that the author is heavily indebted to Protagoras for his general structural approach, whether he is copying the structure of individual works of Protagoras or not; this much the evidence of Diogenes Laertius appears to allow us to say with a fair degree of certainty.

As far as content is concerned, it has seemed clear to many from the evidence of Plato's Protagoras that Δ. Λ. 6 must be related in some way to the thinking of Protagoras; though in what way precisely is uncertain. There are, one soon notices, several arguments shared by the Protagoras and Δ. Λ. 6, and even particular words (εὐφυής, ἑλλανίζειν, ἱκανός); and a common reference to Polyclitus (though--or perhaps because--the details differ) has the ring of authenticity. Assuming, for the sake of argument, that the Protagoras of history is in some measure captured by one or other account, or perhaps by both, what explanation would best fit the evidence? From what Diogenes Laertius tells us, Δ. Λ. 6 (like 1-4) captures in its structure the Protagorean approach to philosophical λόγοι, and if Protagoras was involved, as others were, in the question of the teachability or otherwise of ἀρετή, it seems safe to infer that his discussion of it would have followed the procedural lines (i.e. thesis and counter-thesis) of Δ. Λ. 6. And we do in fact know (if Plato's Protagoras is to count for anything) that Protagoras was indeed involved in the question of the teachability or otherwise of ἀρετή, though only what purport to be his own strongly held views are put forward at length (Prot. 316d-317c). There is, however,

no conflict here. Protagoras merely said, to the best
of our knowledge, that there were two λόγοι on any
question; it was left to others to infer (almost
certainly unfairly) that he felt that each of the two
λόγοι was as cogent as the other. It seems significant,
for example, that in the Theaetetus Plato suggests that
a natural inference of the ἄνθρωπος μέτρον doctrine is
ethical relativism; he does not at any point accuse
Protagoras himself of such relativism. And the Protagoras of the Protagoras is in fact firmly credited with
a belief in traditional moral values (see Levi [I] 297,
Koch 282). So it seems eminently possible that the
Protagoras of history should have held strong personal
views on the teachability of ἀρετή, yet felt as a
philosopher that there was an (inevitable) counter-case
to his own, which should be examined critically and
dispassionately if philosophical progress was to be
made. The final sentence in particular (6.13) rings
true: the author (="any worthy disciple of Protagoras"?)
will evaluate arguments, in circumstances of philosophical dispute, rather than simply propound convictions--
however strong his convictions may happen to be.

    While the atmosphere of debate is less evident
in the latter part of the Δ. Λ., a number of linguistic
expressions scattered throughout the treatise have also
suggested to some the possible influence of Protagoras.
The stress on τὸ ὀρθῶς λέγεν in Δ. Λ. 8, for example,
may be an echo of the Protagorean stress on ὀρθοέπεια,
though the latter might well refer simply to rhetoric,
and the phrase τῶν πραγμάτων ἡ ἀλήθεια (8.1, 12) might
just be an echo of a favourite sophistic (perhaps even
Protagorean) catch-phrase (see nn. on 8.1 [τὰν ἀλάθειαν]

59

and 8.12 [τὰν ἀλάθειαν τῶν πραγμάτων]). At Pl. Prot.
329b 3-4 Socrates talks about Protagoras' willingness
to ἐρωτηθεὶς ἀποκρίνασθαι κατὰ βραχύ (cf. Δ. Λ. 8.1)--
a phrase perhaps used by Protagoras himself to describe
the dialectical atmosphere of such books as Ἀντιλογίαι
and the Τέχνη ἐριστικῶν. And Gomperz was surely right
to point out that the references to καιρός (2.19-20,
3.12) are as likely to go back to Protagoras as to
Gorgias. Similarly, the ionicism κάρτα was a word
used by Protagoras (see n. on 6.7). But such linguistic evidence, if that is what it really is, should at
best be used as a bolster to the arguments from content
and structure; linguistic affinity alone is (notoriously) a poor reason for claiming causal connection.

2. Hippias
        It has frequently been asserted[72] that the
spirit and teachings of Hippias are visible in a number
of passages, if not whole chapters, of the Δ. Λ., but
in recent years an even stronger thesis has emerged,
propounded by Dupréel (passim) and Untersteiner (148-
191), and accepted by Dumont (tr., ad init.): the Δ. Λ.
is basically composed of a series of (relativistic)
theses of a Gorgian nature,[73] and a series of (absolute)
counter-theses of a Hippian nature. The evidence,
however, as I read it, indicates that so strong an
affirmation cannot be endorsed, not least because of
one's doubts about the methodological viability of
accepting at face-value, as Dupréel and Untersteiner
appear to do, passages of the Hippias Maior and Hippias
Minor that are not confirmed in any clear way in any
other, less tendentious, sources. On the strength of
his reading of Hipp. Mai 301b, for example, πρᾶγμα at

1.11 (cf. 3.13) is read by Untersteiner (ad loc.) as
"qualità", σῶμα at 2.1 is read as "[il] manifestarsi
naturale", and 5.10 ff. is said to refer to a 'Hippian'
doctrine of "differenza qualitativa." But the doctrine
of "qualitative difference" that Untersteiner ascribes
to Hippias is one which few will find transparent at
Hipp. Mai. 301b (assuming, for the sake of argument,
that they accept the passage as adequately representa-
tive of Hippias' views), and it seems equally clear
that the same doctrine can be found at Δ. Λ. 1.11,
5.10 ff. et alib. only by the application of a single-
minded determination to excavate it from the text.[74]
Other outstanding examples of such persistence are to
be found at 1.17, where Untersteiner (ad loc.; cf.
Dupréel 207-208)--motivated by his interpretation of
Hipp. Mai. 301b--interprets οὐ λέγω τί ἐστι τὸ ἀγαθόν
as "io non definisco il concetto di bene" and ἀλλ'
ἑκάτερον (after Kranz) as "ma insieme esistono l'uno e
l'altro", and 5.15, where <τὰ> πάντα . . . πῆ ἐστι is
translated (?) "ogni essere è connesso con una qualità".[75] A number of notes ad loc. reflect a similar
conviction: e.g., Δ. Λ. 2 (init.), "il materiale . . .
può dependere anche da Ippia"; 2.9, "sia dai logografi
ionici, sia da Ippia"; Δ. Λ. 6 (init.), it is not
"sound method" that 6.7 ff.--i.e., the counter-thesis--
should be Protagorean in provenance, rather than Hippian, as most scholars believe, says Untersteiner,
since in the previous chapters the opposition was
Gorgias-Hippias; 6.1, the use of the word καινός is
"una nuova conferma che lo spirito di Ippia ha determinato i Dissoi Logoi." And chapters 8 and 9 are
thought to be clear and unequivocal manifestations of

Hippian influence.

For Dupréel also (192 ff.) Δ. Λ. 8 is essentially Hippian; it is an attack upon Gorgias (e.g., 8.4-5, 8.7-8), Protagoras (8.2), or both (8.6). This stems from his belief that in Hippias' eyes all branches of knowledge form a basic unity and fall within the range of competence of a single individual (exemplified by Hippias himself). The omniscience of such a man consists in a knowledge of the φύσις of things--in Dupréel's phrase (195), the "nature of the real." Further evidence of Hippias as the inspiration of chapter 8 he finds in the stress on τὸ κατὰ βραχὺ διαλέγεσθαι, of which he sees an example at Pl. Prot. 315, where Hippias is portrayed as surrounded by questioners (195). Hipp. Min. 368b ff. is referred to as evidence of Hippias' multi-faceted ability (196), as is Hipp. Min. 367cd, with its fourfold use of the phrase ὁ αὐτός (see Δ. Λ. 8.1, <τῶ δ' αὐτῶ> κτλ) (197). Hipp. Min. 370e, 371e are compared with Δ. Λ. 8.8 (197), which is understood in terms of knowledge as the source of power either to act or to refrain from action. Socrates' assertion (Hipp. Min. 372b), "I obviously know nothing" (φαίνομαι οὐδὲν εἰδώς), is read as a riposte to a Hippias who claims to know everything (199), and in the same passage the phrase τῶν . . . πραγμάτων ᾗ ἔχει ἐσφαλμαι is said to be closely comparable with phrases in 8.1 (ibid.). Finally (200), on the strength of Hipp. Min. 372c (οὐ γὰρ πώποτε κτλ), Dupréel claims that in literature of the period words like εὕρημα, εὑρίσκειν, and others of the same root have a strong likelihood of being Hippian in source (cf. Δ. Λ. 9.1), and a doctrine of non-transmutable

substantial entities which he finds at 2.26 is also, he
thinks, Hippian (208).

To take Dupréel's claims first. Even if, for
the sake of argument, it be conceded that the Hippias
Maior and Hippias Minor are accurate sources of information on the philosophical views of Hippias, it seems
far from clear that Hippias ever claims control over
all branches of knowledge, or that all branches of knowledge were thought by him to be a unity;[76] all that we
are told is that he was a polymath, and a man skilled
in many different forms of craftsmanship (Hipp. Min.
368b ff.). Nor, while no doubt being interested in
φύσις in the sense of "the natural world" (see Prot.
315c), is Hippias ever in any clear sense said to be
more interested in "the φύσις of things" than in fact-
collecting (in different terminology: more interested
in connotation than in denotation), or to equate knowledge of the φύσις τῶν ἀπάντων (Δ. Λ. 8.1) with knowledge of πάντα (8.7), and perhaps in that sense to
claim omniscience. As for the phrase ὁ αὐτός, it is in
fact Socrates who at Hipp. Min. 367cd discusses ὁ αὐτός;
Hippias is portrayed as conceding the point only very
grudgingly--and apart from the repeated phrase ὁ αὐτός
the subject-matter has no further apparent relationship
to that of Δ. Λ. 8.1. The reading of Δ. Λ. 8.8 in
terms of action or abstention from action is based upon
an unfortunate reading μέν (for MSS. μή), over which DK
have misled a generation of readers.[77] As for Socrates' assertion of ignorance (Hipp. Min. 372b), it serves
as a riposte to a claim to any degree of knowledge;
nothing in the text suggests that it is a reply to an
omniscience-claim on Hippias' part. And a belief in

individual and really distinct entities (see Δ. Λ. 2.26) is part of the common-sense heritage of the Greeks; to single out Hippias (rather than, say, Socrates) as its star exponent seems gratuitous.

Turning to Untersteiner, one finds that the application of Ockham's razor pares the claim that the Δ. Λ. embodies a set of Hippian counter-theses to a fairly diminutive size. <u>Hipp. Mai</u>. 301b, for example-- a crucial piece of evidence in Untersteiner's case--is, even if for the sake of argument one accepts that it accurately reflects the views of the historical Hippias, far from obviously to be interpreted in the way Untersteiner interprets it.[78] If, as I think, Untersteiner is wrong on this point, not much else remains apart from the evidence provided by Δ. Λ. 8 and 9. To suggest, for example, that certain statements "could" depend on (<u>inter alios</u>) Hippias hardly counts as a serious argument until such-and-such a degree of <u>likelihood</u> of the possibility is offered; and Hippias surely did not have the monopoly of such everyday terms as πρᾶγμα. Similarly, to dub 6.7 ff. as Hippian (with at best a coincidence with certain Protagorean arguments) on grounds of the Gorgian-Hippian nature of the preceding chapters seems to be a flagrant <u>petitio principii</u>, even if one concedes that what has gone before is indeed Gorgian-Hippian; Untersteiner, under the guise of sound methodology, is superimposing a pattern of argument on the text, not discovering one in it.

In discussing chapters 8 and 9 Untersteiner appears at first sight to be on a little firmer ground. Hippias' own prodigious memory, and his stress on

memory-training, is well known,[79] and his wide-ranging
intellectual interests might just conceivably have led
critics (Socrates? See Pl. Euthyd. 293-297) or over-
zealous disciples (the author of the Δ. Λ.?) to take
his (supposed) arguments for polymathy as arguments for
omniscience. What one cannot do, however, as far as I
can see, is to equate claims to polymathy and claims to
omniscience (as Untersteiner appears to do), and argue
that Δ. Λ. 8 is eo ipso Hippian. By reading Hipp. Min.
363d1-4 as an omniscience-claim one could perhaps argue
that it was Hippias himself who made the equation, but
the passage in question seems much more likely to be an
assertion that he treats his audience fairly.[80] As for
Δ. Λ. 9 and the question of μνήμη, Hippias certainly
seems to be the outstanding candidate,[81] if the author
is to be credited with a direct source for his assertions. But why he should be the unique source is not
clear; our testimonia talk only of his prodigious
powers of memory, not of his uniqueness in this regard.

We are left with the linguistic evidence. As I
have suggested already, Untersteiner's interpretation
of Hipp. Mai. 301b is a dubious one, and shaky grounds
for the assertion of πρᾶγμα (Δ. Λ. passim) and σῶμα
(Δ. Λ. 2.1) as 'technical terms' drawn from the
philosophy of Hippias. Words, however, like καινός
(6.1), ἁρμονία (5.12), and ἐξεύρημα (9.1) have a better
claim to the title (see the nn. of Untersteiner ad loc.),
and seem to be much more forcible evidence of Hippian
influence. But their combined strength adds up only to
the fairly modest conclusion that Hippias was one (and
merely one) of a number of thinkers who perhaps influenced the author of the Δ. Λ., and even then (apart from

section 9) his contribution seems to rise little above
the level of verbal echoes. Pace Dupréel and Untersteiner, the Hippias of the Hipp. Mai. and Hipp. Min.
emerges as no philosopher at all; his claim to fame is
founded on his polymathy, rather, his skill in geome-
try[82] and astronomy,[83] and his discovery of mnemonic
techniques. If he had anything of any philosophical
note to say, it had the distinction of being completely
ignored by his contemporaries and successors.

3. Gorgias

Gorgias, like Hippias, has been frequently
credited with influencing particular arguments in the
Δ. Λ., especially in the matter of the concept of καιρός;
but the more recent claims of Dupréel and Untersteiner
(see above, 59) that the entire set of (relativistic)
'theses' of the Δ. Λ. (found with clarity in chapter
1-6) are Gorgian in spirit and content is something new.
      Acceptance or rejection of their view is likely
to turn on one's acceptance or rejection of a generalized 'doctrine of καιρός' in Gorgias: as Untersteiner
puts it, "La morale, l'estetica e la retorica di Gorgia
si fondano tutte su καιρός." That Gorgias had a doctrine
of καιρός in the matter of rhetoric seems clear enough
(Gorgias A 1a, B 13 DK[6]); the καιρός in question will
presumably have been the 'appropriate moment' for the
use of particular rhetorical tropes, flourishes, and the
like. Whether this was extended by him to some all-
embracing philosophical Weltanschauung, however, remains
in my estimation unproven (for some ancient evidence see
Müller 148, n.5). Untersteiner (ad 2.19) following
Rostagni, sees the "Pythagorean" doctrine of καιρός as
a "law of the universe" in which <τὸ> δίκαιον (=καιρός

in another guise) is the blending of opposites by ἁρμονία.
This "law of the universe" Untersteiner equates with
the δίκη or ἀνάγκη of which Aeschylus speaks, and the
latter he takes to involve a doctrine (propounded at
Choe. 461) that "the world is irrational." The conclusion of this (quasi-sorites) argument, he continues, is
that the doctrine of καιρός and the doctrine of the
world's irrationality are one and the same--and are in
fact precisely the 'καιρός' doctrine of Gorgias.

But these arguments are disconcertingly thin.
Rostagni's main sources for a "Pythagorean" doctrine of
καιρός are Dionysius of Halicarnassus De Comp. Verb. 45,
6 ff. Usener-Radermacher and Iamblichus Vita Pythag.
130, 180-182. Of these sources, however, only the
second can be clearly said to venture beyond the sphere
of rhetoric, with its suggestion that in the realm of
human relationships εὐκαιρία and δίκαιον are allied
concepts. Aristotle Met. 1078b 21-23 is, pace Rostagni,
no help to his case; if καιρός, τὸ δίκαιον, and γάμος
are on a par, they are on a conceptual par only, in
that for the Pythagoreans all were reducible to numbers
anyway. In no other sense does Aristotle suggest that
in their eyes καιρός and τὸ δίκαιον were equatable,
still less that καιρός was a "law of the universe." As
for Untersteiner's assertion, on the strength of a
single line of the Choephoroe, that for Aeschylus δίκη/
ἀνάγκη were equated with "irrationality" (or for that
matter his assertion that the Pythagorean δίκαιον and
the Aeschylean δίκη are to be equated), few will be
persuaded by such attempts to excavate 'doctrine' from
the works of playwrights, and fewer still by the doctrine
here excavated. All that has been established with any

firmness, it seems to me, is that the Pythagoreans had
a doctrine of the alliance of εὐκαιρία to δίκαιον in
the matter of human relationships; whether Gorgias himself went so far does not on present evidence appear to
admit of demonstration. The same would appear to be
true a fortiori of the supposedly Gorgian equation
καίρος = δίκαιον = δίκη = the 'irrationality' of the
cosmos.

Turning to other putatively Gorgian elements in
the Δ. Λ., the reference at Δ. Λ. 1 is surely to philosophers such as Protagoras; the existence of a set of
"δισσοὶ λόγοι etici" penned by Gorgias (Untersteiner
[I] 280-281, and n.10) and expounding a "situation
morality" (Dupréel 353) is pure speculation. At 2.19 we
have, in the fragment of poetry there quoted, a generalized doctrine of καιρός, but as far as I can see no
"perfetta corrispondenza con la dottrina gorgiana di
καιρός" (Untersteiner ad loc.; cf. Dupréel 90), unless
of course one has already previously accepted Untersteiner's arguments attributing to him a "doctrine of
καιρός" far transcending rhetoric. As for Δ. Λ. 3, the
chapter as a whole may indeed derive directly from
Xenophon Inst. Cyr. 1.6.26 ff., as Nestlé argues ([I]
39; see Untersteiner ad loc.), but it seems rash to
conclude, as does Nestlé (ibid.), on the strength of
Gorgias frgs. 8 and 23 (DK[6]), that it is Gorgias who is
the source both of the Cyropaedeia passage and of Δ. Λ.
3, since in fr. 23 the "justified deception" relates
specifically to the writing of tragedy, and in fr. 8
the supposed reference to wrestling turns on a highly
unconvincing MS. emendation (αἴσιμα, with Bernays and
Untersteiner, seems much more plausible). To call Δ.

Λ. 3 a "proof" that in the Λ. Λ. the "theses" are Gorgian
(Untersteiner, n. ad Λ. Λ. 3.1) goes far beyond the
evidence--and is the odder for Untersteiner's own denial
of a crucial element in Nestlé's argument, the reading
πλίγμα for αἴσιμα. Finally, Chapter 4, On Truth and
Falsity, Dupréel (92; cf. 296-297) links very unconvinc-
ingly with the Gorgian περὶ τοῦ μὴ ὄντος. Referring to
parts 2 and 3 of Gorgias' treatise, where a distinction
is drawn between what is 'thought' and what is 'given',
ab extra, he claims to find in Λ. Λ. 4 an analogous
distinction between discourse as such and its truth or
falsity. In his own words, "le discours a un sens indé-
pendamment de sa valeur de vérité ou de fausseté." But
Λ. Λ. 4 in fact makes no such claim. All that is
suggested is that verifiable propositions are either
true or false, depending on context; they have no further,
'independent', sense. Nor is it easy to detect a
"Gorgian" doctrine of "the power of λόγος" at 4.8-9
(Dupréel 296-297); what we seem to have rather is a
common or garden 'correspondence' theory of truth.

When all the (supposed) evidence is considered,
the Gorgian influence on the Λ. Λ. that has any serious
degree of likelihood turns out to be very little. At
3.10 the reference to ἀπάτη in τραγωδοποιία is very
likely Gorgian,[84] and the evidence of Meno 95c suggests
that Gorgias figured among the proponents of the thesis
of Λ. Λ. 6,[85] though not that he was the unique proponent thereof, or that the arguments propounded in the
Λ. Λ. were necessarily his particular arguments. And
that, it seems, is about as far as the reasonably solid
evidence allows us to go.

4. Socrates

"Socraticae disciplinae in toto libro certum nullum vestigium", says Wilamowitz ([II] 627; cf. his comments in [I] 295), and more recently Müller (148, n.2). If "certum" means "demonstrably proven", the statement is incontrovertible, but that does not mean that the case is thereby completely closed. Whether the Δ. Λ. was written before the death of Socrates or not, the question still remains whether we do not find in it echoes of Socratic conversational style (e.g., at 1.12 ff.) (Ramage 418 ff.; Kranz 231-232; cf. Taylor 110, 118-121) and/or of philosophical views that are universally accepted as specifically, if not uniquely, Socratic/Platonic (e.g., those found at 4.5) (Taylor passim; Kranz 230-232). The evidence is partly structural, partly linguistic, and partly comparative. On structural grounds it has been argued that 1.12 ff. is 'Socratic' in mood and form, however primitive and unelaborated the expression, and perhaps also 5.9; on linguistic grounds it has been argued that there are echoes of favourite Socratic/Platonic terms at 4.5 (παρῇ), 5.1 ff. (μαίνεσθαι, σωφρονεῖν), and 9.1 (φιλοσοφίαν τε καὶ σοφίαν); on comparative grounds it has been argued that we have 'Socratic' views at 1.17 (οὐ λέγω τί ἐστι), 2.28, 3.17 (poets write to give pleasure, not for truth's sake), 3.2 ff. (deception and the telling of untruths are on occasion justifiable), 4.6 (the 'Liar Paradox' and the question of credibility), 5.15 ("alles (Da)Sein ist an eine Qualität geknüpft" [Kranz 231]), 6 (the problem of the teachability or otherwise of ἀρετή), 7.1 (the deplorable nature of the system of election by lot), 8.4 (the importance, in the different

τέχναι, of the possession of specific knowledge), and
8.9 (knowledge of A entails knowledge of not-A).

To take the comparative evidence first. The
phrase οὐ λέγω κτλ at 1.17 does not appear to be a
generalization (of the form: "I cannot say what the good
is"), but rather an attempt to demarcate once more the
lines of the discussion, in keeping with 1.1; the nature
of τὸ ἀγαθόν, says the author, is a question beyond the
bounds of the present debate. If this interpretation
is correct, nò particular views, Socratic or otherwise,
on essences can be inferred. At 2.28, 3.2, and 3.17,
by contrast, we read statements which other sources (see
nn. ad loc.) strongly suggest to be Socratic/Platonic
(though not necessarily, of course, uniquely so), and
the same would appear to be true of 7.1 ff., 8.4, and
possibly 8.9. As far as 4.6 goes, Socrates had no doubt
felt the force of the 'Liar Paradox' in some philosophically uncomplicated way (see n. ad loc.), but the precise and involved argument of the author of the Δ. Λ.
seems to reflect some other, more elaborate source.
5.15 is probably not Socratic at all; Kranz' translation
is, as far as I can see, backed by no linguistic evidence. As for chapter 6, this has a number of precise
affinities with Plato's Protagoras and Meno in particular, but the arguments that are readily recognizable
seem to be those of Protagoras, rather than those of
Socrates (cf. Heinimann 108, n.14). If the chapter is
'Socratic', it is so in the less strong sense that it
no doubt catches, in the way the Protagoras and Meno
also do, though with less grace and style than they, the
cut-and-thrust of the debate on the topic that exercised
sophists and the Socratic circle alike in the late fifth

century. As far as linguistic evidence goes, that of 5.1 ff. and 9.1 is particularly weak, in that the terminology in question is hardly specifically Socratic, even if it is conceded to be Socratic; and the term φιλοσοφία in particular may only be Platonic (see n. on 9.1, fin.). Stronger evidence, in the estimation of Kranz (230-231), is the use of the verb παρεῖναι (4.5) for the relationship of τὸ ψεῦδος and τὸ ἀλαθές to a λόγος (cf. 4.9, ἀναμέμεικται). The earliest known use of the verb in this sense outside of the Δ. Λ. is found in Socrates' attempt in the Phaedo to explain true predication (see Taylor 109, n.1), where he notoriously concludes that in true propositions subject is related to predicate as particular to Form. Even without a fully-fledged Theory of Forms (which may, of course, have been a specifically Platonic doctrine), however, the notion of παρουσία as a description of the relationship of universal to particular could still perhaps have been proffered by the historical Socrates, since from the beginning he never seems to have doubted the 'absolute' nature of universals (whatever might be said further about their ontological status). So he could just perhaps have been the originator of the Phaedo-like approach to the problem of predication (this time in the matter of both true and false propositions) found in Δ. Λ. 4 (Taylor 109-110). However, the possibility remains that παρουσία was a term that Socrates himself took over from contemporary thought (perhaps even from the author of the Δ. Λ.), as I have suggested in my note ad loc. The truth in the matter we simply do not and perhaps never shall know, and Kranz's claim should be viewed with caution.

The 'structural' evidence seems to me thin. As
Ramage admits (419), the passage 1.12 ff. is "in certain
respects . . . anything but Socratic"; answers to questions are of little interest to the author (so much so
that they are sometimes simply omitted), and they are
undoubtedly "obvious and colorless". I see no reason
therefore for thinking that a bit of dialogue of this
nature should be based upon a memory of some Socratic
conversation; there are no grounds for believing that
Socrates had the monopoly of philosophical conversation
(still less of such dull conversation) in late fifth-
century Athens. One is probably on safer grounds in
attributing the dialectical technique that is found both
in extenso in the Socratic dialogues and here breviter
in the Δ. Λ. to some common source, such as Protagoras
himself (see Gulley 30), who in the words of Diogenes
Laertius τὸ Σωκρατικὸν εἶδος τῶν λόγων πρῶτος ἐκίνησε
(9.53). If Diogenes is correct, one might hypothesize
that the Τέχνη ἐριστικῶν contained lengthy illustrative
passages of conversation between sophists and their
interlocutors and/or that the Ἀντιλογίαι was set out in
the form of a philosophical disputation. The point, if
true, would fit Protagoras' writings only, if Plato is
to be our guide; as Ramage rightly points out, in the
Protagoras the sophist shows little taste for the
dialectical method in public confrontations, in spite of
Socrates' kind remark to the contrary (329b).

I conclude from this discussion, with Trieber
and many others, that the major influence on the author
of the Δ. Λ. is most likely to have been Protagoras,[86]
with some minor influence of Hippias, some even more

minor influence of Gorgias, and the possibility of some
Socratic influence. He was also clearly well-read in
recent ethnographical lore, though the exact sources
cannot be pin-pointed (see my nn. ad 2.9 and passim).
On a possible allusion to Prodicus see n. ad 5.11
[ἁρμονίας κτλ]. As for Platonic dialogues, I see no
evidence (pace Freeman [I] 417, n.a1) that the author
was specifically influenced by any one of them.

5. The Author's Putative Philosophical Position

It has been said that, for all the trappings of
impartiality, the author of the Δ. Λ. cannot disguise
the fact that in the opening chapters at least he himself invariably backs the counter-thesis (or what I have
called in the Commentary the 'difference' thesis) (Joël
1.401, Gomperz [II] 191-192, Levi [I] 296-297, Dupréel
206, Untersteiner ad loc.). As evidence for this Untersteiner cites the fact that in the first four chapters
the counter-thesis "è sempre quello più ampio". But
apart from its basic implausibility (since when has an
argument's length anything to do with its acceptability?),
the argument is in fact false on factual grounds: in
each of the four opening chapters it is in fact the
thesis (in Untersteiner's words the "relativist" case,
or what in the Commentary I have called the 'identity'
thesis) which occupies the larger volume of space (!),
as a glance at the DK text makes clear.

A further argument in favour of the view that
the author invariably backs the counter-thesis (Levi
[I] 296) is the position of the counter-thesis--i.e.,
second in sequence; this is thought to be significant,
in that it is that particular view which as a result is

invariably left ticking over in the reader's mind.
There may be something in this, but against it one
could point out that the thesis invariably propounds
views the factual accuracy of which is open to testing
and observation; and it seems to me very possible that
part of the author's aim is to show that the supposed
counter-thesis more often than not possesses whatever
strength it does thanks to a witting or unwitting misunderstanding of the original thesis--and the point will
be made with particular clarity if the thesis is stated
first in sequence.

Another suggestion (Gulley 25) is that the
author is simply out to imitate Protagoras in "making
the weaker argument the stronger" (Ar. Rhet. 1402a 23).
There may well be something in this, too--particularly
if one follows Levi in stressing the invariable position
of the 'difference' thesis--but we are now a long way
from earlier suggestions that the author 'backs' the
'difference' thesis. On the contrary, the author sees
that the 'difference' thesis is the weaker of the two
(not least because it is based upon a misunderstanding
of the identity-thesis), but for perfectly respectable
propaedeutic reasons (as it seems to me) makes out the
strongest case he can for it; but even that is not to
"make the weaker argument the stronger".

What can be made of specific affirmations in
the Δ. Λ. is unclear. The use of the first person cannot really serve as evidence either way, since it is
constantly used (no doubt as an item in the psychologi-
cal warfare that went with antilogical treatises of
this sort) in defence of thesis and counter-thesis
alike (see 2.18 ff., and passim). There are, however,

stronger statements in favour of both thesis and counter-thesis. To take the counter-thesis first: at 1.11 the original thesis is said to be "astonishing" (θαυμαστόν), and the author appears to throw his weight behind the counter-thesis (ἐγὼ δὲ καὶ αὐτὸς κτλ). The same astonishment (ἐγὼ θαυμάζω) over the thesis is expressed at 2.26, and at 5.6 the proponents of the thesis are flatly said to be in error (οὐκ ὀρθῶς λέγοντι). Similarly, at 6.7 the thesis is said to be "simple-minded" (εὐήθη), and at 6.13 the arguments in its favour are dubbed "insufficient" (οὐκ ἀποχρῶνταί μοι κτλ). At 2.2 the verb πειρασεῦμαι suggests that the thesis is something it takes a conscious effort to defend, and at 3.2 the phrase πρῶτον . . . λεξῶ suggests the fulfilment of a chore--i.e., the defence of the thesis as part of the basic, antilogical structure of the treatise.

Against this, the verb ποτιτίθεμαι ("I side with") of the thesis at 1.2 looks very strong, as does a claim at 2.20 to have "demonstrated" (ἀπέδειξα) the thesis of that chapter. Similar strong claims appear to be found at 4.2 (κἀγὼ τόνδε λέγω) and at 3.7 (ἐγὼ μὲν γὰρ οὐ δοκῶ). The verb πειρᾶσθαι, it should be added--suggesting an effort on the author's part to complete a philosophical assignment, rather than to outline strongly-held beliefs--is used again at 1.17, but this time of the counter-thesis! As for chapter 6, it could be argued that, even if the author opts fiercely for the counter-thesis in this particular instance, little is proved, since it differs in kind from chapters one to five, where it is a 'difference' thesis and an identity-thesis that are in question. As it happens, however, it is made clear at 6.13 that the

76

author is simply doing his best to show the inadequacy
of the arguments used to back the thesis: as he puts it
trenchantly, "I am not saying that ἀρετή is teachable"
(οὐ λέγω ὡς διδακτόν ἐστιν).

What if anything is one to conclude from this?
One possibility is that the author is so "talentlos"
(DK) that he himself fails to see the difference between
an identity-statement and a predicative statement, and
thus fails to notice that the (extreme) thesis attacked
is seldom, if ever, the (moderate) thesis that has just
been defended; in other words, he fails to see the
difference between a genuine and a bogus antithesis.
Another possibility is that he thinks he sees strengths
and weaknesses in the arguments of both thesis and
counter-thesis alike, in spite of their ultimately non-
antithetical nature, and for this reason, while putting
up the best case for both, is unwilling himself to opt
for either. A third possibility is that he is perfectly
aware of the difference between identity-statements and
predicative statements, and perfectly aware that the
(moderate) thesis propounded is not in any sense weak,
but is in fact readily verifiable and in itself unimpeachable. The pseudo-counter-thesis, which is in fact
the antithesis to a thesis never propounded, and is
itself a chaotic jumble of good and bad arguments, is
presented for its propaedeutic value, to instruct the
beginner in the detection of fallacious reasoning. If
the latter possibility is a genuine one, as I think it
is, the author of the Δ. Λ. is not the philosophical
dunce that he has sometimes been made out to be. But
one could not thereby infer that his philosophical
'views' coincide with the 'theses', and only the theses,

here presented. He may quite possibly have believed
that on any given topic two λόγοι (thesis and supposed
counter-thesis) could very well be put forward, each
being, in its own reference-frame, 'true' because each
beams a different search-light on the real; by the
principle of non-contradiction, however, two genuinely
antithetical statements will not at the same time, in
the same circumstances, and relative to the same state
of affairs, both be true (see on this Versényi 21).

Given the lack of convincing evidence one way
or the other, the reader must arbitrate the matter for
himself. In this edition I have stressed the third
possibility, on the simple grounds that it saves the
phenomena as well as any other and at the same time
credits the author with a mild degree of intelligence.

6. The Unity of the Treatise

A glance at the Δ. Λ. reveals at the outset one
disconcerting feature: its (supposedly) 'antilogical'
quality is apparently confined to the first four chapters, with perhaps a truncated example in the fifth.
After that we have a discussion of a well-known topos
in chapter 6 ("Is ἀρετή teachable?"), a strong attack
on the lot-system (chapter 7), an account of the qualities of the paradigmatic orator-statesman (chapter 8),
and a short essay on memory-training (chapter 9). This
has led some to claim that the Δ. Λ. proper consists of
the first four (or perhaps five) chapters only; the
rest is a later, unrelated addition, perhaps by the same
author or perhaps by another. Or the whole thing could
be just a disconnected compilation drawn from various
authors (Freeman [I] 417). But these objections seem

to me fundamentally misconceived. As Taylor (128)
points out, we do not actually know the 'purpose' of
the Δ. Λ.; it can only be at best inferred from the
text itself, and then with diffidence. It is also perhaps unfortunate that most scholars insist on entitling
it the Dissoi Logoi; this is merely a catch-phrase
based on the opening words of the treatise as we have
it. So a second argument, to the effect that because
the first four chapters are in the form of thesis and
counter-thesis the whole must have been planned in such
a form but broke down (either in the author's own mind
or during the period of textual transmission, or in
some measure both) around chapter five is another argument without evidence one way or the other, and the
possibility of either one's being valid should be con-
templated only if arguments for the basic unity of the
treatise--in form and content--are seen to be untenable.

These arguments--well propounded by Kranz (226-
227)[87]--are as follows: the treatise is undoubtedly
structured antithetically in its opening chapters (1-5).
Chapter 6, however, is also antithetical, though this
time the antithesis does not consist of a (supposed)
identity-thesis and a 'difference' thesis. And its
clear connection with 5 lies in the fact that the concepts of σοφία and ἀρετή were very much linked in the
Greek mind (and in the case of one prominent contemporary
thinker--Socrates--perhaps even thought to be identical);
the move from the difference (if any) between σοφία and
ἀμαθία (chapter 5) to the much-discussed question of the
teachability or otherwise of ἀρετή (chapter 6) seems a
particularly natural one. And the same can be said of
chapters 7, 8, and 9. Anyone interested in σοφία/ἀρετή

in public life, as we can assume the Δ. Λ.'s first
readers were, would find it natural to go on from the
question of the teachability of ἀρετή to the question
of the σοφία or otherwise of choosing public officials
by the lot-system (chapter 7), the question of what
constitutes σοφία/ἀρετή in the paradigmatic orator-
statesman (chapter 8), and the role of memory-training
in the schooling of such a statesman (chapter 9). On
this reading, the author is discussing, in what seems
to him the most appropriate manner, topics of current
interest among thinking people in the matter of public
and private morality, and the just and efficient run-
ning of a πόλις. The first six chapters lend themselves
most naturally to an exposition in terms of thesis and
counter-thesis, on the simple grounds that in such
matters articulate cases for and against particular
propositions have been put forward by φιλοσοφοῦντες,
and the author is presumably doing his best to sketch,
for his Doric-speaking audience, the intellectual give-
and-take on such matters to be found in some important
cultural centre such as Athens. The same can even be
said for chapter 7, though it looks at this stage as
though the author's own views are starting to get the
better of him (as seems also very possible in the case
of chapters 8 and 9; see Untersteiner [II] 169, following Kranz). However, it seems not impossible that in
this particular matter he genuinely felt that all that
the proponents of the thesis ever did say in its favour
was that it was ἀγαθὸν καὶ δαμοτικὸν κάρτα (7.5), and
that to outline their argument so summarily was not in
fact to misrepresent it. In which case it would be
fair to say that here too we are looking at another

instance of thesis and counter-thesis, no different in
kind from those that preceded. Chapter 8 is less easy
to account for, in that it is hard to believe that the
author had not heard counter-arguments to so paradoxical
a thesis. On reflection, however, it is perhaps not
wholly beyond belief. A near-contemporary Platonic
dialogue, the Euthydemus, also offered no easy answers
to similar claims to omniscience, stemming from a
similar set of equivocations. So it seems not impossible
that the author, never perhaps having heard anyone say
that the claim was based largely on an unequivocal use
of the words πᾶς, ὀρθῶς, and δεῖ, felt that the para-
doxical-looking thesis was in fact soundly based.
Alternatively, he may have felt that the ambiguities
embedded in it (and sensed by him to be embedded in it)
would have the same propaedeutic value for his readers
as the technique of thesis and counter-thesis on other
topics--i.e., they would generate serious thought on an
important matter. (A third possibility--an irresponsible
'eristic' thesis for its own sake--seems to me so dis-
sonant with the basically serious philosophical tone of
the rest of the treatise that it can be passed over.)
Those who believe, with Diels, that the author of the
Δ. Λ. is "talentlos" will probably opt for the first
alternative; but the second, it seems to me, cannot be
discounted. No one has ever believed that the sophists
in Plato's Euthydemus are fooled by their own bad arguments; the whole point is that they are smart enough
not to be fooled, though not perhaps (in Socrates' eyes)
philosophically astute enough or morally sound enough to
abandon sophistry for Socraticism. If anyone, they
would no doubt have exploited the third possibility

mentioned above. But the author of the Δ. Λ. differs
from them in being both clever and apparently serious,
and for this reason I am myself inclined to favour the
possibility of a worthwhile propaedeutic purpose in the
writing of Δ. Λ. 8. Such a purpose would, of course,
be wholly compatible with the further apparent fact
that as the treatise progresses the author warms to his
subject, and his own views start to emerge more and
more clearly (especially in chapters 7 to 9). It is a
feature which all lecturers among the readership of
this book will recognize that they share or have at one
time or another shared with our unknown sophistic author!

Notes

[1] Die Fragmente der Vorsokratiker[6], edd. H.
Diels and W. Kranz (Dublin/Zürich 1966) 2. 405-416.

[2] Op. cit. 617.

[3] Stiftsbibliothek, Zeitz. This MS. Fabricius
consulted directly. See edit., 617.

[4] Bodleian Library, Oxford. This MS. Fabricius
knew only indirectly (see Kochalsky 5).

[5] 1.12 ἕροιτο Meib. ἄροιτο Ciz.; 1.16 ἀσθενέουσι
ταῦτα ποιὲν Meib. ἀσθενεῦντι ταῦτα ποιεῦν Ciz.; 2.1 τὸ
πρᾶγμα Meib. τὸ σῶμα Ciz.; ἐγκαταφαγὲν Meib. πιὲν καὶ
φαγὲν Ciz.

[6] 5.9 ταῦτα N. Meib. (in vers. lat. autem
'eadem') ταὐτά Fabr.; 2.19 ὄψει Meib. ὄψῃ Fabr.

[7] 3.5 totam civitatem expugnare N. captam urbem
reddere libertati Fabr.

[8] 1.8 τὰ νεωστί N. (in n.) τὰ νεότατι Fabr. (in

textu idem N.); 2.28 ἄν καλόν N. δ' ἄν καλόν Fabr.; 3.14
καταυτόν N. κατά ταύτόν Fabr.; 4.2 τόν δέ λόγω N. τῶδε
λόγω Fabr.; 4.4 Μίμας N. μύστας Fabr.; 5.9 ἐπ' ἄρτεος
(in textu) N. ἐπ' ἀργεος Fabr.; 5.15 ἐστί N. ἐντι Fabr.;
ἤν O [ἤν] St N. ἤεν Fabr.; 6.12 οὖ N. (in not.) οὐ
Fabr.; οὕτως περί N. οὕτως. περί Fabr.
In each instance the requisite change in the Latin
translation is made.

[9] E.g., 5.3 μέζον καί μῆόν; 6.12 ἐντι.

[10] E.g., 1.2 ἐπιμελής (N. in not.); 1.5 κατέσθεσθαι; 4.4 ἄν λέγοιμεν (N. in not.); 4.4 ἀλαθές (N. in
not.).

[11] E.g., 3.11 βιαίως (susp. Fabr. in not.);
3.14 κατά ταύτόν; 3.16 καττωϋτό; 4.1-2 τῶδε λόγω; 4.4
μύστας; 4.6 ἀλαθές τι πόκα; 5.15 ἐντι; 6.3 εἶεν (=ἤεν,
ut vid. e not.); 8.12 ὅς γάρ.
The readings at 3.11 and 3.16 are, however, attributed
to Heringa, without mention of Fabricius.

[12] 1.8 τά νεώτατα; 1.8 ᾇ τοι; 2.26 ἅ τις καλά
νομίζει, λαμβάνεν, πάντα καί (sic punct.); 5.9 καί ἔτι
ἄτερος ὁ λόγος (in not., in text. autem om. ὁ); 5.9
πότερον ἐν δέοντι; 6.12 ἐντι (antea autem Fabr.); 6.12
ἤλεγται; 7.2 καττωϋτό.

[13] 2.17 ἔρια; 2.19 διαθρῶν.

[14] 2.13 κανών; 2.18 καλλειφθῆμεν; 3.11 βιαίως
(antea autem susp. Fabr.); 3.16 καττωϋτό (antea autem
Fabr.); 5.12 σᾶκος καί σάκος (in text.).

[15] See his notes ad loc. on 1.7 καί τοῦτο δέ;
1.7 καί τοί ἄλλοι κτλ; 1.13 τῶς συγγενέας ἤδη κτλ; 1.14
ἄγε καί δή κτλ; 1.16 τοῦτο γάρ τοῖς ἀσθενέουσι κτλ; 2.2
κάγώ πειρασεῦμαι κτλ; 2.6 χρυσία περιάπτεσθαι; 2.11
λαβόντι (ad fin.); 3.8 τά δέ κοινά κτλ; 4.1 ὧν ὁ μέν
φατί; 4.1 τοί δέ τόν αύτόν κτλ; 4.8 ούκῶν διαφέρει κτλ;
6.7 ἅ καί αὐτός κτλ; 7.4 τώς τοξότας κτλ; 8.1 ἀνδρός
. . . καί ἀλέγεσθαι; 8.6 περί πάντων κτλ; 9.2 ἐάν
προσέχῃς κτλ; 9.5 πυριλάμπη.

[16] E.g., 1.8 ᾇ τοι; 1.13 καὶ μεγάλα. ἄρα κτλ; 2.18 καλλειφθῆμεν; 2.19 διαθρῶν; 2.26 λέγοντι; 2.26 ἃ τις καλά κτλ (ut punct. Koen) vers. North autem in not.; 2.28 οἳ; 3.11 βιαίως; 3.16 καττωῦτό (vers. North in not.); 5.9 καὶ ἔτι ἅτερος <ὁ?> λόγος; 5.9 πότερον ἐν δέοντι; 7.2 καττωῦτό.

[17] 3.11 καὶ τὸ βίᾳ ῥέξαι τοῦτο δικαιότατον vi facere hoc certe res magis aequa fuit; 3.14 κατὰ ταὐτόν eodem modo; 4.1-2 αὖ κἀγώ. τῷδε λόγῳ* igitur ipse illud primum ajo; 4.4 μύστας* initiatus; 9.3 μελέται, αἴ κα ἀκούσῃς si mediteris assidue audiendo. (Asterisks indicate a difference in text between Meibom and Fabricius, as well as a difference in translation.)

[18] 5.15 ergo; 6.3 posset; 6.11 evaserit.

[19] 3.5 captam civitatem reddere libertati.

[20] 1.8 τὰ νεώτατα πρῶτον ἐρῶ ut recentissima primum commemorem; 2.17 ἔρια ἐργάζεσθαι lanificio operam dare; 6.12 οὐκὶ ἀκούομες non auscultantes; 6.13 ἤλεγταί μοι κτλ si sermonem quem primum dixi, redargui, principium, medium ac finem habes.

[21] At 1.14 it is not clear whether 'aliud' has been accidentally omitted from his translation, but it seems probable, given that he has retained the phrase ἄλλο τι, though changing the punctuation of the sentence.

[22] 1.8 νεώτατα; 1.16 καὶ κακόν; 2.17 ἔρια; 2.18 κα λειφθῆμεν; 2.19 διαθρῶν; 2.26 κα*; 3.11 βιαίως; 4.4 λέγοιμεν, μύστας, ἀλαθές; 4.6 ἀλαθῆ τις; 5.9 καὶ ἔτι ἅτερος κτλ; 6.12 ἐντι; 6.12 οὐκὶ ἀκούομες; 6.13 ἤλεγταί μοι; 7.2 καττωῦτό; 7.4 τυχών; 8.5 περὶ πάντων τῶν ἐόντων ἐντι*; 8.12 ἐπίσταται. (Asterisks indicate the occasions on which Mullach acknowledges his debt to Orelli; in all the other instances his acknowledgements to North, Koen, Valckenaer, etc., are clearly drawn from Orelli's notes.)

[23] 1.8 ἄν τοί Ἕλλανες; 1.14 ἄλλο τι ἢ κτλ; 2.11 παρά; 3.16 ἔξεστιν; 4.1 ἐν οἷς κἀγώ; 4.6 καὶ τὸ πρᾶγμα; 5.8 αἱ; 5.15 τῶ (= τῶς?), λέγοντας, ἔν τι;

6.7 ἅ ἕκαστος αὐτῶν; 9.2 δι' ὧ κτλ; 9.3 δεύτερον δὲ διὰ τῷ μελετᾶν; 9.5 πυριλάμπην.

[24] 1.6 ταῦτα, πάντα; 2.16 ἐργάσασθαι; 2.16 θέλοι; 2.27 ἄν; 2.28 καλὰ ἀπάγαγον; 2.28 αἰσχρὸν ἄγαγε; 3.15 ἀξιοῦντι; 3.16 τὸ αὐτό; 4.2 λέγεται; 4.6 ἂν εἴη; 4.6 ἀποκρίναιτό κα; 4.8 τοῖς δυνασταῖς; 5.3 ἂν εἴη; 5.5 ταὐτά; 5.6 τοὶ τοίνυν; 5.7 διαφέρει; 5.10 ποτιθεῖναι; 5.12 σακὸς καὶ σάκος; 5.14 ἂν εἴη; 5.15 ἦμεν ἔν; 6.3 ἦσαν; 6.8 ἦσαν; 6.11 ἔμαθε; 6.13 μέσον; 7.2 καὶ γὰρ; 7.2 ἂν ἐρωτῷη; 7.3 διακλαρώσομεν καὶ ἀναγκάσομεν; 8.3 λέγεν, καὶ περί; 8.6 δεῖ λέγεν; 8.6 [τὼς] διακωλύεν; 8.7-8 ἐκεῖνα δὲ πάντα πότε δεῖ πράσσεν ἐπιστασεῖται. διὰ τοῦτο χρή κἂν μὴ ἐπίστηται αὐλέν, σκοπὲν αἶκα δέῃ τοῦτο πράσσεν; 8.9 ἐτεροῖα; 8.12 εὐπετὴς <τούτῳ> ὁ λόγος; 8.13 ὡς δ' ἐν βραχεῖ εἰπέν; 9.2 τοιοῦτο; 9.4 ἔπειτα δ' εἰδῆς.

[25] For two among many examples see 1.14 and 1.17, and the more precise translation of διάλεξις as "disputatio" (in this he agrees with Fabricius; North, Meibom, and Orelli translate the term as "dissertatio").

[26] Throughout his notes he refers constantly to 'codd.' and 'cod.', meaning apparently "the (unemended) text printed by Orelli", rather than (as the unsuspecting might naturally take it) "manuscripts I have consulted" or "a manuscript I have consulted".

[27] ἐστί is printed by Stephanus, North, and Meibom. But if, on this occasion, Mullach has glanced at one or other of them, he has still omitted to look at Fabricius and Orelli. One suspects that the truth is much more simple: he simply misread Orelli, and then generalized from his (mis-) reading.

[28] See Weber (I) 33.

[29] Ibid.

[30] Ibid.

[31] Ibid.

32 6.9 ἔν<α> τιν<ά>; 6.11 κα πολλά.

33 See also Mutschmann 244, n.1; 277, n.1, and passim.

34 Mutschmann 244, n.1.

35 Mutschmann, ibid.; Diels, Fragmente³, introd. n. to Dialexeis.

36 DK⁶, introd. n. to Dialexeis.

37 In Fleckeisens Jahrb. Suppl.-Bd. 13, 543 ff. Surprisingly, Weber claims that his introduction of Doricisms has been made "mit schonender, vielleicht allzu schonender Hand hergestellt" (34), but his text belies the claim, as a cursory glance will quickly reveal.

38 Mutschmann 277, n.1.

39 See the Diels, Fragmente² (1907) app. crit. ad 1.7 καττωυτό (1st edit. καὶ τοῦτο), 3.11 βιαίως, 3.13 ὁμολογησοῦντι (1st edit. ὁμολογοῦντι), 7.2 ὀψοποιῇ.

40 According to Kranz (223), Diels and Wilamowitz established a text between them around 1900. It is to the conjectures of Wilamowitz that stem from around that date, or at any rate from after 1889, that Diels refers in his app. crit. (Weber's references to Wilamowitz, by contrast, are references to the Wilamowitz of the Commentariolum of 1889.)

41 See my article, "Matthew de Varis and the Dissoi Logoi", CQ 22.1 (1972) 195-198.

42 Mario Untersteiner (I) 148-191.

43 Jean-Paul Dumont, Les Sophistes (Paris 1969) 232-246.

44 Mind 77 (1968) 155-167; reprinted in The Older

Sophists, ed. Rosamond Kent Sprague (University of South
Carolina Press 1972) 279-293.

[45] For several much-inspected MSS. I have relied
on the collations of earlier scholars and editors of the
text: Fabricius, Blass, Schanz, Trieber, Weber, Diels,
Mutschmann, and Kochalsky. Fl.2, Yl.2, Vl.2, and T I
inspected personally, and M S E in microfilm.

[46] It is true that the MS. is quite late (1534)
and has proportionately more doricisms in it than any
other major MSS. except Pl.2 (suggesting that it may
have been largely 'edited' back into Doric), and the
fact that it reads ὁ αὐτός at 4.6 and καὶ ἀγαθὸν at 7.5
seems on the face of it good reason for locating it in
the group that I have dubbed ζ. Against this, however,
we must place the fact that it is no later than several
other good MSS. (B P2.4.6); that, proportionately speaking, it has no more doricisms than Pl.2, and in fact
rather less; and that several elementary possibilities
for scribal emendation in favour of Doric forms are
passed over (e.g., in the first three chapters alone,
2.7 ποιεῖν [Pl.2 ποιέν], 2.11 and 17 τοὺς [Pl.2 τὼς],
3.6 ἐπιορκεῖν [Pl.2 ἐπιορκέν], 3.17 ἡδονάς [Pl.2
ἀδονάς]). Secondly, if P3 belongs to a group descended
from the last hyparchetype, it is extremely difficult
to account for its unique Ionic form σοφίη at 5.7, 6.1,
and 6.7. And it is also--apart from the common reading
ποιεῦν at 1.16 (in all major MSS. except that of the
first family)--unique in all MSS. except P2 for its ευ-
form readings πειρασεῦμαι and ποιεῦντι (2.2, 2.28).
The latter two forms one could, no doubt, ascribe to
the emendational zeal of the scribe, Nicolaus Sophianus,
in the light of the earlier forms ποιεῦν (1.6) and
συγκαλεσεῦντες (2.26), though the existence of similar
ευ- forms in a MS. belonging to the first family--a
family that P3 is clearly unaware of--makes this hypothesis a weak one. What one surely cannot do, however, is
ascribe the three uses of the purely Ionic form σοφίη
to scribal emendation, without stretching credulity
beyond all limits. And yet it seems equally difficult
to ascribe them to γ or ζ either! For had they been
found in γ, it seems unimaginable that all three uses
would then have vanished without trace in ε, ζ, and η.
     These difficulties lead me to sympathize with
Weber, who placed P3--with a question mark--in the first
family, and Trieber, who did the same, though with care

to assert that its descent was not directly from the
archetype. But this cannot be right either. For P3
has lacunae at 1.3 and 2.13 that are found in all MSS.
except those of the first family! So I hypothesize
the existence of a small but important family, parented
by a MS. that I call β, which seems to have been the
closest approximation to α after δ and from which P3
was copied (with or without a little extra doricizing
on the part of Sophianus). Even by the time of β a
considerable amount of scribal atticization had no
doubt occurred, from which δ was still relatively free
(e.g., 1.1 τοί Pl.2 οἱ rel., 1.5 σίδαρον Pl σίδηρον
rel., 2.7 ποιέν Pl.2 ποιεῖν rel., 2.11 and 17 τὼς Pl.2
τοὺς rel., etc), and lacunae were starting to appear
(1.3, 2.13, and the three in chapter 8), but the crucial
ionicisms of 5.7, 6.1, and 6.7 were still there, as well
as a few specifically dialectal Doric ευ- forms. This
makes β in my estimation a crucial MS., and the fact
that it is written from β makes P3 (pace DK and Mutschmann; see my n.1 ad 5.7), along with Pl.2, one of the
three best sources we have for the text of the Δ. Λ.

[47] See esp. E. Zeller, Kl. Schr. 1 (Berlin 1910)
115-135, and on the Protagoras specifically, 120-122.

[48] Mazzarino's redating appears to be tentatively accepted by Martano (288); but he has no comment
on the worth of Mazzarino's arguments, other than to
say that he finds them "acute" (283, n.1).

[49] The date proposed by Th. Gomperz (Die Apolo-
gie der Heilkunst [Leipzig 1910] 153), somewhere between
the platonic and post-platonic epochs, must be rejected
(cf. Untersteiner [II] 168). As Pohlenz sees (72), 1.8
makes good sense if the document was written some time
between the end of the Peloponnesian War and the beginning of the Corinthian War (394).

[50] Some evidence for this possibility is the
fact that the Suda numbers among the writings of Sextus
of Chaeronea σκεπτικὰ βιβλία δέκα. See Mullach 2.
xxxiii.

[51] See Trieber 210, n.2.

[52] See Trieber 210, n.3.

[53] 150-151. See also Bergk (II) 120-121.

[54] For caustic (and deserved) criticism of the thesis see Bergk (II) 120-122.

[55] If 'Schuster' is understood in its particular sense, no conclusion at all can be drawn; if in its general sense (an 'incompetent'), we simply have a tautology.

[56] The view is accepted by Pohlenz, 77.

[57] See also A. Rüstow 25 f., with Gomperz's criticisms, (II) 179, n.366a; J. L. Fischer 36; K. Freeman (I) 417.

[58] Ibid. He also, it should be said, finds traces of the influence of Hippias (127).

[59] Untersteiner (I) 149; (II) 161-172; Dupréel, 190 ff. Cf. also Dal Pra 45. A slight variant is provided by Zeppi 132-134, who sees the treatise as a Hippian-inspired attack on Protagoras.

[60] Zeller (I) 177 (a compiler from the works of Protagoras); Zeller (II) 1333, n.1 (a compiler from "various Sophistic writings"); Nestlé 439 ff. (a compiler from various sophistic sources, pre-eminently Protagoras, Gorgias, and Hippias). For further refs. see Untersteiner (II) 170, n.3.

[61] It should be noticed, however, that Kranz does not think it possible to call the author an adherent of any particular 'school' of thought: "Vielmehr hat dieser Sophisten- und Sokratesschüler eine eigene selbständige Arbeit angefertigt, so wenig auch die Einzelgedanken auf eigenem Boden gewachsen sind."

[62] See also Minar 64, who calls the assertion of D. L. "highly improbable", and attributes it to "the popular re-action to the Pythagoreans."

^{63} E.g., σοφίη, κάρτα, εἶπαι, οἶδας, ζώειν, διαιρεῦμαι, ποτιτιθεῖ, etc.

^{64} E.g., ἐστι passim (elsewhere ἐντί); ἂν 3.2, 6.4, and perhaps 3.7, 4.2 (elsewhere κα). (The forms are also, of course, Ionic.)

^{65} ποιεῦν (1.6) and ἀξιδοντι (3.15) seem to me clearly scribal errors. See my nn. ad loc.

^{66} For evidence of Pythagorean opposition to the lot-system see D. L. 8.34, Iambl. V. P. 260, Rostagni 175-176; contra, however, Minar 64.

^{67} For a reply to the unconvincing suggestion (Bergk [II] 130-133, Nestlé 437) that the author was perhaps of Cyprian origin see Taylor 94, n.1. Gomperz, more convincingly, suggests Syracuse ([II] 151, n.321). Wilamowitz' suggestion ([V] 2. 432) that the author was from Cyrene is backed by no evidence.

^{68} While it is tempting to see in the Δ. Λ. one of those "Manuals of Eristic" of which Aristotle speaks (De Soph. El. 183b 37), this idea too must ultimately be rejected, on the grounds that only the first half really comes near fitting the description. Whatever the author's plans for a dispassionate pro/contra exposition, the plan appears to break down as he warms to his subject (see Gaiser 53)--and that, it seems to me, is very characteristic of a lecture (!), and perhaps a lecture prepared under certain pressures of time. As far as the aim of the lecture is concerned, I am tempted to agree with Gaiser (59) that it was to instruct the "uninitiate" (cf. 4.4) in the ἀρεταί, τέχναι, and σοφία involved in the life of a public speaker (see 7.1 ff., 8, 9). The technique of instruction is a series of mind-limbering exercises (Δ. Λ. 1-4), at which any future rhetorician will need to be adept, but gradually the tone becomes more openly didactic. As I have suggested above, what we seem to have in the Δ. Λ. is part of a set of extensive notes to the lecture, not really intended for publication. If the lecturer distributed copies of such notes to his audience (see Guthrie 3.316), it is easy to see how the treatise could have (accidentally) survived.

[69] The unpolished nature of the Δ. Λ. is, I think, self-evident. While it might plausibly be argued that the co-existence of forms like ἐστι/ἐντί and κα/ἄν stems rather from an atticizing MS. tradition than from the author's own carelessness, the tedious connective καίs and τοίνυνs were clearly there from the beginning (see esp. Δ. Λ. 1.3 ff.), as I think were features like the change of subject at 4.6. And the constant use of καττωὐτό suggests strongly that we are looking at short-hand versions of arguments that could be expanded on the appropriate occasion.

[70] For litt. on the subject see Zeller (II) 1. 1334, n., and Untersteiner (II) 170, n.3. Giannantoni's comment (262) that the "tono compilatorio" of the treatise "annulla il problema della ricerca delle fonti" is unacceptable.

[71] See below, n.87.

[72] See, e.g., Dümmler 250-251, 259, Trieber 236 ff., Rüstow 26, 58, Nestlé (II) 509, Taylor 127, Gomperz 172, 179, Pohlenz 77, Levi 300-301, Kranz 229.

[73] For Dupréel (192), Gorgias and Protagoras combined.

[74] At 1.11 πρᾶγμα simply means "reality", a word which subsequent discussion (both here and in the rest of the treatise) makes clear covers events, actions, and states of affairs. The word was very possibly used in the same 'general' sense by Protagoras (see Isoc. Helena 1, Diog. Laert. 9.51), and occurs frequently with the same wide extension in Plato; see, e.g., Pl. Euthyd. 283e9, 284d1, 286a5, 286a7, Protag. 349b3, 4, 349c1, 330c1 ff., and cf. Ar. Top. passim. At 5.10 τὰ πράγματα = "things", in the apparent sense of "meanings"; cf. the subsequent discussion (5.11-14).

[75] Dupréel's translation of the passage (211) is, as far as I know, unique. τί ἡ τὰ πάντα ἐστιν; he reads as predicative ("cet homme est-il une chose ou est-il toutes choses?"), and, apparently reading ὢν for ὧν in the final sentence, concludes: "si l'homme est

tout, il est en quelque façon". But in this he fails
to distinguish between πάντα and τὰ πάντα, and between
τί and ἕν τι, and there is no evidence from what has
preceded to suggest that the proponent of the thesis
of 5.5 is committed to the further, bizarre thesis that,
in existing at all, "quelque chose est tout" (in
another translation [95] Dupréel translates the clause
much more accurately as "puisqu'il a dit que toutes les
choses sont la même chose"; presumably in the former
instance he understood ταὐτά <ἧμεν> as predicative, when
an identity-assertion appears to be in fact in question).

[76] On the value or otherwise of Hipp. Mai. 301b
in particular see below, n.78.

[77] Nothing in the app. crit. suggests that μέν
is the emendation of Diels himself; the fact that all
the MSS. read μή is (astonishingly) passed over in
silence.

[78] Quite apart from the fact that Pl. Hipp. Mai.
301b has not won universal acceptance as a criticism
stemming from the genuine Hippias (DK[6] still exclude it;
for the status quaestionis see Untersteiner, Sofisti 8
[86] c2, n.), it seems much too strong to say that at
Δ. Λ. 1.17 the author "rifiuta la definizione" (n. ad
loc.); he merely prescinds from it, and confines himself
to what he takes to be the problem posed in 1.1. Whatever his views (if any) on definition were, they do not
appear in the Δ. Λ. And as for the phrase σώματα τῆς
οὐσίας πεφυκότα (Hipp. Mai. 301b), this surely means,
not "manifestazioni naturali dell' essere", but rather
"natural bodies" (such as sun and moon) or "natural
masses" (such as earth and sea) comprising part of 'the
real'; cf. Tarrant ad loc.

[79] See Hippias A 2, 1; A 5a DK[6].

[80] While it is no doubt possible to read the
clause ἀποκρινόμενον τῷ βουλομένῳ ὅ τι ἂν τις ἐρωτᾷ as
a claim to omniscience, the whole sentence seems much
more naturally understood as meaning simply that Hippias
is ready to read (or deliver from memory?) his set
pieces and answer any questions concerning them that
people might care to put--not any questions on any
imaginable topic.

[81] For the refs. see n. 79 above.

[82] Hippias B 21, B 12 DK[6].

[83] See Pl. Hipp. Mai. 285b, Hipp. Min. 367c, Prot. 315c; and cf. Levi 300.

[84] For the sentiment see Gorgias B 11 #10, B 23 DK[6]; cf. Madyda 56 ff., Dupréel 91, Untersteiner ad loc. For a suggestion that it might be an echo of Simonides (ap. Plut. Glor. Ath. 3.346 F) see Nestlé (II) 318 ff., 324; Levi (I) 302 (with litt.); Untersteiner ad loc.

[85] See especially 6.1 (καινός, οὔτε διδακτόν), 6.3 (διδάσκαλοί κα κτλ), 6.6.
6.1 καινός: see Gorgias B 11a DK[6], in which both the terms καινός and ἀληθής are used and in a remarkably similar fashion to their use at Δ. Λ. 6.1: εἰ μὲν γὰρ ἀνοήτους, καινός ὁ λόγος, ἀλλ᾽ οὐκ ἀληθής. The chance that we are looking here at an echo of a peculiarly Gorgian rhetorical mannerism (of the form, perhaps, "It's new, yes—but is it true?") seems to me a high one.
οὔτε διδακτόν: see Pl. Meno 95c: Γοργίου μάλιστα . . . ταῦτα ἄγαμαι, ὅτι οὐκ ἄν ποτε αὐτοῦ τοῦτο ἀκούσαις ὑπισχνουμένου [sc. διδάσκαλον εἶναι ἀρετῆς]. The clear indication seems to be that Sophists themselves (particularly Gorgias) found the question a problematic one, and the view appears to be corroborated by what we find in chapter 6 of the Δ. Λ. (Guthrie, however [3.45; cf. 3.271 f.], suspects that Gorgias' disclaimer is "a little disingenuous".)
6.3 διδάσκαλοί κα κτλ: the word to stress is ἀποδεδεγμένοι, the point being that, whatever the pretensions of certain σοφισταί, they had not won acceptance as teachers of ἀρετή; compare also Meno 89e, 95b-96c. If Meno 95c is a trustworthy account, we might tentatively infer therefrom (with Müller 226, n.2) that Δ. Λ. 6.3 is connected--even if 'indirectly'--with Gorgias.
6.6 With the whole sentence compare Pl. Prot. 327a ff., Laches 185e, Hippocr. De Arte 4, and, more succinctly, the remarkably similar claim of Isocrates (a direct echo?): ἄλλοι δέ τινες οὐδενί πώποτε συγγενόμενοι τῶν σοφιστῶν καί λέγειν καί πολιτεύεσθαι δεινοί γεγόνασιν (Contra Soph. 14; cf. Pohlenz 201, n.4). A favourite

example in antiquity was Themistocles; see Xen. <u>Mem</u>.
4.2.2, Thuc. 1.138.3, with Nestlé (II) 445 and Untersteiner <u>ad loc</u>. As Müller points out (226, n.2),
Isocrates was a pupil of Gorgias, and we might just
possibly have here a statement of one of the master's
views (cf. Pl. <u>Meno</u> 95c).

[86] See Trieber 232-236, with Gomperz (II) 162,
187, 191-192; Levi 300; Rittelmeyer 11; Gigon 252 f.;
Heinimann 111, n.30; Gaiser 52; and for further litt.
Untersteiner (II) 171, n.12, to which should be added
Versényi 18, Gulley 31.

[87] For the extreme counter-case see Pohlenz 72-
74, for whom the Δ. Λ. is a note-book compilation, by a
student, of a sophist's course of lectures. No particular unity is therefore to be expected (cf. Gomperz [II]
139; and Zeller [II] 1. 1333, n.1, followed by Nestlé
[II] 437-438, for whom the Δ. Λ. is a student's compilation of several different sophistic writings [cf. Freeman (I) 417]). Levi, too ([I] 294-295), sees the
treatise as a hodge-podge of unconnected parts.

TEXT AND TRANSLATION

SIGLA

(DK)

B*	P	Berol. Phill. 1518	1542
C		Ciz. 70	1556
E		Escor. T-1-16	s. 16
F1		Laurent. 85, 19	s. 16
F2*	F	" 85, 24	s. 15/16
H	H	Vesont. F. 19	s. 16
L		Leidensis	s. 16/17
M		Merton. 304	s. 15
P1*	E	Paris. 1964	s. 15
P2*		" 1967	s. 16
P3*	A	" 1963	1534
P4*	C	" 2081	s. 16
P5		" suppl. 133	s. 17
P6*	B	" 1965	s. 16
Q		Ottobon. 21	1541
R*	K	Regiomont. 16^b 12	s. 14/15
S		Savil. gr. 1	s. 16
T		Taurin. gr. 12	s. 16
V1	W	Marc. 4, 26	s. 15
V2*	V	" 262	s. 15
Y1		Vatic. 1338	s. 16
Y2		" 217	s. 16
Z		Monac. 79	s. 16

Fabr.	Fabricius
Kr.	Kranz
Ma.	Matthaei
Meib.	Meibom
Mull.	Mullach
N.	North
Or.	Orelli
Sch.	Schanz
St	Stephanus
Tch.	Teichmüller
Tr.	Trieber
Voss.	Vossianus
Wil.	Wilamowitz

N.B. Formae doricae in textum a Weber illatae in apparatu critico non notantur.

COMPENDIA GENERALIA

O	omnes codices
*	codex inter optimos aestimandus
rel.	reliqui codices inter optimos aestimandi

ΔΙΣΣΟΙ ΛΟΓΟΙ (DIALEXEIS)

1. Περὶ ἀγαθῶ καὶ κακῶ

   (1) δισσοὶ λόγοι λέγονται ἐν τᾶ Ἑλλάδι ὑπὸ τῶν φιλοσοφούντων περὶ τῶ ἀγαθῶ καὶ τῶ κακῶ. τοὶ μὲν γὰρ
λέγοντι ὡς ἄλλο μέν ἐστι τὸ ἀγαθόν, ἄλλο δὲ τὸ
5 κακόν· τοὶ δὲ ὡς τὸ αὐτό ἐστι, καὶ τοῖς μὲν ἀγαθὸν
εἴη, τοῖς δὲ κακόν, καὶ τῷ αὐτῷ ἀνθρώπῳ τοτὲ μὲν
ἀγαθόν, τοτὲ δὲ κακόν. (2) ἐγὼ δὲ καὶ αὐτὸς τοῖσδε
ποτιτίθεμαι. σκέψομαι δὲ ἐκ τῶ ἀνθρωπίνω βίω, ᾧ
ἐπιμελὲς βρώσιός τε καὶ πόσιος καὶ ἀφροδισίων.
10 ταῦτα γὰρ ἀσθενοῦντι μὲν κακόν, ὑγιαίνοντι δὲ καὶ
δεομένῳ ἀγαθόν. (3) καὶ ἀκρασία τοίνυν τούτων τοῖς
μὲν ἀκρατέσι κακόν, τοῖς δὲ πωλεῦντι ταῦτα καὶ
μισθαρνέοντι ἀγαθόν. νόσος τοίνυν τοῖς μὲν ἀσθενεῦντι
κακόν, τοῖς δὲ ἰατροῖς ἀγαθόν. ὁ τοίνυν θάνατος
15 τοῖς μὲν ἀποθανοῦσι κακόν, τοῖς δ' ἐνταφιοπώλαις καὶ
τυμβοποιοῖς ἀγαθόν. (4) γεωργία τε καλῶς ἐξενείκασα
τὼς καρπὼς τοῖς μὲν γεωργοῖς ἀγαθόν, τοῖς δὲ ἐμπόροις
κακόν. τὰς τοίνυν ὁλκάδας συντρίβεσθαι καὶ παρα-
θραύεσθαι τῷ μὲν ναυκλήρῳ κακόν, τοῖς δὲ ναυπαγοῖς

   Post Sexti Empirici subscriptionem, δωρικῆς διαλέκτου ἐντεῦθεν ἕως τοῦ τέλους. ζητεῖται δὲ εἰ καὶ τὸ
παρὸν σύγγραμμα Σέξτειόν ἐστιν O praeter Ἰωνικὴ διάλεκτος ἢ παροῦσα τυγχάνει P2 ἰωνικῆς διαλέκτου ἐντεῦθεν
ἕως τέλους P1 Q Ἀνωνύμου τινὸς Διαλέξεις Δωρικῇ διαλέκτῳ, Περὶ τοῦ ἀγαθοῦ καὶ τοῦ κακοῦ, κτλ St 1 Tit.
om. Pl.2 genet. in -οῦ rel. Περὶ τῶ ἀγαθῶ καὶ τῶ κακῶ
St 2 τῶ super τῆι Pl τᾷ Mull. 3 genet. in ῶ Fl R V2
in ᾧ et ter in ῶ B Vl ῶ super οῦ Pl -οῦ P2 rel. / τοὶ
Pl.2 τοῖς B οἱ rel. 4 λέγουσι super λέγοντι Pl 5 τοὶ

1. On good and bad

(1) On the matter of what is good and what is bad
contrasting arguments are put forward in Greece by
educated people: some say that what is good and what is
bad are two different things, others that they are the
same thing, and that the same thing is good for some
but bad for others, or at one time good and at another
time bad for the same person. (2) For myself, I side
with the latter group, and I shall examine the view by
reference to human life, with its concern for food and
drink and sex. For these things are bad for those who
are sick, but good for the person who is healthy and
needs them. (3) Or again, lack of restraint in these
matters is bad for those who lack restraint, but good
for those who sell these commodities and make money out
of them. And illness is bad for the sick but good for
the doctors. And death is bad for those who die, but
good for the undertakers and the grave-diggers. (4)
Farming also, when it makes a handsome success of pro-
ducing crops, is good for the farmers, but bad for the
merchants. And it is bad for the ship-owner if his
merchant-ships are involved in a collision or get
smashed up, but good for the shipbuilders. (5) Further-

Pl.2 St τοῖς rel. 6 [εἴη] Wil. 8 genet. in ω vel φ O
praeter ου super ω P̄l.2 / ῷ Wil. ὧν O 9 ἐπιμελής H
10 ταύτά Tr. / κακόν Pl.2 κακά ἐστι(ν) r̄el. 11 ἀγαθόν
P̄l.2 ἀγαθά rel. 12 τοῖς δὲ πωλεῦντι -- ἀσθενεῦντι
κακόν Pl.2 om. rel̄. 18 περιθραύεσθαι Pl.2 19 ναυπη-
γοῖς B P2

ἀγαθόν. (5) ἔτι <δὲ> τὸν σίδαρον κατέσθεσθαι καὶ
ἀμβλύνεσθαι καὶ συντρίβεσθαι τοῖς μὲν ἄλλοις κακόν,
τῷ δὲ χαλκῆ ἀγαθόν. καὶ μὰν τὸν κέραμον παραθραύεσ-
θαι τοῖς μὲν ἄλλοις κακόν, τοῖς δὲ κεραμεῦσιν ἀγαθόν.
5 τὰ δὲ ὑποδήματα κατατρίβεσθαι καὶ διαρρήγνυσθαι τοῖς
μὲν ἄλλοις κακόν, τῷ δὲ σκυτῆ ἀγαθόν. (6) ἐν τοίνυν
τοῖς ἀγῶσι τοῖς γυμνικοῖς καὶ τοῖς μωσικοῖς καὶ τοῖς
πολεμικοῖς, αὐτίκα ἐν τῷ γυμνικῷ τῷ σταδιοδρόμῳ, ἁ
νίκα τῷ μὲν νικῶντι ἀγαθόν, τοῖς δὲ ἡσσαμένοις
10 κακόν. (7) καττωύτὸ δὲ καὶ τοὶ παλαισταὶ καὶ
πύκται καὶ τοὶ ἄλλοι πάντες μωσικοί· αὐτίκα ἁ
κιθαρῳδία τῷ μὲν νικῶντι ἀγαθόν, τοῖς δὲ ἡσσαμένοις
κακόν. (8) ἔν τε τῷ πολέμῳ (καὶ τὰ νεώτατα πρῶτον
ἐρῶ) ἁ τῶν Λακεδαιμονίων νίκα ἃν ἐνίκων Ἀθηναίως
15 καὶ τὼς συμμάχως Λακεδαιμονίοις μὲν ἀγαθόν, Ἀθηναίοις δὲ καὶ τοῖς συμμάχοις κακόν· ἅ τε νίκα ἃν
τοὶ Ἕλλανες τὸν Πέρσαν ἐνίκασαν τοῖς μὲν Ἕλλασιν
ἀγαθόν, τοῖς δὲ βαρβάροις κακόν. (9) ἁ τοίνυν τοῦ
Ἰλίου αἵρεσις τοῖς μὲν Ἀχαίοις ἀγαθόν, τοῖς δὲ
20 Τρωσὶ κακόν. καδδὲ ταὐτὸν καὶ τὰ τῶν Θηβαίων καὶ
τὰ τῶν Ἀργείων πάθη. (10) καὶ ἁ τῶν Κενταύρων καὶ

---

1 <δὲ> Voss. <δὴ> Tr. / σίδαρον Pl σίδηρον rel. /
κατεσθίεσθαι Fabr. 7 γυμνικοῖς Blass. γυμναστικοῖς O
8 πολεμικοῖς <καττωύτό> Tr. / αὐτίκα -- σταδιοδρόμῳ
post κακόν transp. Wil. / τῶν σταδιοδρόμων Sch. 9 δὲ St
δ' O 10 καττωύτὸ Matth. de Varis καὶ τοῦτο O καττωῦτὸ
vel καδδὲ ταυτὸ Or. καττοῦτο Weber / τοὶ παλαισταὶ καὶ
πύκται καὶ τοὶ ἄλλοι πάντες μωσικοί· αὐτίκα ἁ κιθαρῳδία
O praeter μουσικοί Pl.2 ὁ κιθαρῳδὸς Pl.2 'aut delendum
v. ἄλλοι, aut legendum καὶ τοὶ ἄλλοι πάντες (scil.
γυμναστικοὶ vel ἀθληταὶ) καὶ μωσικοί, vel etiam καὶ
ἀθληταὶ πάντες καὶ μωσικοί' Or. τῷ παλαιστᾷ καὶ πύκτᾳ
καὶ τοῖς ἄλλοις πᾶσιν <ἔν τε τῷ> μωσικῷ ἁ νίκα Wil.
item praeter ἄλλοις ἕν τε <τῷ> Diels 12 τῷ κιθαρῳδῷ
Wil. ἁ κιθαρῳδίας Diels <ἁ νίκα> ἁ κιθαρῳδίας Kr.
13 πολεμικῷ Tr. / τὰ P2 τᾶ (τᾷ) rel. / νεώτατα Koen

more, it is bad for everyone else, but good for the
blacksmiths if a tool corrodes or loses its sharp edge
or gets broken to pieces. And undoubtedly it is bad
for everyone else, but good for the potters if pottery
gets smashed. And it is bad for everyone else, but good
for the cobbler if footwear wears out or gets ripped
apart. (6) Again, when it comes to contests, be they
gymnastic, or artistic, or military--for example, when
it comes to games (i.e., foot-races)--victory is good
for the winner, but bad for the losers. (7) And the
same is also true for wrestlers and boxers and all
those who take part in artistic contests as well; for
example, lyre-playing is good for the winner, but bad
for the losers. (8) And in the matter of war (I shall
speak first of the most recent events) the Spartan
victory over the Athenians and their allies was good for
the Spartans, but bad for the Athenians and their allies;
and the victory which the Greeks won over the Persians
was good for the Greeks, but bad for the non-Greeks.
(9) Again, the capture of Troy was good for the Achaeans,
but bad for the Trojans. And the same holds for what
happened to the Thebans and to the Argives. (10) And

νεώτατοι M S νεότητι Pl.2 νεότατι rel. νεωστὶ N. <u>14</u> ἀ
τῶν Koen αὐτῶν O αὐτίκα susp. Tr. / ἀν Weber ἐν ᾇ O /
<τὼς> Ἀθηναίως St <u>15</u> τοὺς Pl.2 / συμμάχως C St ω
super ου B V2 συμμάχους rel. / Ἀθηναίοις δὲ καὶ om.
Pl.2 <u>16</u> τοῖς δὲ συμμάχοις Pl.2 / ἀν τοι Schaefer ἀν
τοι Pl.2 ἀν τε B Fabr. ἀν τε rel. ᾇ τοι Koen <u>18</u> ἡ
super ἀ Pl ἡ eras. P2 <u>20</u> ταύτὸ St / Θηβαίων καὶ τὰ τῶν
om. B / <τοῖς μὲν Θηβαίοις ἀγαθόν, τοῖς δ' Ἀργείοις
κακόν.> post Ἀργείων πάθη add. Blass

Λαπιθᾶν μάχη τοῖς μὲν Λαπίθαις ἀγαθόν, τοῖς δὲ
Κενταύροις κακόν. καὶ μὰν καὶ ἃ τῶν θεῶν καὶ
Γιγάντων λεγομένα μάχα καὶ νίκα τοῖς μὲν θεοῖς
ἀγαθόν, τοῖς δὲ Γίγασι κακόν. (11) ἄλλος δὲ λόγος
5 λέγεται ὡς ἄλλο μὲν τἀγαθὸν εἴη, ἄλλο δὲ τὸ κακόν,
διαφέρον ὥσπερ καὶ τὤνυμα οὕτω καὶ τὸ πρᾶγμα. ἐγὼ
δὲ καὶ αὐτὸς τοῦτον διαιρεῦμαι τὸν τρόπον. δοκῶ
γὰρ οὐδὲ διάδαλον ἦμεν ποῖον ἀγαθὸν καὶ ποῖον
κακόν, αἰ τὸ αὐτὸ καὶ μὴ ἄλλο ἑκάτερον εἴη· καὶ
10 γὰρ θαυμαστόν κ' εἴη. (12) οἶμαι δὲ οὐδέ κ' αὐτὸν
ἔχεν ἀποκρίνασθαι, αἴ τις [αὐτὸν] ἔροιτο τὸν ταῦτα
λέγοντα· "εἶπον δή μοι, ἤδη τι τὼς γονέας ἀγαθὸν
ἐποίησας;" φαίη κα· "καὶ πολλὰ καὶ μεγάλα." "τὺ
ἄρα κακά καὶ μεγάλα καὶ πολλὰ τούτοις ὀφείλεις,
15 αἴπερ τωὐτόν ἐστι τὸ ἀγαθὸν τῷ κακῷ. (13) τί δέ,
τὼς συγγενέας ἤδη τι ἀγαθὸν ἐποίησας; τὼς ἄρα
συγγενέας κακὸν ἐποίεις. τί δέ, τὼς ἐχθρὼς ἤδη
κακῶς ἐποίησας; καὶ πολλὰ καὶ μέγιστα ἄρα ἀγαθὰ
ἐποίησας. (14) ἄγε δή μοι καὶ τόδε ἀπόκριναι·
20 ἄλλο τι ἢ τὼς πτωχὼς οἰκτείρεις ὅτι πολλὰ καὶ κακὰ

---

1 Λαπιθᾶν (ὦν super ᾶν) P1 Λαπιθῶν St Or. / μάχα
τοῖς Mull. 3 [καὶ νίκα] Wil. 5 τὸ ἀγαθὸν Blass
7 αὐτὸς B P1.2 R αὐτὸ rel. / διερεῦμαι P2 8 οὐδὲ P1.2
οὐ rel. / οὐ διάδαλόν <κ> Blass οὗ κα διάδαλον Tr. οὐδέ
κα δᾶλον susp. Diels 9 εἴη O praeter ἦεν P1.2 ἦς Wil.
10 κ' εἴη St εἴη P2 κείη rel. / οὐδέν Or. 11 ἔχεν P1.2
ἔσχεν vel ἔσχον rel. / [αὐτὸν] Diels αὐτὸν αὐτὸν P6 V2
[αὐ] τὸν αὐτὸν Friedländer 12 ἤδη τι τοὺς γονέας ἀγαθὸν
ἐποίησας; O praeter τὼς P1.2.4.6 V2 τύ τι τοὶ γονέες
ἀγαθὸν ἐποίησαν; W. Schulze post ἐποίησας; add. 'ναί.'
vel 'μάλιστα.' Or. 13 σὺ P3 τὸ P1.2 / κακά [καὶ] Wil.
15 δαί P1.2 δή Tr. 16 post ἐποίησας; "<καὶ πολλὰ καὶ
μεγάλα>." Diels 17 δαί P1.2 δή Tr. / ἤδη κακόν P1.2
ἤδη <τι> κακόν Tr. 18 καὶ πολλὰ καὶ μέγιστα ἄρα P1.2
καὶ πολλὰ καὶ μεγάλα ἄρα rel. καὶ πολλὰ καὶ μεγάλα.
καὶ πολλὰ καὶ μεγάλα ἄρα Blass "καὶ πολλὰ καὶ <μεγάλα>."

the battle between the Lapiths and the Centaurs was good
for the Lapiths, but bad for the Centaurs. And it is
certainly the case that the fabled battle of the gods
and Giants, and its victorious outcome, was good for the
gods, but bad for the Giants. (11) Another view is that
what is good is one thing and what is bad is another
thing; as the name differs, so likewise does the reality.
I myself also distinguish the two in the above-mentioned
manner. For I think it not even clear what sort of
thing would be good and what sort of thing bad if each
of the two were the same thing and not different things;
the situation would be an astonishing one indeed. (12)
And I think that the man who says the above-mentioned
things would not even be able to make a reply if someone
were to put the following question: "Tell me now, did
you ever before now do to your parents anything that was
good?" He might say, "Yes, I did a great deal that
was <u>very</u> good." "In that case you ought to do them a
great deal that is very <u>bad</u>, if what is good and what is
bad are the same thing. (13) Tell me, did you ever
before now do to your relatives anything that was good?
In such a case you were doing them something bad. Or
tell me, did you ever before now do harm to your enemies? In such a case you did them a great deal that
was very beneficial. (14) And please answer me this as
well: Are you not in the position of pitying beggars
because they are in a very bad way and also (contrariwise)

---

¹μέγιστα ἄρα Diels <u>19</u> ἄγε <καί> δή St / ἀπόκριναι ἄλλο,
τί N. ἀπόκριναι ἄλλο τι Or. <u>20</u> πολλά καί κακά ἔχοντι
Diels πολλά καί μεγάλα ἔχοντι O πολλά καί μεγάλα κακά
ἔχοντι; N. (antea Matth. de Varis) πολλά καί μεγάλα
ἔχοντι κακά Mull.

ἔχοντι, πάλιν εὐδαιμονίζεις ὅτι πολλὰ καὶ ἀγαθὰ
πράσσοντι, αἵπερ τωὐτὸ κακὸν καὶ ἀγαθόν;" (15) τὸν
δὲ βασιλῆ τὸν μέγαν οὐδὲν κωλύει ὁμοίως διακεῖσθαι
τοῖς πτωχοῖς. τὰ γὰρ πολλὰ καὶ μεγάλα ἀγαθὰ αὐτῷ
5 πολλὰ κακὰ καὶ μεγάλα ἐστίν, αἴ γα τωὐτόν ἐστιν
ἀγαθὸν καὶ κακόν. καὶ τάδε μὲν περὶ τῶ παντὸς
εἰρήσθω. (16) εἶμι δὲ καὶ καθ' ἕκαστον ἀρξάμενος ἀπὸ
τῶ ἐσθίεν καὶ πῖνεν καὶ ἀφροδισιάζεν. τωὐτὸ γὰρ
τοῖς ἀσθενεῦντι ταῦτα ποιὲν ἀγαθὸν ἐστιν [αὐτοῖς],
10 αἵπερ τωὐτόν ἐστιν ἀγαθὸν καὶ κακόν. καὶ τοῖς
νοσέοντι κακὸν ἐστι τὸ νοσεῖν καὶ ἀγαθόν, αἵπερ
τωὐτόν ἐστι τὸ ἀγαθὸν τῷ κακῷ. (17) καδδὲ τόδε καὶ
τἆλλα πάντα τὰ ἐν τῷ ἔμπροσθεν λόγῳ εἴρηται. καὶ οὐ
λέγω τί ἐστι τὸ ἀγαθόν, ἀλλὰ τοῦτο πειρῶμαι διδάσ-
15 κειν, ὡς οὐ τωὐτόν εἴη κακὸν καὶ ἀγαθόν, ἀλλ' ἄλλο
ἑκάτερον.

2. Περὶ καλοῦ καὶ αἰσχροῦ

(1) λέγονται δὲ καὶ περὶ τῶ καλῶ καὶ αἰσχρῶ δισσοὶ
λόγοι. τοὶ μὲν γάρ φαντι ἄλλο μὲν ἦμεν τὸ καλόν,
20 ἄλλο δὲ τὸ αἰσχρόν, διαφέρον ὥσπερ καὶ τὤνυμα οὕτω
καὶ τὸ σῶμα· τοὶ δὲ τωὐτὸ καλὸν καὶ αἰσχρόν. (2)

1 ἔχοντι, πάλιν scripsi ἔχοντι· πάλιν O ἔχοντι; ἢ [πάλιν?]
N. ἔχοντι <κακά, τὼς δὲ πλουσίως> πάλιν Mull. ἔχοντι;
<. . . τὼς ἄρα προωχῶς> πάλιν Blass ἔχοντι <καὶ> πάλιν
Sch. ἔχοντι; <πῶς οὐ τὼς πτωχὼς> πάλιν Wil. / <πλουσίως>
εὐδαιμονίζεις susp. N. / πολλὰ καὶ μεγάλα ἀγαθὰ Weber
2 τωὐτόν καὶ κακόν St   3 βασιλῆ Pl.2 βασιλῆα rel.
4 πολλὰ καὶ μεγάλα κακά Wil.   5 αἴ γα Diels αἶκα O αἵπερ
Blass   6 τῶν πάντων Wil.   7 καὶ om. P2 / καὶ <ἐπὶ τὰ>
καθ' Blass   8 τῶ F2 Pl R τῶν rel. / ἐσθίειν Pl ἔσθειν
Wil. / τωὐτὸ (vel ταυτὸ) Or. τοῦτο O ταῦτα Mull. οὕτω
Wil. <κατ>τωυτὸ Tr. / [γάρ] Tr.   9 ἀσθενέουσι St εὐσθε-
νέουσι Tr. / ἀσθενεῦντι <ποιὲν κακόν, καὶ πάλιν> ταῦτα

congratulating them for being well off, if the same
thing is good and bad?" (15) And there is nothing to
stop the King of Persia from being in the same condition
as beggars. For what is for him a great deal of good is
also a great deal of evil, if the same thing is good and
evil. And we can assume that these things have been
said for every case. (16) However, I shall also go
though each individual case, beginning with eating and
drinking and sexual intercourse. For, in the same way
as has been mentioned above, if the same thing is good
and bad, it is good for those who are ill should they
do these things. And being sick is bad for the sick and
also good for them if what is good and what is bad are
the same thing. (17) And for all else that has been
mentioned in the above argument this holds good. Not
that I am saying what the good is; I am trying rather
to point out that it is not the same thing which is bad
and good, but that each is different from the other.

2. On seemly and shameful

(1) Contrasting arguments are also put forward on
what is seemly and shameful. For some say that what is
seemly and what is shameful are two different things;
as the name differs, so likewise does the reality.
Others, however, say that the same thing is both seemly

Blass / [ταῦτα] Or. πάντα Mull. τὸ Tr. / ποιὲν F2 Pl.2
ποιεῦν rel. praeter πϊεῦν Fl ποιέουσι Wil. εὐσθενὲν Tr. /
[αὐτοῖς?] Tr. αὐτοῖς <καὶ κακόν> Or. 11 νοσέουσι St
13 οὐ om. P2 15 [εἴη] W. Schulze / τὸ κακὸν καὶ τἀγαθόν
Diels 16 <ἄλλο> Blass 17 Tit. om. Pl.2 κακοῦ pro καλοῦ
Β Περὶ τῶ καλῶ καὶ αἰσχρῶ St Περὶ καλῶ καὶ αἰσχρῶ Fabric.
18 <τῶ> αἰσχρῶ Tr. 21 σῶμα Ο πρᾶγμα St

κἀγὼ πειρασεῦμαι τόνδε τὸν τρόπον ἐξαγεύμενος.
αὐτίκα γὰρ παιδὶ ὡραίῳ ἐραστᾷ μὲν χρηστῷ χαρίζεσθαι
καλόν, μὴ ἐραστᾷ δὲ καλῷ αἰσχρόν. (3) καὶ τὰς
γυναῖκας λοῦσθαι ἔνδοι καλόν, ἐν παλαίστρᾳ δὲ αἰσχρόν,
5 ἀλλὰ τοῖς ἀνδράσιν ἐν παλαίστρᾳ καὶ ἐν γυμνασίῳ
καλόν. (4) καὶ συνίμεν τῷ ἀνδρὶ ἐν ἀσυχίᾳ μὲν
καλόν, ὅπου τοίχοις κρυφθήσεται, ἔξω δὲ αἰσχρόν,
ὅπου τις ὄψεται. (5) καὶ τῷ μὲν αὐτᾶς συνίμεν ἀνδρὶ
καλόν, ἀλλοτρίῳ δὲ αἴσχιστον. καὶ τῷ γε ἀνδρὶ τᾷ
10 μὲν ἑαυτῶ γυναικὶ συνίμεν καλόν, ἀλλοτρίᾳ δὲ αἰσχρόν.
(6) καὶ κοσμεῖσθαι καὶ ψιμυθίῳ χρίεσθαι καὶ χρυσία
περιάπτεσθαι τῷ μὲν ἀνδρὶ αἰσχρόν, τᾷ δὲ γυναικὶ καλόν.
(7) καὶ τὼς μὲν φίλως εὖ ποιὲν καλόν, τὼς δὲ ἐχθρὼς
αἰσχρόν. καὶ τὼς μὲν πολεμίως φεύγεν αἰσχρόν, τὼς
15 δὲ ἐν σταδίῳ ἀγωνιστὰς καλόν. (8) καὶ τὼς μὲν φίλως
καὶ τὼς πολίτας φονεύεν αἰσχρόν, τὼς δὲ πολεμίως
καλόν. καὶ τάδε μὲν περὶ πάντων. (9) εἶμι δ' <ἐφ'>
ἃ ταὶ πόλιές τε αἰσχρὰ ἄγηνται καὶ τὰ ἔθνεα. αὐτίκα
Λακεδαιμονίοις τὰς κόρας γυμνάζεσθαι <καὶ> ἀχειριδώ-
20 τως καὶ ἀχίτωνας παρέρπεν καλόν, Ἴωσι δὲ αἰσχρόν.

1 πειρασεῦμαι P3 πειρασοῦμαι rel. post πειρασεῦμαι susp.
excidisse δεικνύεν vel simile quid Or. / τοῦτον τὸν
τρόπον H / ἐξαγούμενος Pl 2 παιδὶ Blass παιδίῳ O /
χρηστῷ Pl.2 χρηστῷ μὲν rel. [χρηστῷ] Wil. 3 μὴ ἐραστᾷ
δὲ ἢ κακῷ Blass ἐραστᾷ δὲ μὴ καλῷ Rohde ἐραστᾷ δὲ μὴ
[καλῷ] Wil. ἐραστᾷ δὲ μὴ χρηστῷ Weber (χρηστῷ antea N.
Sch.) μὴ ἐραστᾷ δὲ [καλῷ] Diels 4 ἔνδοι Vahlen ἔνιοι
Pl.2 ἔνδον rel. 8 τὸ St / αὐτᾶς N. αὐτᾶς O αὐτᾶς
Diels 9 αἴσχιστον F2 Pl.3 R Vl αἴσχιστον ex αἰσχρόν Z
αἴσχιστον ad mrg. V2 αἰσχρόν rel. / τῷ γ' ἀνδρὶ Diels 10
αὐτῶ Wil. 11 ψιμυθίῳ Pl.2 ψιμμυθίῳ rel. 12 τᾷ μὲν
Weber 13 ποιὲν Pl.2 ποιεῖν rel. 15 ἀνταγωνιστὰς Or.
16 φονεύεν Pl.2 φονευεν (~ et ' super υ) R φονεῦεν rel.
17 καὶ -- πάντων om. P2 / <ἐφ'> St 18 [τε] Wil. 19 <καὶ>
ἀχειριδώτως Blass

and shameful. (2) For my part, I shall attempt an
exposition of the matter along the following lines: for
example, it is seemly for a boy in the flower of his
growth to gratify a respectable lover, but it is shameful for a handsome boy to gratify one who is <u>not</u> his
lover. (3) And it is seemly for women to wash indoors,
but shameful to do it in a wrestling school; but for men
it is seemly to wash in a wrestling-school or gymnasium.
(4) And to have sexual intercourse with one's husband
in private, where one will be concealed from view by
walls, is seemly: to do it outside, however, where somebody will see, is shameful. (5) And it is seemly to
have sexual intercourse with one's own husband, but very
shameful with someone else's. Yes--and for the husband
too it is seemly to have sexual intercourse with his own
wife, but shameful with someone else's. (6) And for the
husband it is shameful to adorn himself and smear himself with white lead and wear gold ornaments, but for
the wife it is seemly. (7) And it is seemly to treat
one's friends kindly, but shameful to treat one's enemies
in such a way. And it is shameful to run away from one's
enemies, but seemly to run away from one's competitors
in a stadium. (8) And it is shameful to slaughter those
who are friends or fellow-citizens, but seemly to
slaughter one's enemies. And the above points apply to
every case. (9) However, I shall go on to what cities
and nations consider shameful. To Spartans, for example,
it is seemly that girls should exercise naked or walk
around bare-armed or without a tunic, but to Ionians
this is shameful. (10) And <in Sparta> it is seemly

108

(10) καὶ τὼς παῖδας μὴ μανθάνειν μωσικά καὶ γράμματα
καλόν, "Ιωσι δ' αἰσχρὸν μὴ ἐπίστασθαι ταῦτα πάντα.
(11) Θεσσαλοῖσι δὲ καλὸν τὼς ἴππως ἐκ τᾶς ἀγέλας
λαβόντι αὐτῷ δαμάσαι καὶ τὼς ὀρέας, βῶν τε λαβόντι
5 αὐτῷ σφάξαι καὶ ἐκδεῖραι καὶ κατακόψαι, ἐν Σικελίᾳ
δὲ αἰσχρὸν καὶ δώλων ἔργα. (12) Μακεδόσι δὲ καλὸν
δοκεῖ ἦμεν τὰς κόρας, πρὶν ἀνδρὶ γάμασθαι, ἔρασθαι
καὶ ἀνδρὶ συγγίγνεσθαι, ἐπεὶ δέ κα γάμηται, αἰσχρόν·
"Ελλασι δ' ἄμφω αἰσχρόν. (13) τοῖς δὲ Θραξὶ κόσμος
10 τὰς κόρας στίζεσθαι, τοῖς δ' ἄλλοις τιμωρία τὰ
στίγματα τοῖς ἀδικέοντι. τοὶ δὲ Σκύθαι καλὸν
νομίζοντι ὃς ἄνδρα <κα> κατακανὼν ἐκδείρας τὰν κεφα-
λὰν τὸ μὲν κόμιον πρὸ τοῦ ἴππου φορῇ, τὸ δ' ὀστέον
χρυσώσας καὶ ἀργυρώσας πίνῃ ἐξ αὐτοῦ καὶ σπένδῃ τοῖς
15 θεοῖς· ἐν δὲ τοῖς "Ελλασιν οὐδέ κ' ἐς τὰν αὐτὰν
οἰκίαν συνεισελθεῖν βούλοιτό τις τοιαῦτα ποιήσαντι.
(14) Μασσαγέται δὲ τὼς γονέας κατακόψαντες κατέσθοντι, καὶ τάφος κάλλιστος δοκεῖ ἦμεν ἐν τοῖς
τέκνοις τέθαφθαι, ἐν δὲ τᾷ Ἑλλάδι αἴ τις ταῦτα
20 ποιήσαι ἐξελαθεὶς ἐκ τῆς Ἑλλάδος κακῶς κα ἀποθάνοι
ὡς αἰσχρὰ καὶ δεινὰ ποιέων. (15) τοὶ δὲ Πέρσαι

1 καὶ <τήνοις> τὼς παῖδας Wil. καὶ <τοῖς μὲν> τὼς παῖδας
Diels / μοσικάν (ἀ super ἀν) P2 μωσικάν Weber 2 [πάντα]
Bergk 3 ἐν Θεσσαλοῖσι Or. παρὰ Θ. Mull., Bergk / τὼς P1.2
τάς rel. 4 αὐτῷ Blass -ὼς O / βῶς St 5 αὐτῷ Blass αὐτὼς
O praeter αὐτός P2 6 δέ om. B F2 7 [ἀνδρὶ] γάμασθαι
Wil. / ἔρασθαι scripsi ἐρᾶσθαι O 8 δέ κα γάμηται Blass
δὲ καὶ γαμεῖται O 10 τοῖς δ' ἄλλοις -- ἀδικέοντι P1.2
om. rel. / τιμωρία Weber τιμωρίαν O 12 ὃς ἄνδρα <κα>
scripsi ὃς <κ'> ἄνδρα Blass / κατακανὼν Blass κατκτανὼν
P1 κατακτανῶν P2 κανῶν Z L St κτανῶν B R N. 13 προκόμιον
Blass / πρὸς B / φορῇ Blass φορεῖ rel. praeter φορεῖν P2
14 χρυσώσας καὶ ἀργυρώσας O χρυσώσας ἢ ἀργυρώσας Wil.
χρυσώσας <ἢ> καὶ ἀργυρώσας Diels / πίνη P1.2 πίνει rel. /
σπένδῃ Blass σπένδει O 16 βούλοιτό τις Blass (susp.
antea Ma.) βούλοιτ' ἄν τις O βούλοιτ' οὔ τις Tr. / τοιαῦτα

that boys should <u>not</u> learn arts or letters, but to
Ionians it is shameful not to know all these things.
(11) Among Thessalians it is seemly for a man first to
select the horses from the herd and then train them and
the mules <u>himself</u>, and seemly for a man first to select
a steer and then slaughter, skin, and cut it up <u>himself</u>;
in Sicily, however, such activities are shameful, and
the work of slaves. (12) To Macedonians it appears to
be seemly that girls should love and have intercourse
with a man before marrying a man, but shameful to do
this once they are married. To Greeks both practices
are shameful. (13) The Thracians count it an adornment
that their girls tattoo themselves, but in the eyes of
everyone else tattoo-marks are a punishment for wrong-
doers. And the Scythians consider it seemly that, after
killing a man, one should on the one hand scalp him and
carry the frontal hair on one's horse's brow and on the
other hand gild or silver over the skull and drink from
it and offer libations to the gods; among the Greeks no
one would want to go into the same house as a person who
had done that sort of thing. (14) Massagetes cut up
their parents and then eat them, and it seems to them an
especially seemly form of entombment to be buried inside
one's children; if a person did this in Greece he would
be driven out of Greece and die a miserable death for
doing things that are shameful and horrible. (15) The

O τῷ ταῦτα Diels <u>17</u> τὼς C V2 St τοὺς rel. / κατέσθοντι
O praeter κατέσθονται Pl.2 κατεσθίοντι Or. <u>18</u> κάκιστος
Pl.2 <u>19</u> τᾷ Pl.3 St τῶ P2 R V2 τῷ B / αἴ Pl.2 ἄν rel.
<u>20</u> ποιῆσαι Blass ποιήσῃ vel ποιήσῃ O praeter ποιήσας (η
super α) P2 / [ἐκ τῆς Ἑλλάδος] Wil. / κακῶς <κα> Blass
κακά O [κακά] <κα> Sch. / ἀποθάνοι Pl.2 ἀποθάνῃ vel
ἀποθάνῃ rel.

κοσμεῖσθαί τε ὥσπερ τὰς γυναῖκας καὶ τὼς ἄνδρας
καλὸν νομίζοντι, καὶ τᾷ θυγατρὶ καὶ τᾷ ματρὶ καὶ τᾷ
ἀδελφᾷ συνίμεν, τοὶ δὲ Ἕλλανες καὶ αἰσχρὰ καὶ
παράνομα. (16) Λυδοῖς τοίνυν τὰς κόρας πορνευθείσας
5 καὶ ἀργύριον ἐνεργάσασθαι καὶ οὕτω γάμασθαι καλὸν
δοκεῖ ἦμεν, ἐν δὲ τοῖς Ἕλλασιν οὐδείς κα θέλοι
γᾶμαι. (17) Αἰγύπτιοί τε οὐ ταὐτὰ νομίζοντι καλὰ
τοῖς ἄλλοις· τῇδε μὲν γὰρ γυναῖκας ὑφαίνειν καὶ
ἐργάζεσθαι καλόν, ἀλλὰ τηνεῖ τὼς ἄνδρας, τὰς δὲ γυναῖκας
10 πράσσεν ἅπερ τῇδε τοὶ ἄνδρες. τὸν παλὸν δεύειν ταῖς
χερσί, τὸν δὲ σῖτον τοῖς ποσί, τήνοις καλόν, ἀλλ᾽
ἀμὶν τὸ ἐναντίον. (18) οἶμαι δ᾽, αἴ τις τὰ αἰσχρὰ
ἐς ἕν κελεύοι συνενεῖκαι πάντας ἀνθρώπως ἃ ἕκαστοι
νομίζοντι, καὶ πάλιν ἐξ ἀθρόων τούτων τὰ καλὰ λαβὲν
15 ἃ ἕκαστοι ἅγηνται, οὐδέν κα λειφθῆμεν, ἀλλὰ πάντας
πάντα διαλαβέν. οὐ γὰρ πάντες ταὐτὰ νομίζοντι.
(19) παρεξοῦμαι δὲ καὶ ποίημά τι·
    καὶ γὰρ τὸν ἄλλον ὧδε θνητοῖσιν νόμον
    ὄψῃ διαιρῶν· οὐδὲν ἦν πάντῃ καλὸν
20   οὐδ᾽ αἰσχρόν, ἀλλὰ ταῦτ᾽ ἐποίησεν λαβὼν
    ὁ καιρὸς αἰσχρὰ καὶ διαλλάξας καλά.

---

1 [τε] Diels 2 ματρί L St μητρί rel. 3 δὲ L St δ᾽ rel.
5 ἐνεργάσασθαι Weber ἐνεργήσασθαι O ἐργάσασθαι Mull. /
οὕτως Diels 6 θέλοι Pl.2 θέλει rel. 7 γᾶμαι Blass
γαμᾶν O γαμῆν Ma. γαμέν Tr. 8 τοῖς ἄλλοις <Ἕλλασιν>
susp. Valckenaer / <τὰς> γυναῖκας Wil. / ὑφαίνεν N.
ὑφαῖνεν Fabric. 9 <ἔρια> ἐργάζεσθαι Valckenaer / καλὸν
om. Or. (per error. typograph.?) / τὼς Pl.2 τούς rel.
10 πράσσειν Or. πρᾶσσεν Tr. / δεύεν Tr. 11 δὲ Pl.2 om.
rel. / ἀλλ᾽ ἀμὶν Pl(?) ἀλλ᾽ ἅμιν P2 ἀλλὰ μιν vel ἀλλάμιν
rel. ἀλλ᾽ ἀμῖν St 12 αἴ Wil. ἂν O / αἰσχρά N. καλά O
13 κελεύοι Pl.2 κελεύῃ vel κελεύη rel. κελεύσῃ Tr. /
ἀνθρώπως Pl.2 ἀνθρώπους rel. 14 τούτων Weber τοι O
[τοι] Wil. / καλὰ N. αἰσχρά O 15 οὐδέν O οὐδὲ ἕν Diels
κα λειφθῆμεν Matth. de Varis καλυφθεῖμεν (ἦ super εῖ)
R καλλειφθῆμεν Pl Heringa καλυφθῆμεν rel. καταλειφθῆμεν

Persians consider it seemly for men, too, to adorn themselves, like women, and to have sexual intercourse with
their daughter or mother or sister; the Greeks consider
such actions shameful and unlawful. (16) Again, to
Lydians it appears seemly that girls should prostitute
themselves to earn money, and in that way get married;
among the Greeks no one would be willing to marry any
such girl. (17) And Egyptians differ from everyone else
in their views on what is seemly. For here it appears
seemly that women should weave and do manual work, but
there it appears seemly that men should do such things
and that women should do what men do here. Kneading clay
with the hands, or dough with the feet, is for them
seemly, but for us just the opposite. (18) I think
that if one were to order all mankind to bring together
into a single pile all that each individual considered
shameful, and then again to take from this mass what each
thought seemly, nothing would be left, but they would
all, severally, take away everything. For not everyone
has the same views. (19) I shall bring forward as additional evidence some verses:

> "For if you make this distinction you will see
> the other law that holds for mortal men: there is
> nothing that is in every respect seemly or shameful,
> but the Right Moment takes the same things and
> makes them shameful and then changes them round
> and makes them seemly."

N. <κα> καλλειφθῆμεν Weber διαλαβέν O praeter διαλαβεῖν
Pl.2 <κα> διαλαβέν Tr. 18 τιν᾽ ἄλλον τόνδε Nauck /
θνητοῖσιν E L Valckenaer θνητοῖσι rel. 19 ὄψῃ Pl.2
Fabric. ὄψη E (ει super η) R ὄψει rel. ὄψει Meib. (per
error. typograph.?) / διαιρῶν O διαθρῶν Valckenaer
διαρθρῶν susp. Nauck / ἤν Nauck ἄν O ὄν Cobet / κακόν
P2 20 ταῦτ᾽ Valckenaer ταῦτ᾽ O πάντ᾽ Wil. / ἐποίησεν L
Valckenaer ἐποίησε rel.

(20) ὡς δὲ τὸ σύνολον εἶπαι, πάντα καιρῷ μὲν καλά
ἐντι, ἐν ἀκαιρίᾳ δ' αἰσχρά. τί ὧν διεπραξάμην; ἔφαν
ἀποδείξειν ταὐτά αἰσχρά καὶ καλά ἐόντα, καὶ ἀπέδειξα
ἐν τούτοις πᾶσι. (21) λέγεται δὲ καὶ περὶ τῶ αἰσχρῶ
5 καὶ καλῶ ὡς ἄλλο ἑκάτερον εἴη. ἐπεὶ αἴ τις ἐρωτάσαι
τὼς λέγοντας ὡς τὸ αὐτὸ πρᾶγμα αἰσχρὸν καὶ καλόν
ἐστιν, αἴ ποκά τι αὐτοῖς καλὸν ἔργασται, αἰσχρὸν
ὁμολογησοῦντι, αἴπερ τωὐτὸν καὶ τὸ αἰσχρὸν καὶ τὸ
καλόν. (22) καὶ αἴ τινά γα καλὸν οἴδαντι ἄνδρα,
10 τοῦτον καὶ αἰσχρὸν τὸν αὐτόν. καὶ αἴ τινά γα λευκόν,
καὶ μέλανα τοῦτον τὸν αὐτόν. καὶ <αἴ> καλόν γ' ἐστι
τὼς θεὼς σέβεσθαι, καὶ αἰσχρὸν ἄρα τὼς θεὼς σέβεσθαι,
αἴπερ τωὐτὸν αἰσχρὸν καὶ καλόν ἐστι. (23) καὶ τάδε
μὲν περὶ ἀπάντων εἰρήσθω μοι· τρέψομαι δὲ ἐπὶ τὸν
15 λόγον αὐτῶν ὃν λέγοντι. (24) αἱ γὰρ τὰν γυναῖκα
καλόν ἐστι κοσμεῖσθαι, τὰν γυναῖκα αἰσχρὸν κοσμεῖσθαι, αἴπερ τωὐτὸν αἰσχρὸν καὶ καλόν· καὶ τἆλλα κατὰ
τωὐτόν. (25) ἐν Λακεδαίμονί ἐστι καλὸν τὰς παῖδας
γυμνάζεσθαι, ἐν Λακεδαίμονί ἐστιν αἰσχρὸν τὰς παῖδας
20 γυμνάζεσθαι, καὶ τἆλλα οὕτως. (26) λέγοντι δὲ ὡς αἴ
τινες τὰ αἰσχρά ἐκ τῶν ἐθνέων πάντοθεν συνενείκαιεν,
ἔπειτα συγκαλέσαντες κελεύοιεν ἃ τις καλά νομίζοι

1 εἶπαι Pl.2 εἰπὲν St εἶπεν rel. / καλά μὲν καλά Pl.2
2 [ἐν] Wil. / τί δ' ὧν Or. 3 ἀποδείξειν O ἀποδείξεν N.
ἀποδείξεν Fabr. ἀποδειξὲν Weber / ἐόντα F2 ὄντα rel.
5 <τῶ> καλῶ Blass / ἐρωτάσαι O ἐρωτάσῃ St ἐρωτάσῃ N.
7 εἴργασται L Meib. / <καὶ> αἰσχρὸν Wil. 8 ὁμολογη-
γοῦντι Pl ὁμολογοῦντι P2 9 γα (ex τά) Pl τα P2 om. St
10 κα λευκόν St λευκόν Or. 11 καὶ <αἴ> scripsi καὶ
Diels 12 ἄρα vel ἄρ O αὖ Wil. 14 περὶ O praeter πρὸς
Pl πρὸ P2 / τῶν λόγων P2 16 <καὶ> αἰσχρὸν Diels 18 ἐν
Λ. -- γυμνάζεσθαι om. B 20 λέγοντι Pl.2 Matth. de
Varis λέγονται rel. 21 συνενείκαι <τὼς ἀνθρώπως?> Sch.
22 συγκαλέσαντες Blass συγκαλεσοῦντες vel συγκαλεσεῦντες
O συγκαλέοντας Or. / νομίζοι Pl νομίζει P2 (quod susp.
et Matth. de Varis) νομίζεν rel.

(20) To put the matter generally, all things are seemly
when done at the right moment, but shameful when done
at the wrong moment. What then have I managed to do?
I said I would demonstrate that the same things are
shameful and seemly, and I demonstrated it in all the
above-mentioned cases. (21) It is also said, when
what is shameful and what seemly is under discussion,
that each differs from the other. For if one were to
ask those who say that the same thing is shameful and
seemly whether any seemly thing has ever been done by
them, they will have to agree that what they did was
shameful, if what is shameful and what is seemly are
the same thing. (22) And if they know that a particular man is handsome, they know that this same man is
also ugly; and if white, also black. And if it is
seemly to treat the gods with respect, it is also shameful to treat the gods with respect, if the same thing
is shameful and seemly. (23) And it can be assumed that
I have made the same point in each and every instance.
Turning to their <specific> argument: (24) If it is
seemly for a woman to adorn herself, it is shameful for
a woman to adorn herself, if the same thing is shameful
and seemly. And this applies to all the other cases:
(25) In Sparta it is seemly for girls to exercise naked,
in Sparta it is shameful for girls to exercise naked--
and similarly in all the other instances. (26) They say
that if some people were to bring together from every
part of the world those things that are shameful, and
were then to call people together and command them to
take what each considered seemly, everything would be
taken away as seemly. I personally profess my astonishment if things that were shameful when they were brought

λαμβάνεν πάντα κα ἐν καλῷ ἀπενειχθῆμεν. ἐγὼ θαυμάζω
αἰ τὰ αἰσχρὰ συνενεχθέντα καλὰ ἐσεῖται, καὶ οὐχ
οἷάπερ ἦνθεν. (27) αἰ γοῦν ἵππως ἢ βῶς ἢ ὄϊς ἢ
ἀνθρώπως ἄγαγον, οὐκ ἄλλο τί κα ἀπᾶγον· ἐπεὶ οὐδ᾽ αἰ
5 χρυσὸν ἤνεικαν, χαλκὸν [ἀπήνεικαν], οὐδ᾽ αἰ ἀργύριον
ἤνεικαν, μόλιβδόν κα ἀπέφερον. (28) ἀντὶ δ᾽ ἄρα τῶν
αἰσχρῶν καλὰ ἀπάγοντι; φέρε δή, αἰ ἄρα τις αἰσχρὸν
ἄγαγε, τοῦτον αὖ <κα> καλὸν ἀπάγαγε; ποιητὰς δὲ
μάρτυρας ἐπάγονται, <οἳ> ποτὶ ἀδονὰν οὐ ποτ᾽ ἀλάθειαν
10 ποιεῦντι.

3. Περὶ δικαίου καὶ ἀδίκου

(1) δισσοὶ δὲ λόγοι λέγονται καὶ περὶ τῶ δικαίω
καὶ τῶ ἀδίκω, καὶ τοὶ μὲν ἄλλο ἦμεν τὸ δίκαιον,
ἄλλο δὲ τὸ ἄδικον, τοὶ δὲ τωὐτὸ δίκαιον καὶ ἄδικον·
15 καὶ ἐγὼ τούτῳ πειρασοῦμαι τιμωρέν. (2) καὶ πρῶτον
μὲν ψεύδεσθαι ὡς δίκαιόν ἐστι λεξῶ καὶ ἐξαπατᾶν.
τὼς μὲν πολεμίως ταῦτα ποιέν αἰσχρὸν καὶ πονηρὸν

---

1 κα Or. καὶ O κε Matth. de Varis καν Ma. / ἀπενεχθῆμεν
Ē Fabr. / ἐγὼν Koen ἐγὼ <δὲ> Blass κήγὼ Tr. 2
συνενεχθέντα L Z St συνενειχθέντα rel. Fabr. / ἐσεῖται
Pl.2 R St ἐσσεῖται rel. Fabr. 4 ἀπᾶγον Wil. ἀπάγον P4.6
V2 ἀπάγαγον rel. / οὐδ᾽ αἰ Pl.2 Matth. de Varis οὐδὲ rel.
οὐδὲ αἰ Meib. 5 χαλκὸν <ἂν> Mull. χαλκόν <κα> Blass /
[ἀπήνεικαν] Wil. / οὐδ᾽ αἰ Weber (antea Matth. de Varis)
οὐδ᾽ ἂν Pl.2 οὐδὲ αἰ Meib. / ἄργυρον Blass 6
μόλυβδόν Mull. 7 ἀπάγοντι; Wil. (quaest. sig. Ma.)
ἀπαγαγόντι O ἀπάγαγον Mull. κ᾽ ἀπάγαγον; Ma. / αἰσχρὸν
<ἄνδρα> Diels 8 ἄγαγε Mull. ἀπάγαγε O / τοῦτον --
ἀπάγαγε om. P2 7 τοῦτο M S <ταύτὸν> τοῦτο Wil. / αὖ <κα>
καλὸν scripsi (post Diels) δ᾽ ἂν καλὸν F2 Pl.4.6 R ἂν
καλὸν rel. δὴ καὶ οὐ καλὸν κ᾽ Ma. ἄρα καλὸν Wil. καὶ
αἰσχρὸν susp. Weber, qui δὴ καὶ οὐ καλὸν in text. δ᾽ αὖ
<κα> καλὸν Diels / ἀπάγαγε O ἀπάγει; Wil. ἀπάγε; Diels
9 <οἳ> Or. / ποτ᾽ O ποτὶ Kr. / <τὰ ποιήματα> ποιέοντι
T̄r. 10 ποιεῦντι P3 ποιοῦντι rel. 11 Tit. Περὶ δικαίου
καὶ ἀδίκου O praeter Περὶ τῶ δικαίω καὶ τῶ ἀδίκω St Περὶ

together are going to turn out to be seemly, and not
the sort of things they were when they came.   (27)
Certainly if they had brought horses or cattle or sheep
or people they would not have taken something else away.
For they would not even have taken brass away if they
had brought gold, nor lead if they had brought silver
coin.   (28) Do they really then take away things that
are seemly in place of the shameful that they brought?
Come now, if someone had brought along an ugly man,
would he have taken him away handsome instead?   They
also adduce as witnesses poets--who write their poetry
to give pleasure, not to propound truth.

3. On just and unjust

(1) Contrasting arguments are also put forward on
the matter of what is just and what is unjust.   Some
say that what is just and what is unjust are two different things, others that the same thing is just and
unjust.   For my part, I shall attempt to bolster the
latter view.   (2) And I shall say first of all that it
is just to tell lies and to deceive.   Opponents of this
view might say that doing these things to one's enemies
is shameful and base; yet they would not say that it is
shameful and base to do them to those whom one holds
very dear--parents, for example.   For if it were

δικάιω καὶ ἀδίκω Or. 13 τῶ ἀδίκω P3 περὶ τῶ ἀδίκω rel.
14 τωὐτόν P3 15 τοῦτο P4.6 V2 τούτοις Sch. τούτῳ <τῷ
λόγῳ> Tr. / πειρασοῦμαι P1.2 πειράσομαι rel. 16 <τὸ>
ψεύδεσθαι Fabr. / δίκαιόν om. P1.2 / ἔστι καὶ ἔστι P1.2 /
<τὸ> ἐξαπατᾶν Fabr. 17 ταῦτα <μὴ> ποιὲν αἰσχρὸν Blass
ταῦτα ποιὲν <καλὸν καὶ δίκαιον, τὼς δὲ φίλως> αἰσχρὸν
Diels / <κα> καὶ πονηρὸν Tr.

116

ἂν ἐξείποιεν· τὼς δὲ φιλτάτως οὕ· αὐτίκα τὼς γονέας·
αἱ γὰρ δέοι τὸν πατέρα ἢ τὰν ματέρα φάρμακον πιὲν
καὶ φαγέν, καὶ μὴ θέλοι, οὐ δίκαιόν ἐστι καὶ ἐν τῷ
ῥοφήματι καὶ ἐν τῷ ποτῷ δόμεν καὶ μὴ φάμεν ἐνῆμεν;
5 (3) οὐκῶν ἤδη ψεύδεσθαι καὶ ἐξαπατᾶν τὼς γονέας καὶ
κλέπτεν μὰν τὰ τῶν φίλων καὶ βιῆσθαι τὼς φιλτάτως
δίκαιον. (4) αὐτίκα αἴ τις λυπηθείς τι τῶν οἰκηΐων
καὶ ἀχθεσθεὶς μέλλοι αὐτὸν διαφθείρεν ἢ ξίφει ἢ
σχοινίῳ ἢ ἄλλῳ τινι, δίκαιόν ἐστι ταῦτα κλέψαι, αἱ
10 δύναιτο, αἱ δὲ ὑστερίξαι καὶ ἔχοντα καταλάβοι,
ἀφελέσθαι βίᾳ; (5) ἀνδραποδίξασθαι δὲ πῶς οὐ δίκαιον
τὼς πολεμίως, αἴ τις δύναιτο ἐλὼν πόλιν ὅλαν ἀποδόσθαι; τοιχωρυχὲν δὲ τὰ τῶν πολιτῶν κοινὰ οἰκήματα
δίκαιον φαίνεται. αἱ γὰρ ὁ πατὴρ ἐπὶ θανάτῳ, κατεσ-
15 τασιασμένος ὑπὸ τῶν ἐχθρῶν, δεδεμένος εἴη, ἆρα οὐ
δίκαιον διορύξαντα κλέψαι καὶ σῶσαι τὸν πατέρα;
(6) ἐπιορκὲν δέ· αἴ τις ὑπὸ τῶν πολεμίων λαφθεὶς
ὑποδέξαιτο ὀμνύων ἦ μὰν ἀφεθεὶς τὰν πόλιν προδώσεν,
ἆρα οὗτος δίκαιά <κα> ποιήσαι εὐορκήσας; (7) ἐγὼ
20 μὲν γὰρ οὐ δοκῶ, ἀλλὰ μᾶλλον τὰν πόλιν καὶ τὼς φίλως
καὶ τὰ ἱερὰ σῶσαι <ἂν τὰ> πατρῷα ἐπιορκήσας. ἤδη

1 αἱ ἐξείη ποιέν Blass [ἂν] ἐξείποιεν Tr. ἂν 'falsch'
Kr. / ἐξείποιεν· <πῶς δὲ τὼς πολεμίως,> τὼς δὲ φιλτάτως
Diels / οὕ; Blass, Diels 2 ματέρα St μητέρα Pl.2
compend. rel. / φάρμακόν τι St / πιὲν καὶ φαγέν O
praeter ποιὲν καὶ φαγὲν P2 ἐγκαταφαγὲν St πιὲν ἢ φαγὲν
Blass 3 ἐντὶ P3 / καὶ . . . καὶ O ἢ . . . ἢ susp. Diels
5 οὐκῶν scripsi (susp. antea Matth. de Varis) οὔκων vel
οὔκουν O οὐκοῦν Mull. / οὐκοῦν <δίκαιον> ἤδη Diels /
τὼς γονέας. καὶ κλέπτει punct. Diels 7 αἱ [τις]
λυπηθείς τις Wil. / οἰκήων Pl.2 οἰκήων rel. 8 καὶ O ἢ
Wil. / αὐτὸν St αὐτόν O 10 ὑστερήσαι P2 11 βίᾳ O
βίᾳ; Fabr. 12 [τὼς πολεμίως] Wil. / <καὶ> αἴ τις Diels
13 πολιτᾶν Tr. 14 κατεστασιασμένα Fabr. 17 ἐπιορκὲν
Pl.2 ἐπιορκεῖν rel. (volebat τὸ ἐπιορκεῖν R) / ἐπιορκὲν
δέ· αἴ τις punct. Mull. (simil. intell. in vers. lat.

necessary that one's father or mother should consume
some medicament (whether in solid or liquid form), but
he or she was unwilling, is it not just to give them the
medicament in their food or in their drink and not say
that it is in it? (3) So it is already clear that it
is just to tell lies and to deceive one's parents, and
for that matter to steal the property of one's friends
and use violence on those whom one holds very dear.
(4) For example, if some member of one's household had
been brought to grief in some way and were on the point
of doing away with himself with a sword or rope or some
other implement, it is just to steal these implements,
should one be able to, or, should one arrive late on
the scene and come upon him with the implement in his
hand, to take it away from him by force. (5) And
surely it is just to enslave one's enemies, should one
prove able to capture an entire city and sell it into
slavery? And breaking into buildings which are the
public property of one's fellow-citizens appears to be
just. For if one's father has been overpowered by his
enemies and jailed, under sentence of death, is it not
just to break in through the wall and steal one's father
away and so save him? (6) Or take oath-breaking. If
a man were captured by the enemy and undertook on oath
to betray his city if they set him free, would this man
be acting justly if he kept his oath? (7) I for my
part do not think so, but rather that he would save his
city and his friends and the ancestral temples by

N.) ἐπιορκεῖν δὲ αἴ τις O ἐπιορκὲν δέ, αἴ τις Fabr.   19
αἴα Pl.2 / οὕτως (ος super ως) Pl.2 / <κα> Ma. / ποιησεῖ
Wil.   20 [γὰρ] Wil.   21 σῶσαι <ἄν> scripsi σῶσαι St
σῶσαι rel. σῶσας Sch.   / <κα Diels, τά> Matth. de Varis,
Blass

118

ἆρα δίκαιον καί τό ἐπιορκεῖν. καί τό ἱεροσυλέν·
(8) τά μέν ἴδια τῶν πόλεων ἑῶ, τά δέ κοινά τᾶς
Ἑλλάδος, τά ἐκ Δελφῶν καί τά ἐξ Ὀλυμπίας, μέλλοντος
τῶ βαρβάρω τάν Ἑλλάδα λαβέν καί τᾶς σωτηρίας ἐν
5 χρήμασιν ἐούσας, οὐ δίκαιον λαβεῖν καί χρῆσθαι ἐς
τόν πόλεμον; (9) φονεύεν δέ τώς φιλτάτως δίκαιον,
ἐπεί καί Ὀρέστας καί Ἀλκμαίων· καί ὁ θεός ἔχρησε
δίκαια αὐτῶ ποιῆσαι. (10) ἐπί δέ τάς τέχνας τρέψομαι
καί τά τῶν ποιητῶν. ἐν γάρ τραγωδοποιίᾳ καί ζωγραφίᾳ
10 ὅστις πλεῖστα ἐξαπατῇ ὅμοια τοῖς ἀληθινοῖς ποιέων,
οὗτος ἄριστος. (11) θέλω δέ καί ποιημάτων παλαιοτέρων
μαρτύριον ἐπαγαγέσθαι. Κλεοβουλίνης·
    ἄνδρ' εἶδον κλέπτοντα καί ἐξαπατῶντα βιαίως,
    καί τό βίᾳ ῥέξαι τοῦτο δικαιότατον.
15 (12) ἦν πάλαι ταῦτα· Αἰσχύλου δέ ταῦτα·
    ἀπάτης δικαίας οὐκ ἀποστατεῖ θεός·
    ψευδῶν δέ καιρόν ἔσθ' ὅπου τιμῇ θεός.
(13) λέγεται δέ καί τῷδε ἀντίος λόγος ὡς ἄλλο τό
δίκαιον καί τό ἄδικόν ἐστιν, διαφέρον ὥσπερ καί
20 τὤνυμα οὕτω καί τό πρᾶγμα. ἐπεί αἴ τις ἐρωτάσαι τώς

---

1 ἐπιορκέν Fabr. 2 τῆς Pl.2 / Ἑλλάδος <λέγω?> Or. 4 τήν
Pl.2 / λαβέν vel λαβῆν Ο λαβεῖν Diels 5 λαβεῖν Ο λαβῆν
Fabr. 7 Ἀλκμάν Blass 8 αὐτῶ Blass αὐτῶ Pl.2 R V2 αὐτῷ
B Vl αὐτώς St 9 καί τά τῶν Diels καί ταῦτα Ο / ποιητᾶν
Tr. 10 ὅστις <κα> Blass / πλεῖστα <κα> Tr. / ἀλαθινοῖς
(ex ἀληθινοῖς) P2 11 ποιημάτων παλαιοτέρων Diels
ποιήματα τῶν παλαιοτέρων Ο 12 μαρτυριῶν Pl.2 μαρτύρων
Bergk 13 ἀρπάζοντα (pro ἐξαπατῶντα) susp. Or. / βιαίως
Matth. de Varis βία· ὡς Ο βίᾳ· ὡς St βίᾳ ὡς Crusius
δικαίως susp. Bergk 14 ῥύξαι B Vl / δικαιότατ' ἦν Blass
15 ἦν πάλαι Ο ἦν. παλαιά Blass ἐν πάλαι (= ἐν πάλᾳ) Wil.
παλαιοτέρων μέν susp. Weber / [Αἰσχύλου δέ ταῦτα] Wil.
16 ἀποστατεῖ ἀπο in fin. col. Pl / θεός· <καί·> ψευδῶν
Diels 17 ὅπου Hermann ὅποι Ο / τιμᾷ Or. (susp. antea
Matth. de Varis) / ἔσθ' ὅτ' ἐν τιμῇ θεῶν Thiersch 19
ἐστιν Pl.2 ἐστι rel. 20 ἐρωτάσαι Pl.2 Fabr. ἐρωτῆσαι
rel. ἐρωτῆσαι St

breaking his oath. So it is already clear that oath-
breaking too is just. And temple-robbery as well.
(8) I am excluding those temples which are the private
possessions of particular cities; but is it not just
to take and use for war-purposes those temples which
are the public property of Greece--those of Delphi and
Olympia--if the foreign invader is on the point of
capturing Greece, and if preservation depends on money?
(9) And it is just to slaughter those who are dearest,
since both Orestes and Alcmaeon did--and the god
declared that they had acted justly. (10) I shall
turn to the arts--particularly the compositions of poets.
For in the writing of tragedies and in painting the
best person is the one who deceives the most in creating
things that are <u>like</u> the real thing. (11) And I want
to adduce evidence from older poetry, like that of
Cleobuline:

    I saw a man stealing and deceiving by force,
    And gaining his ends by force in this way was
        a very just action.

(12) These lines were in existence a long time ago.
The next are from Aeschylus:

    God does not stand aloof from just deception.
    There are occasions when God respects an
        opportune moment for lies.

(13) To this view also there is an opposing view, to
the effect that what is just and what is unjust are
different things; as the name differs, so likewise
does the reality. For if one were to ask those who
say that the same thing is just and unjust whether they

λέγοντας ὡς τὸ αὐτὸ ἐστιν ἄδικον καὶ δίκαιον, αἱ ἤδη
τι δίκαιον περὶ τὼς γονέας ἔπραξαν, ὁμολογησοῦντι.
καὶ ἄδικον ἄρα. τὸ γὰρ αὐτὸ ἄδικον καὶ δίκαιον
ὁμολογέοντι ἦμεν. (14) φέρε ἄλλο δέ· αἴ τινα
5 γινώσκει δίκαιον ἄνδρα, καὶ ἄδικον ἄρα τὸν αὐτὸν
(καὶ μέγαν τοίνυν καὶ μικρὸν κατὰ τωὐτόν). καίτοι
πολλὰ ἀδικήσας ἀποθανέτω <ἄτε θανάτω ἄξια
δια?>πραξάμενος. (15) καὶ περὶ μὲν τούτων ἄλις.
εἶμι δὲ ἐφ' ἃ λέγοντες ἀξιοῦντι τὸ αὐτὸ καὶ δίκαιον
10 καὶ ἄδικον ἀποδεικνύεν. (16) τὸ γὰρ κλέπτεν τὰ τῶν
πολεμίων δίκαιον, καὶ ἄδικον ἀποδεικνύεν τοῦτ' αὐτό,
αἴ κ' ἀληθὴς ὁ τήνων λόγος, καὶ τἆλλα καττωὐτό.
(17) τέχνας δὲ ἐπάγονται ἐν αἷς οὐκ ἔστι τὸ δίκαιον
καὶ τὸ ἄδικον. καὶ τοὶ ποιηταὶ οὗτοι ποτ' ἀλάθειαν
15 ἀλλὰ ποτὶ τὰς ἀδονὰς τῶν ἀνθρώπων τὰ ποιήματα
ποιέοντι.

---

1 αἱ ἤδη Wil. αἴ κα δή Ο αἴ <πο>κα δή Blass 2 ὁμολογησοῦντι Matth. de Varis ὁμολογοσοῦντι Pl ὁμολογοῦντι
rel. 4 ἄλλο Diels ἄλλον Ο / δέ Ο δή Diels / ἃν Or.
5 γινώσκει L γινώσκη vel γινώσκη rel. γινώσκεις Diels
6 καὶ μέγα (sc. ἀδικοῦντα) καὶ μικρὸν καττωὐτὸ susp. Or. /
κατὰ τωυτὸν P3 κάτ τωὐτόν Matth. de Varis κατὰ ταὐτόν
F2 Pl.2 R Vl Fabr. κατ' αὐτὸν Η καταυτὸν Z St τὰ κατ'
αὐτὸν P6 V2 / καὶ τοι πολλὰ Ο καὶ τοι <ὁ> πολλὰ Diels,
qui susp. καττόδε ὁ πολλὰ vel καττωυτὸν ὁ πολλὰ, καὶ <αἱ
Friedländer λέγοιτο> "πολλὰ Kr. 7 "πολλὰ ἀδικήσας
ἀποθανέτω" Kr. / ἀποθανέτω Ο praeter ἀποθανέτω ἀποθανέτω
C P6 V2 ἀποθανέτω. ἀποθανέτω Y1.2 post ἀποθανέτω susp.
lac. unius lin. Sch. / ἀποθανέτω <ἄτε θανάτω ἄξια
δια?>πραξάμενος scripsi ἀποθανέτω πραξάμενος Ο praeter
C P6 V2 Y1.2 (v. supra) ἀποθανέτω, ἀποθανέτω <πολλὰ καὶ
δίκαια δια>πραξάμενος Blass καὶ τοι <ὁ?> πολλὰ ἀδικήσας
ἀποθανέτω, <καὶ πάλιν <ὁ?> πολλὰ δίκαια ἐργασ>άμενος
Sch. ἀποθανέτω <ὁ πολλὰ καὶ δίκαια τὸν> πρα <ἔργα>ξά-
μενος Wil. ἀποθανέτω <καὶ πολλὰ καὶ δίκαια δια>πραξάμενος
Diels ἀποθανέτω," ἀποθανέτω <καὶ πολλὰ καὶ δίκαια

had ever up to then performed any just action towards
their parents, they will say Yes. But in that case it
was also an <u>unjust</u> action; for they concede that the
same thing is just and unjust. (14) Or take another
point. If somebody knows that some man is just, he
in that case knows that the same man is <u>unjust</u> and by
the same token big and small. But if a man <u>has</u> been
very <u>unjust</u> in his actions he ought to be executed!--
For he has brought about <a situation that warrants
death?>. (15) Let that suffice for these points. I
shall turn to the <specific> arguments they use when
they claim that they can demonstrate that the same thing
is both just and unjust. (16) For, if what they say
is true, <the fact? to demonstrate?> that stealing the
enemy's possessions is just is to demonstrate that this
very action is <u>unjust</u>; and likewise for all the other
cases. (17) They adduce as evidence arts in which what
is just and what is unjust have no place. And poets
never write their poems to propound truth but to give
pleasure.

δια>πραξάμενος Kr. <u>9</u> ἀξιοῦντι Mull. ἀξιδοντι O ἀξιδωντι
St ἀξιῶοντι Blass ἀξιῶντι Wil. <u>10</u> τὸ γὰρ κλέπτεν --
ἀποδεικνύεν bis B Vl <u>11</u> [ἀποδεικνύεν] Blass <κ>
ἀποδείκνυεν (antea ἀποδεικνύει) Wil. / ἀποδεικνύεν τοῦτ᾽
αὐτό scripsi ἀποδεικνύεν, τοῦτ᾽ αὐτό O ἀποδεικνύεν. τοῦτ᾽
αὐτό. St ἀποδεικνύεν ῥᾴδιον (vel tale quid) τοῦτ᾽ αὐτό N.
<ἔξεστιν> ἀποδεικνύεν τὸ αὐτό Mull. <κ> ἀποδεικνύεν
τοῦτο τωὐτό Diels <u>12</u> αἱ γ᾽ Blass / ἀληθὴς <ῆς> Wil.
<u>14</u> οὗτοι Blass οὕτο vel οὕτό O praeter καὶ τὸ P3 οὕτι
St οὔτε Or. οὐ [τὸ] Sch. οὔ τι Tr. / ποτὶ Kr. / ἀλάθειαν
Pl ἀλήθειαν rel. <u>15</u> ἀδονάς Pl.2 ἡδονάς rel. <u>16</u>
ποιέοιντο St

4. Περὶ ἀλαθείας καὶ ψευδέος

(1) λέγονται δὲ καὶ περὶ τῶ ψευδέος καὶ τῶ
ἀλαθέος δισσοὶ λόγοι, ὧν ὁ μέν φατι ἄλλον μὲν τὸν
ψεύσταν ἦμεν λόγον, ἄλλον δὲ τὸν ἀλαθῆ· τοὶ δὲ τὸν
5 αὐτὸν αὖ. (2) κἀγὼ τόνδε λέγω· πρῶτον μὲν ὅτι τοῖς
αὐτοῖς ὀνόμασι λέγονται· ἔπειτα δέ, ὅταν λόγος
ῥηθῇ, αἱ μὲν ὡς <ἂν?> λέγηται ὁ λόγος οὕτω γεγένηται, ἀλαθὴς ὁ λόγος, αἱ δὲ μὴ γεγένηται, ψευδὴς ὁ
αὐτὸς λόγος. (3) αὐτίκα κατηγορεῖ ἱεροσυλίαν τω·
10 αἴ γ' ἐγένετο τὦργον, ἀλαθὴς ὁ λόγος· αἱ δὲ μὴ
ἐγένετο, ψεύστας. καὶ τῶ ἀπολογουμένω ὥς γε ὁ
λόγος. καὶ τά γε δικαστήρια τὸν αὐτὸν λόγον καὶ
ψεύσταν καὶ ἀλαθῆ κρίνοντι. (4) ἐπεί τοι καὶ ἐξῆς
καθήμενοι αἱ λέγοιμεν "μύστας εἰμί," τὸ αὐτὸ μὲν
15 πάντες ἐροῦμεν, ἀλαθὴς δὲ μόνος ἐγώ, ἐπεὶ καὶ εἰμί.
(5) δᾶλον ὧν ὅτι ὁ αὐτὸς λόγος, ὅταν μὲν αὐτῷ παρῇ
τὸ ψεῦδος, ψεύστας ἐστίν, ὅταν δὲ τὸ ἀλαθές, ἀλαθὴς
(ὥσπερ καὶ ἄνθρωπος τὸ αὐτό, καὶ παῖς καὶ νεανίσκος

1 Tit. Περὶ ἀλαθείας καὶ ψευδέος F2 Περὶ ἀληθείας καὶ
ψεύδους rel. Περὶ τῶ ψευδέος καὶ τᾶς ἀλαθείας St 2 τῶ
vel τῷ O praeter τᾶς P3 St 3 ἀλαθέος Diels ἀλαθείας
P3.4 ἀληθείας rel. τῶ ἀλαθέος vel τῆς ἀλαθείης Matth.
de Varis / τοὶ μὲν φατι Or. 4 ὁ δὲ Wil. / τοὶ δὲ τὸν
αὐτὸν αὖ. κάγὼ Blass τοὶ δὲ τὸν αὐτὸν. αὖ καγώ· (vel
αὖ. κάγώ·) O τοὶ δὲ, ὧν κάγώ, τὸν αὐτὸν Or. τοὶ δὲ τὸν
αὐτόν, ἐν οἷς κάγὼ Mull. 5 τὸ δὲ λέγω vel τὸ δὲ λόγω
N. τώδε λόγω Fabr. τῶδε λόγω Or. τῷδε <τῷ> λόγω
<πειρασοῦμαι τιμωρέν> Tr. 6 λέγοντι susp. Diels /
ἔπειτα -- γένηται ad mrg. P4 / ὅκκα Wil. 7 αἱ P3 ἂν
rel. / <ἂν?> λέγηται scripsi λέγεται Mull. <κα> λέγηται
Blass / γεγένηται Blass (<γε>γένηται ad mrg. P4) γένηται
O 8 ἀλαθὴς P3 ἀληθὴς rel. / αἱ P3 ἂν rel. / γεγένηται
Blass γένηται O 9 κατηγορεῖς B St / τῳ St 10 αἴ γ'
Diels αἴκ' O αἱ μὲν Blass / αἱ γεγένηται, αἱ δὲ μὴ γεγένη-
ται susp. Diels 11 ὥς γε ὁ O ὠυτὸς Wil. 12 γε O δὲ
susp. Diels 13 ἀλαθῆ P3.4 ἀληθῆ rel. / ἐπεί τοι [καὶ]
Wil. ἔπειτα τοὶ Diels / καὶ ἐξῆς O κατεξῆς vel καθεξῆς
Bergk αἱ ἐξῆς Wil. [καὶ] ἐξῆς Diels 14 καθήμενοι [αἱ] Wil.

4. On truth and falsehood

(1) Contrasting arguments are also put forward on what is true and what is false. The one view affirms that the true statement and the false statement are different things; the other group affirms that the two statements are on the contrary the same. (2) I for my part also hold the latter view: first, because the two statements are expressed in the same words; and next, because whenever a statement is made, if the event has taken place in the way indicated by the statement, the statement is true; but if the event has not taken place in the way indicated, the same statement is false. (3) For example, suppose a statement consists of an accusation against somebody of temple-robbery. If the act did in fact take place, the statement is true; if not, the statement is false. And likewise with the statement of the man defending himself against the charge. And lawcourts in fact judge the same statement to be both true and false. (4) For the fact is, even if, sitting next to one another in a row, we were <as a group> to say, "I am an initiate", we shall all be saying the same thing, but only I shall be telling the truth, since only I am an initiate. (5) It is clear, then, that the same statement is false when the false is present to it, and true when the true is present to it (just as a person is the same person, though at one time a child, at another a youth, at another an adult,

---

αἱ O ἂν N. / λέγοιμεν N. λέγοι μὲν Yl.2 λέγοιμι (εν super μι) P4 λέγοιμι rel. / μύστας O praeter μύμας L Z Μίμας St Μύστας Mull. Σιμμίας Blass Μίλτας Bergk Σίμων Tch. 15 ἀληθὲς N. ἀλαθὲς Or.

καὶ ἀνήρ καὶ γέρων, ἐστίν). (6) λέγεται δὲ καὶ ὡς
ἄλλος εἴη ὁ ψεύστας λόγος, ἄλλος δὲ ὁ ἀλαθής,
διαφέρων τὤνυμα <ὥσπερ καὶ τὸ πρᾶγμα>. αἰ γάρ τις
ἐρωτάσαι τὼς λέγοντας ὡς ὁ αὐτὸς λόγος εἴη ψεύστας
5 καὶ ἀλαθὴς ὅν αὐτοί λέγοντι, πότερος ἐστιν· αἰ μὲν
"ψεύστας," δᾶλον ὅτι δύο εἴη· αἰ δ' "ἀλαθὴς" ἀποκρίναιτο, καὶ ψεύστας ὁ αὐτὸς οὗτος. καὶ <αἰ> ἀλαθές
τί ποκα εἶπεν ἢ ἐξεμαρτύρησε, καὶ ψευδῆ ἄρα τὰ αὐτὰ
ταῦτα. καὶ αἴ τινα ἄνδρα ἀλαθῆ οἶδε, καὶ ψεύσταν
10 τὸν αὐτόν. (7) ἐκ δὲ τῶ λόγω λέγοντι ταῦτα, ὅτι
γενομένω μὲν τῶ πράγματος ἀλαθῆ τὸν λόγον, ἀγενήτω
δὲ ψεύσταν. οὔκων διαφέρει <ἐρέσθαι>   (8) αὖθις
τὼς δικαστάς ὅ τι κρίνοιντο (οὐ γάρ πάρεντι τοῖς
πράγμασιν). (9) ὁμολογέοντι δὲ καὶ αὐτοί, ᾧ μὲν τὸ
15 ψεῦδος ἀναμέμεικται, ψεύσταν ἦμεν, ᾧ δὲ τὸ ἀλαθές,
ἀλαθῆ. τοῦτο δὲ ὅλον διαφέρει.

     5. (1) "ταύτά τοί μαινόμενοι καὶ τοί σωφρονοῦν-
τες καὶ τοί σοφοί καὶ τοί ἀμαθεῖς καὶ λέγοντι καὶ

---

3 <ὥσπερ καὶ τὸ πρᾶγμα> Diels <οὕτω καὶ πρᾶγμα> N. <καὶ
τὸ πρᾶγμα> Mull. <ὥσπερ καὶ> τὤνυμα <οὕτω καὶ τὸ πρᾶγμα>
Blass [διαφέρων τὤνυμα] Sch. διαφέρων <τὸ πρᾶγμα ὥσπερ
καὶ> τὤνυμα Wil.   4 ὁ om. P4.6 V2 6 δᾶλον P3 St δῆλον
rel. / <ἄν> εἴη Mull. <κ> εἴη Blass ἐντί Wil. / "ἀλαθὴς"
ἀποκρίναιτο, καὶ Weber ἀλαθὴς ἀποκρίναιτο, καὶ O praeter
ἀποκρίναιντο P3 ἀλαθής, ἀποκρίναιτο καὶ Or. ἀλαθής,
ἀποκρίναιτό κα Mull. ἀλαθής, [ἀποκρίναιτο] καὶ Sch.
7 καὶ <αἰ> Blass καὶ Diels (καὶ <εἰ> susp. antea Matth.
de Varis) / ἀλαθῆ τις N. ἀλαθῆ τίς Sch.   8 ποκα vel
πόκα O praeter πόλα L πόκα e πόλα Z πολλὰ St N.   9 ἀληθῆ
P4 10 ἐν δὲ τῶ λόγω susp. N. / λόγου <λέγοντι> Diels
11 ἀγεννήτω P4 12 ψεύσταν <νομίζοντι> Tr. ψεύσταν
<τοί δικασταί κρίνοντι> Weber / οὔκων Or. / <ἐρέσθαι>
αὖθις scripsi 13 τοῖς δικασταῖς Mull. τοί δικασταί
Sch. / ὅ τι κρίνοντι Sch. ὅ τι <κα> κρίνωντι Weber /
οὔκων διαφέρει. αὖθις τὼς δικαστάς, ὅτι τὸν αὐτὸν λόγον
καὶ ψεύσταν καὶ ἀλαθῆ κρίνοντι Blass οὔκων διαφέρει

and at another an old man). (6) It is also said that the false statement is different from the true statement; as the name differs, so likewise does the reality. For if anyone were to ask those who say that the same statement is false and true which of the two their own statement is, if the reply were "false", it is clear that a true statement and a false statement are two different things, but if he were to reply "true" then this same statement is also false. And if at any time he said something true or testified that something was true, then he also testified that these same things were false. And if he knows that a certain man is an honest man, he knows the same man is a liar. (7) And in accord with their thesis they say that a statement is true if (8) the event to which it refers took place, but false if it did not. It is therefore important to ask jurymen in their turn what their judgment is (jurymen, of course, not being personally present at the events). (9) Even they themselves agree that that with which the false is intermingled is false, and that that with which the true is intermingled is true. But this view is totally different <from their original thesis>.

5. (1) "The demented, the sane, the wise and the ignorant both say and do the same things. (2) First of

<αὐτῶν τῶνυμα, ἀλλὰ τὸ πρᾶγμα. (8) ἐρωτᾶσαι δέ κά τις> αὖθις τὼς δικαστάς, ὅ τι κρίνοντι Diels οὔκων διαφέρει; <καὶ> αὖθις τὼς δικαστὰς ὅτι κρίνοντι Gomperz 15 ἀναμέμεικται Blass ἀναμέμικται Ο / ὦ Diels (per error. typograph.?) 16 lac. post διαφέρει Diels (item ut app. antea N.) 17 Sect. nov. distinxit N. / "ταὐτά (or. recta 5.1-5) Diels ταὐτά N. ταυτα vel ταυτα Ο <λέγοντι δέ τινες ὡς> ταὐτά Blass ταὐτά -- καὶ οὐκ ἐντί post 4.5 transp. esse put. N.

πράσσοντι. (2) καὶ πρᾶτον μὲν ὀνομάζοντι ταὐτά, γᾶν
καὶ ἄνθρωπον καὶ ἵππον καὶ πῦρ καὶ τἆλλα πάντα.
καὶ ποιέοντι ταὐτά, κάθηνται καὶ ἔσθοντι καὶ πίνοντι
καὶ κατάκεινται, καὶ τἆλλα καττωύτό. (3) καὶ μάν
5 καὶ τὸ αὐτὸ πρᾶγμα καὶ μέζον καὶ μῆόν ἐστι καὶ
πλέον καὶ ἔλασσον καὶ βαρύτερον καὶ κουφότερον.
οὕτω γὰρ ἐντι ταὐτὰ πάντα. (4) τὸ τάλαυτόν ἐστι
βαρύτερον τῆς μνᾶς καὶ κουφότερον τῶν δύο ταλάντων·
τωὐτὸν ἄρα καὶ κουφότερον καὶ βαρύτερον. (5) καὶ
10 ζώει ὁ αὐτὸς ἄνθρωπος καὶ οὐ ζώει, καὶ ταὐτὰ ἔστι
καὶ οὐκ ἔστι· τὰ γὰρ τῇδ' ἐόντα ἐν τῇ Λιβύᾳ οὐκ
ἔστιν, οὐδέ γε τὰ ἐν Λιβύᾳ ἐν Κύπρῳ. καὶ τἆλλα
κατὰ τὸν αὐτὸν λόγον. οὐκῶν καὶ ἐντὶ τὰ πράγματα
καὶ οὐκ ἐντί." (6) τοὶ τῆνα λέγοντες, τὼς μαινο-
15 μένως καὶ τὼς σοφὼς καὶ τὼς ἀμαθεῖς τωὐτὰ διαπράσ-
σεσθαι καὶ λέγεν, καὶ τἆλλα <τὰ> ἐπόμενα τῷ λόγῳ,
οὐκ ὀρθῶς λέγοντι. (7) αἰ γάρ τις αὐτὼς ἐρωτάσαι
αἰ διαφέρει μανία σωφροσύνης καὶ σοφίη ἀμαθίης,
φαντί· "ναί." (8) εὖ γὰρ καὶ ἐξ ὧν πράσσοντι

---

1 ταὐτά Meib. ταῦτα O (bis)   4 καὶ κατάκεινται post
κάθηνται transp. Wil.   5 τωὖτō Meib. / μεῖζον L St
μεῖόν L St   7 [οὕτω -- πάντα] Wil. / ἐντι Diels εἴη O
<ἄν> εἴη Mull. <κ> εἴη Blass <κα> εἴη Tr. / ταὐτά Meib.
(antea susp. Matth. de Varis) ταῦτα O   8 κωφότερον Tr.
9 post βαρύτερον susp. ὥσπερ -- ἐστίν (4.5) collocand.
Wil. lac. susp. Diels   10 καὶ ταὐτά Mull. κατταυτά O
praeter κατ' αὐτά Υl.2 St καὶ αὐτά N.   11 τεῖδε Bergk /
ἐόντα P3 ὄντα rel. / τᾷ P3 τῇ rel.   12 ἐντὶ P3 / οὐδέ γα
Tr. / <τᾷ> Λιβύᾳ Tr.   13 οὐκῶν P3 οὐκοῦν rel. / καὶ
ἔστι τὰ πράγματα καὶ οὐκ ἔστι Wil.   14 τοὶ τῆνα Diels
τοί τινες O τοὶ τοίνυν Mull. / [τὼς μαινομένως -- λέγεν]
in prima edit. Diels / inter τὼς et μαινομένως ind. ad
mrg. (al. man., ut vid.) τεμνομένως καὶ B (in textu E)

all they call things by the same name: 'earth', 'man',
'horse', 'fire', and everything else. And they do the
same things: they sit, eat, drink, lie down, and so on,
in the same way. (3) What is more, the same thing is
also both bigger and smaller, and more and less, and
heavier and lighter. For in those respects all objects
are the same. (4) The talent is heavier than the mina
and lighter than two talents; the same thing then is
both lighter and heavier. (5) And the same man is alive
and is not alive; and the same things exist (are the
case) and do not exist (are not the case). For what
exists (is the case) here does not exist (is not the
case) in Libya; nor does what exists (is what is the
case) in Libya exist (turn out to be the case) in Cyprus.
And so on in all other instances, using the same argument. Consequently, things both exist (are the case)
and do not exist (are not the case)". (6) Those who
say this--that the demented and the wise and the ignorant
do and say the same things, and all the other things
that follow from the argument--are in error. (7) For
if one were to ask them if dementedness differs from
sanity or wisdom from ignorance, they say "Yes". (8)
For it is quite obvious, even from the actions of each

μαινομένως καί <τὼς σωφρονοῦντας καί> τὼς σοφῶς Blass
15 τωὐτά P3 ταύτά rel.   16 <τά> Blass / ἐπόμενα F2
P3.4 ἐπόμνα vel ἐπόμνα rel.   17 ἐν γάρ τις αὐτὸς P4.6
V2 / ἐρωτάσαι Fabr. ἐρωτάσας Ο 18 διαφέρει P3 V2
διαφέρη vel διαφέρη rel. / σοφίη P3 σοφία rel. /
ἀμαθίας Or. 19 [ναί] Diels / εὖ Ο οὐ (-- ὁμολογησοῦντι;) susp. Diels

ἑκάτεροι δᾶλοί ἐντι ὡς ὁμολογησοῦντι. οὔκων, καὶ
<αἱ> ταὐτὰ πράσσοντι, καὶ τοὶ σοφοὶ μαίνονται καὶ
τοὶ μαινόμενοι σοφοὶ καὶ πάντα συνταράσσονται.
(9) καὶ ἐπακτέος ὁ λόγος πότερον [οἷον] ἐν δέοντι
5 τοὶ σωφρονοῦντες λέγοντι ἢ τοὶ μαινόμενοι. ἀλλὰ
γὰρ φαντι ὡς ταὐτὰ μὲν λέγοντι, ὅταν τις αὐτὼς
ἐρωτῇ· ἀλλὰ τοὶ μὲν σοφοὶ ἐν τῷ δέοντι, τοὶ δὲ
μαινόμενοι ᾇ οὐ δεῖ. (10) καὶ τοῦτο λέγοντες
δοκοῦντι μικρὸν ποτιθῆναι <τὸ> ᾇ δεῖ καὶ μὴ δεῖ,
10 ὥστε μηκέτι τὸ αὐτὸ ἦμεν. (11) ἐγὼ δὲ οὐ πράγματος
τοσούτω ποτιτεθέντος ἀλλοιοῦσθαι δοκῶ τὰ πράγματα,
ἀλλ' ἁρμονίας διαλλαγείσας· ὥσπερ "Γλαῦκος" καὶ
"γλαυκός" καὶ "Ξάνθος" καὶ "ξανθός" καὶ "Ξοῦθος" καὶ
"ξουθός." (12) ταῦτα μὲν τὴν ἁρμονίαν ἀλλάξαντα
15 διήνεικαν, τὰ δὲ μακρῶς καὶ βραχυτέρως ῥηθέντα,
"Τύρος" καὶ "τυρός," "σάκος" καὶ "σακός," ἄτερα δὲ
γράμματα διαλλάξαντα, "κάρτος" καὶ "κρατός," "ὄνος"
καὶ "νόος." (13) ἐπεὶ ὦν οὐκ ἀφαιρεθέντος οὐδενὸς
τοσοῦτον διαφέρει, τί δή, αἵ τις ἢ ποτιτιθεῖ τι ἢ

---

1 οὔκων scripsi οὐκῶν P3 οὐκοῦν rel. / καὶ <αἱ> scripsi
ἂν N. (in edit. alt.; in prima edit. utrum αἴ an ἂν
legendum haud clarum) αἱ Mull. (antea susp. Matth. de
Varis) 2 ταῦτα E Y2 (ut vid.) N. / τοὶ om. Or. (per
error. typograph.?) 4 ἐπακτέος Wil. ἐπ' ἄργεος F2 ἐπ'
ἄγεος P4.6 ἐπάρτεος vel ἐπ' ἄρτεος rel. ἐπερωτέος vel ἐπ'
ἀρτίου vel ἐπαρτής susp. N. ἔτι ἄτερος Koen ἐπάργεμος
Blass / πότερον F2 R St καὶ πότερον P4 V2 πρότερον rel.
πότεροι susp. Diels / [οἷον] Koen ὦν Wil. / ἐν τῷ δέοντι
Koen 6 ταὐτὰ Fabr. ταῦτα O ταῦτα N. (in vers. lat.
autem ⌐eadem') / ὅκα τις αὐτὼς ἐρωτῇ post φαντι transp.
Wil. 8 ᾇ οὐ Blass αἱ οὐ O αἱ μὴ Tr. 9 ποτιθεῖναι Mull.
ποτιθέμεν Ma. ποττιθέμεν Blass / <τὸ> Diels / ᾇ Blass
αἱ O / καὶ <αἱ> μὴ Or. 10 ὥστε <οὔ> St <οὐχ> ὥστε
Blass / ἦμεν O ᾗ Wil. / δὲ O μὰν Wil. / οὐ πράγματος O
οὐχ ὅτι Blass 11 τοσοῦτον Wil. / ποτιτεθέντος P3
προστεθέντος rel. / πράγματα O ὀνύματα Tr. 14 τὰν St
τὴν O [τὰν] Or. 15 διήνεγκαν Fabr. 16 τύρος καὶ τῦρος

group, that they will grant this point. So even if they do the same things (as the demented do) the wise are not demented, nor the demented wise, nor is everything turned into confusion. (9) And one ought to bring up the question whether it is those who are sane or those who are demented who speak at the right moment. For whenever one asks them they say that the two groups say the same things, only the wise say them at the right moment and the demented at moments when it is not proper. (10) And in saying this they seem to me to have added the small phrases "when it is proper" and "when it is not proper", with the result that it is no longer the same thing. (11) I myself do not think that things are altered by the addition of such qualifications, but rather when an accent is altered. For example: "Γλαῦκος" (Glaucus) and "γλαυκός" (green), or "Ξάνθος" (Xanthus) and "ξανθός" (blonde), or "Ξοῦθος" (Xuthus) and "ξουθός" (nimble). (12) The above differed by a difference in the placing of the accent: the following by being spoken with longer or shorter vowel-lengths: "Τύρος" (Tyre) and "τυρός" (cheese), "σάκος" (shield) and "σακός" (enclosure), and yet others by a change in the ordering of their letters: "κάρτος" (strength) and "κρατός" (of a head), "ὄνος" (ass) and "νόος" (mind). (13) Since, therefore, there is such a difference when nothing is taken away, what if in that case somebody does either add something or take some-

---

Wil. / σάκος καὶ σακός Weber σάκκος καὶ σάκκος (sic) L St σάκκος καὶ σάκος Z σάκος καὶ σάκκος rel. σᾰκος (scutum) καὶ σᾱκος (saccum) Heringa σακὸς (i.e., σηκός) καὶ σάκος Mull. σάκος καὶ σᾶκος Wil. / ἕτερα P3 17 κρατός Wil. κράτος O 18 ὧν (ex οὖν) P3 οὖν rel. 19 ἤ O τι Diels / ποτιτίθητι Diels

ἀφαιρεῖ; καὶ τοῦτο δείξω οἷόν ἐστιν. (14) αἴ τις
ἀπὸ τῶν δέκα ἕν ἀφέλοι, οὐκέτι δέκα οὐδὲ ἕν <ἄν>
εἴη, καὶ τἆλλα καττωύτό. (15) τὸ δὲ τὸν αὐτὸν
ἄνθρωπον καὶ ἦμεν καὶ μὴ ἦμεν, ἐρωτῶ· "τί ἢ τὰ πάντα
5 ἐστιν;" οὐκῶν αἴ τις μὴ φαίη ἦμεν, ψεύδεται "τὰ
πάντα" εἰπών. ταῦτα πάντα ὤν πῃ ἐστι.

6. (1) λέγεται δέ τις λόγος οὔτ' ἀλαθής οὔτε καινὸς
ὅτι ἄρα σοφίη καὶ ἀρετά οὔτε διδακτὸν εἴη οὔτε
μαθητόν. τοὶ δὲ ταῦτα λέγοντες ταῖσδε ἀποδείξεσι
10 χρῶνται· (2) ὡς οὐχ οἷόν τε εἴη, αἴ τι ἄλλῳ παραδοίης, τοῦτο αὐτὸν ἔτι ἔχειν. μία μὲν δὴ αὔτα.
(3) ἄλλα δὲ ὡς, αἰ διδακτὸν ἦν, διδάσκαλοί κα
ἀποδεδεγμένοι ἦν, ὡς τᾶς μωσικᾶς. (4) τρίτα δὲ
ὡς τοὶ ἐν τᾷ Ἑλλάδι γενόμενοι σοφοὶ ἄνδρες τὰ αὐτῶν
15 τέκνα ἄν ἐδίδαξαν καὶ τὼς φίλως. (5) τετάρτα δὲ ὅτι
ἤδη τινὲς παρὰ σοφιστὰς ἐλθόντες οὐδὲν ὠφέληθεν.

_____

1 ἐντι Meib. 2 ἀφέλοι <ἢ τοῖς δέκα ἕν ποτθείη>, οὔ κ'
ἔτι Diels / οὔ κ' ἔτι Ma. οὔ κα ἔτι Bergk / <ἄν> εἴη L
Mull. <κ> εἴη Blass 3 καττωύτό Meib. καττοῦτο O / τοὺς
δὲ susp. Mull. 4 ἦμεν <λέγοντας> ἐρωτῶ susp. Mull. /
<ἕν> τι ἢ Mull. <ἄλλο> τι ἢ Blass <πῇ> ἢ Wil. 5 φαίη
ἦμεν καὶ μὴ ἦμεν susp. N. μὴ φαίη ἦμεν <ἕν> Mull. πῇ
φαίη ἦμεν Wil. / ψεύδονται Wil. / "τὰ πάντα" scripsi τὰ
πάντα O <τὸ τί καὶ> τὰ πάντα Diels 6 εἰπών Mull.
εἰπόντες O / ταύτα πάντα (vel πάντως) N. ταύτα. πάντα
Diels ταῦτα. <τὰ> πάντα H. Gomperz / ὤν vel ὤν O susp.
ὅ N. ὤν Dupréel (ut vid.: v. Les Sophistes 211) / πῇ Or.
susp. μή N. πῇ Diels / ἔστι Weber (antea susp. N.) ἔστι
O ἐντι Fabr. ἐστίν Wil. / ψεύδεται. τὰ δὲ πάντα
πάντεσσι ταύτά, πάντα ὤν πῃ ἐστί susp. Blass 7 Tit.
Περὶ τᾶς σοφίας καὶ τᾶς ἀρετᾶς, αἰ διδακτὸν suppl. St /
ἀλαθής P3 St ἀληθής rel. / καινὸς (ε super αι) R Sch.
κενὸς rel. ἱκανὸς Shorey 8 ὅτι St τίς O ὡς Matth. de
Varis / σοφίη P3 σοφία rel. 9 μαθατόν Fabr. 10 τ'
Mull. / αἴ τι P4.6 ἄν rel. ἄ κ' Wil. τι post ἄλλῳ Sch.
11 τοῦτο αὐτὸν P4.6 τοῦτο αὐτό rel. ταῦτ' αὐτόν Wil. /
ἔχεν N. 12 διδασκαλικά St 13 ἀποδεδογμένην St ἀποδεδεγ-

thing away? I shall give an example of the sort of
thing I mean. (14) If a man were to take away one from
ten, there would no longer be ten or even one, and so
on in the same way in all other instances. (15) As for
the affirmation that the same man exists and does not
exist I ask, "Does he exist in some particular respect
or in every respect?" Thus, if anyone denies that the
man in question exists, he is making the mistake of
asserting "in every respect". The conclusion is that
all these things exist in some way.

  6. On whether wisdom and moral excellence are teachable

  (1) There is a certain view put forward which is
neither true nor new, to the effect that wisdom and
moral excellence can be neither taught nor learnt.
Those who say this use the following proofs: (2) That it
is impossible, if you impart something to some other
person, for you to retain possession of that thing. This
is one proof. (3) Another is that, had wisdom and moral
excellence been able to be taught, there would have
existed recognized teachers of them--the way there have
been recognized teachers of the arts. (4) A third proof
is that those men in Greece who became wise would have
taught this wisdom to their own children and their
friends. (5) A fourth proof is that before now there

μένην Meib. / [ἦν] St ἦεν Fabr. εἶεν (in text., in
adnot. autem ἦεν, cum Fabr.) Or. ἦσαν Mull. 14 αὐτῶν St
αὑτῶν O 15 τέχναν W. Schulze / ἂν O κα Ma. [ἂν] W.
Schulze / καὶ τὼς φίλως L (ad mrg.) St καὶ πῶς φίλωσι
(vel φίλως) rel. τῶν φίλων vel τὰ τῶν φίλων susp. Sch.
κα τὼς φίλως W. Schulze κα καὶ τὼς φίλως Friedländer
16 παρά St περί O

(6) πέμπτα δὲ ὅτι πολλοὶ οὐ συγγενόμενοι σοφισταῖς
ἄξιοι λόγω γεγένηνται.   (7) ἐγὼ δὲ κάρτα εὐήθη
νομίζω τόνδε τὸν λόγον· γινώσκω γὰρ τὼς διδασκάλως
γράμματα διδάσκοντας ἃ καὶ αὐτὸς ἐπιστάμενος
5 τυγχάνει, καὶ κιθαριστὰς κιθαρίζεν. πρὸς δὲ τὰν
δευτέραν ἀπόδειξιν, ὡς ἄρα οὐκ ἐντὶ διδάσκαλοι
ἀποδεδεγμένοι, τί μὰν τοὶ σοφισταὶ διδάσκοντι ἀλλ'
ἢ σοφίην καὶ ἀρετάν;   (8) [ἢ] τί δὲ Ἀναξαγόρειοι
καὶ Πυθαγόρειοι ἦεν;   τὸ δὲ τρίτον, ἐδίδαξε Πολύ-
10 κλειτος τὸν υἱὸν ἀνδριάντας ποιεῖν.   (9) καὶ ἂν μέν
τις μὴ διδάξῃ, οὐ σαμῆον· αἱ δ' ἔστι διδάξαι,
τεκμάριον ὅτι δυνατόν ἐστι διδάξαι.   (10) τέταρτον
δὲ αἱ μή τοι παρὰ σοφῶν σοφιστῶν σοφοὶ γίνονται.
καὶ γὰρ γράμματα πολλοὶ οὐκ ἔμαθον μαθόντες.   (11)
15 ἔστι δέ τις καὶ φύσις, ᾇ δή τις μὴ μαθὼν παρὰ
σοφιστᾶν ἱκανὸς ἐγένετο, εὐφυὴς καὶ γενόμενος, ῥαδίως
συναρπάξαι τὰ πολλά, ὀλίγα μαθὼν παρ' ὧνπερ καὶ τὰ
ὀνύματα μανθάνομεν· καὶ τούτων τι ἤτοι πλέον ἤτοι

---

4 διδάσκοντας ἃ Ο διδάσκεν τὰ κα Diels / καὶ αὐτὼς Matth.
de Varis καὶ αὐτὸς <ἕκαστος> vel καὶ αὐτῶν <ἕκαστος> Or.
[καὶ] <ἕκαστος> αὐτῶν Mull. καὶ αὐτός <τις> Weber /
ἐπισταμένως Matth. de Varis 5 τυγχάνειν Matth. de Varis
τυγχάνῃ Diels subinde lac. susp. Tr.   7 ἀποδεδειγμένοι
V2 / διδάσκοντι; ἀλλ' Weber διδάσκοντι ἀλλ' Diels 8
σοφίην P3 σοφίαν rel. / [ἢ] Wil. / δὲ Ο δαὶ Weber δὴ Tr.
9 ἦεν Ο ἦσαν Mull. ἦν Blass 10 ποιεῖν (ex ποιεῖν) P3 /
ἂν scripsi αἱ Ο 11 διδάξαι Blass ἐδίδαξε Diels / σαμῆον
P3 Meib. σαμῆον rel. σαμεῖον Gomperz (antea susp. Matth.
de Varis) / δ' ἔστι vel δ' ἐστί Ο praeter δ' ἔστιν L Z δ'
ἐστίν St δ' ἐντὶν Fabr. δ' ἐντὶ Mull. δέ τις Blass δ' ἕν τι
(antea δ' εἶς τις) Wil. δ' εἶς τις Diels ἐνά τινά
Gomperz / διδάσκεν susp. N. ἐδίδαξε Wil.   12 τεκμάριον
P3 τεκμήριον rel. / ἐντι Fabr.   13 αἱ μή τοι E St αἱ μὴ
τοὶ rel. / [σοφῶν] Blass / σοφιστῶν <μαθόντες> Blass
σοφιστᾶν Tr. / γίνονται, καὶ [γὰρ] Wil.   15 τι Sch. /
post φύσις. add. πέμπτον δέ Tr. / ᾇ δὴ Diels αἱ δὲ Ο
αἱ γὰρ Weber / ἔμαθε Mull.   16 σοφιστῶν St / ἐγένετο,
εὐφυὴς Blass (idemque in vers. lat. subintell. Fabr.

have been people who frequented sophists and gained no
benefit. (6) A fifth proof is that a large number of
people who did not associate with sophists have become
eminent. (7) I myself consider this line of reasoning
exceedingly simple-minded. For I know that teachers <u>do</u>
teach those letters which each one happens to possess
himself, and that harp-players <u>do</u> teach people how to
play the harp. As for the second proof--that there do
not in fact exist acknowledged teachers--what in that
case do the <u>sophists</u> teach, if not wisdom and moral
excellence? (8) And what were the followers of Anaxagoras and Pythagoras? As for the third proof, Polyclitus
<u>did</u> teach his son how to make statues. (9) Even if an
individual man does <u>not</u> teach <his own wisdom> nothing
will have been proved; but if he <u>is</u> able to teach it,
there is your proof that it is <u>possible</u> to do so. (10)
The fourth point <is valid only> if those in question
do not become wise after associating with <u>skilled</u> sophists. <I say <u>skilled</u>> because a lot of people do <u>not</u>
learn their letters, even though they have taken a
course in them. (11) There is also an important natural
talent whereby a person becomes capable, without having
learned his competence from sophists, of comprehending
the greater part <of a subject> with ease (provided he
is also naturally well-endowed), after learning <only?>
a small part <of it> from those from whom we also learn
words. And some of these latter things (be it a greater
or smaller number) one person learns from his father and

Or.) ἐγένετο εὐφυὴς O / κα Blass [καὶ] Wil. γα Diels
<u>17</u> συνάρπαξε Sch. / κα πολλά Gomperz / μαθὼν παρ' ὦνπερ
vel μαθών· παρ' ὦνπερ O μαθών, παρ' ὦνπερ O / τὰ ὠνύματα
P3 <u>18</u> de ἤτοι . . . ἤτοι dub. Wil. <ἐν>τι τοί πλέον,
<ἐντί> δ' οἱ susp. Diels

ἔλασσον, ὁ μὲν παρὰ πατρὸς ὁ δὲ παρὰ ματρός. (12)
αἱ δέ τῳ μὴ πιστόν ἐστι τὰ ὀνύματα μανθάνεν ἀμέ,
ἀλλ' ἐπισταμένως ἅμα γίνεσθαι, γνώτω ἐκ τῶνδε· αἴ τις
εὐθὺς γενόμενον παιδίον ἐς Πέρσας ἀποπέμψαι καί

5 τηνεῖ τράφοι, κωφὸν Ἑλλάδος φωνᾶς, περσίζοι κα· αἴ
τις τηνόθεν τῇδε κομίζοι, ἑλλανίζοι κα. οὕτω
μανθάνομεν τὰ ὀνύματα, καὶ τὼς διδασκάλως οὐκ
ἴσαμες. (13) οὕτω λέλεκταί μοι ὁ λόγος, καὶ ἔχεις
ἀρχὴν καὶ τέλος καὶ μέσαν· καὶ οὐ λέγω ὡς διδακτόν

10 ἐστιν, ἀλλ' οὐκ ἀποχρῶντί μοι τῆναι ταὶ ἀποδείξιες.

7. (1) λέγοντι δέ τινες τῶν δαμαγορούντων ὡς χρὴ
τὰς ἀρχὰς ἀπὸ κλάρω γίνεσθαι, οὐ βέλτιστα ταῦτα
νομίζοντες. (2) αἱ γάρ τις αὐτὸν ἐρωτῴη τὸν ταῦτα
λέγοντα, "τί δὴ σὺ τοῖς οἰκέταις οὐκ ἀπὸ κλήρω τὰ

15 ἔργα προστάσσεις, ὅπως ὁ μὲν ζευγηλάτας, αἴ κ' ὀψοποιὸς λάχῃ, ὀψοποιῇ, ὁ δὲ ὀψοποιὸς ζευγηλατῇ, καὶ
τἄλλα κατὰ τωὐτό; (3) καὶ πῶς οὐ καὶ τὼς χαλκῆας
καὶ τὼς σκυτῆας συναγαγόντες καὶ τέκτονας καὶ
χρυσοχόας διεκλαρώσαμεν καὶ ἠναγκάσαμεν ἂν χ' ἕκαστος

1 ματρός F2 St μητρός P3 per compend. rel. 2 ἐντι
Fabr. / τὰ ὠνύματα P3 τώνύματα susp. Weber / μανθάνειν
Or. / ἀμέ Koen ἄμε B P3.4.6 R Vl ἅμα rel. 3 αἴ τι Blass
6 τεῖδε Bergk / κομίξαι Wil. 7 τὰ ὠνύματα P3 / οὐκ
ἴσαμες Blass οὐκί ἄμες L St οὐκί ἄμες rel. (ἄμες ex ἄμες
B) οὐκί ἄμες; Fabr. οὐκί ἀκούομες Koen οὔτι ἀκούομες Tr.
8 οὕτω Diels οὐ Ο οὖ N. [οὐ] Koen / λέλεκται Ο ἤλεγκται
Koen 9 μέσαν P3 μέσην rel. / μέσον Mull. καὶ μέσον καὶ
τέλος Rohde / διδακτός L St 10 ἀλλ' οὐκ Diels ἀλλ' ὅτι
οὐκ F2 ἀλλ' ὅτι rel. / αἱ Matth. de Varis ταὶ Ο praeter
Yl.2 qui om. / ἀποδείξεις St 11 δαμαγορούντων P3 Tr.
δημαγορούντων rel. 13 αἱ P3 Tr. εἱ rel. καὶ Mull. /
<ἂν> ἐρωτῴη Mull. / [τὸν ταῦτα λέγοντα] Diels 14 τὺ
Tr. / κλάρω St 15 προστάσσεις L Matth. de Varis
προστάσσῃς rel. 16 ὀψοποιῇ Matth. de Varis ὀψοποιᾷ Ο
ὀψοποιᾷ St 17 κατὰ τωὐτό Koen κατά τοῦτο Ο κάτ τοῦτο

another from his mother. (12) And if someone is not
convinced that we learn our words, but feels sure we
are born knowing them, let him ascertain the truth from
the following evidence: should a person send a child to
Persia immediately it was born and have it brought up
there without ever hearing the speech of Greece, the
child would speak Persian; should one bring the child
from Persia to Greece, the child would speak Greek.
That is the way we learn words, and we do not know who
it was who taught us. (13) With that my argument is
completed, and you have its beginning, end, and middle.
I am not saying that wisdom and moral excellence are
teachable, but that the above-mentioned proofs do not
satisfy me.

7. (1) Some of the public speakers say that offices
should be assigned by lot; but this opinion of theirs
is not a very good one. (2) If only somebody would ask
him (i.e., the man who says this), "Why in that case
don't you assign your household slaves their jobs by
lot, so that the ox-driver, if he draws the job of cook
as his lot, will cook, while the cook will drive oxen,
and so on in all other instances? (3) And why don't we
bring together smiths and cobblers, carpenters and gold-
smiths, and assign them jobs by lot, forcing them to
perform whatever craft each one draws by lot, not the

Matth. de Varis καττωύτό Diels / καὶ τὼς Ο praeter P4.6
Y1.2 qui om. καί / χαλκῆας P3 χαλκέας rel. ὁ χαλκεὺς οὑ
ad mrg. B 18 σκυτῆας P3 σκυτέας rel. 19 χρυσοχόους
Or. / διεκλαρώσαμεν Meib. διεκληρώσαμεν Ο διακλαρώσομεν
Mull. διεκλαρώσαμες Weber / ἀναγκάσομεν Mull. ἀναγκάσαμες
Weber / ἂν χ' N. ἀνάσχ' vel simile quid Ο (ἀ ἀν χ' ad mrg.
L) ἂν ἂν χ' Matth. de Varis

λάχῃ τέχναν ἐργάζεσθαι, ἀλλὰ μὴ ἂν ἐπίσταται;" (4)
τωὐτὸν δὲ καὶ ἐν ἀγῶσι τᾶς μωσικᾶς διακλαρῶσαι τὼς
ἀγωνιστὰς καὶ ὅ τι χ'ἔκαστος [κα] λάχῃ ἀγωνίζεσθαι·
αὐλητὰς κιθαριεῖται τυχὸν καὶ κιθαρῳδὸς αὐλήσει·
5 καὶ ἐν τῷ πολεμῷ [τὼς] τοξότας καὶ [τὼς] ὁπλίτας
ἱππασεῖται, ὁ δ' ἱππεὺς τοξεύσει, ὥστε πάντες ἃ οὐκ
ἐπίστανται οὐδὲ δύνανται [οὐδὲ] πραξοῦντι. (5)
λέγοντι δὲ καὶ ἀγαθὸν ἦμεν καὶ δαμοτικὸν κάρτα· ἐγὼ
ἥκιστα νομίζω δαμοτικόν. ἐντὶ γὰρ ἐν ταῖς πόλεσι
10 μισόδαμοι ἄνθρωποι, ὧν αἴ κα τύχῃ ὁ κύαμος ἀπολοῦντι
τὸν δᾶμον. (6) ἀλλὰ χρὴ τὸν δᾶμον αὐτὸν ὁρῶντα
αἱρεῖσθαι πάντας τὼς εὔνως αὐτῷ, καὶ τὼς ἐπιταδείως
στραταγέν, ἀτέρως δὲ νομοφυλακέν καὶ τἆλλα.

8. (1) <τῶ δ' αὐτῶ> ἀνδρὸς καὶ τᾶς αὐτᾶς τέχνας
15 νομίζω κατὰ βραχύ τε δύνασθαι διαλέγεσθαι, καὶ <τὰν>
ἀλάθειαν τῶν πραγμάτων ἐπίστασθαι, καὶ δικάσασθαι
ὀρθῶς, καὶ δαμαγορεῖν οἷόν τ' ἦμεν, καὶ λόγων τέχνας
ἐπίστασθαι, καὶ περὶ φύσιος τῶν ἀπάντων ὥς τε ἔχει
καὶ ὡς ἐγένετο, διδάσκεν. (2) καὶ πρῶτον μὲν ὁ
20 περὶ φύσιος τῶν ἀπάντων εἰδὼς πῶς οὐ δυνασεῖται

---

1 ἂν P3 St (ἂν ex ἄν ut vid. R) ἄν rel. 2 τοὺς B R Vl
3 [κα] λάχῃ Blass καὶ λάχῃ L Z St 4 κιθαριεῖται scripsi
κιθαριζέτω O κιθαριξεῖ Wil. / τυχὼν Or. / κιθαρωδὸν P6
5 [τὼς] τοξότας καὶ [τὼς] ὁπλίτας Wil. ὁ τοξότας καὶ ὁ
ὁπλίτας vel art. om. Or. / τὼς ὁπλίτας <καὶ τὼς ἱππέας·
καὶ ὁ μὲν τοξότας ὁπλιτευσεῖ, ὁ δ' ὁπλίτας> ἱππασεῖται
Blass 6 ὁ δὲ N. 7 [οὐδὲ] Sch. (susp. antea Matth. de
Varis) οὐδὲν <ἧσσον> Tr. τάδε Morel <ᾷ> οὐ δεῖ susp.
Diels 8 καὶ ἀγαθὸν F2 R ἀγαθὸν rel. / δογματικὸν P3 /
δαμοτικὸν· κάρτα St / ἐγὼ <δ> Blass 13 καὶ τἆλλα
<ἐπιστατέν> Blass καὶ τἆλλα <καττωὐτὸ> Sch. post τἆλλα
lac. pauc. litt. O praeter L St 14 <τῶ δ' αὐτῶ> ἀνδρὸς
scripsi <τῶ αὐτῶ> ἀνδρὸς Blass ἄνδρα susp. N; / καὶ τᾶς
αὐτᾶς Blass κατὰ τὰς αὐτὰς O 15 διαλέγεσθαι N. καὶ

craft of which each has expert knowledge?" (4) Likewise in the case of artistic contests: one could make
the contestants draw lots, and each compete in whatever
contest he draws. A flute-player will perhaps be play-
ing the harp, or a harpist the flute. And in war an
archer or hoplite will be a cavalryman, and a cavalryman will be an archer; with the result that everyone
will be doing things of which they have neither the
knowledge nor the capability. (5) And they say that
this is a good method, and exceedingly democratic. I
personally consider it the least democratic of all
methods. For there are in cities men who hate the
people (demos), and if ever the lot falls to them they
will destroy the people (demos). (6) But the people
itself ought to keep watch and elect all those who are
well-disposed towards itself, and ought to choose as its
army-commanders those who are suitable for the job, and
to choose others to serve as guardians of the law, and
so on.

8. (1) I consider it a characteristic of the same
man and of the same art to be able to converse in brief
questions and answers, to know the truth of things, to
plead one's cause correctly, to be able to speak in
public, to have an understanding of argument-skills,
and to teach people about the nature of everything--
both how everything is and how it came into being. (2)
First of all, will not the man who knows about the nature

ἀλέγεσθαι Ο καὶ <κατὰ μακρὸν> διαλέγεσθαι Or. καὶ <διὰ
μακρῶν> διαλέγεσθαι Mull. / <τὰν> ἀλάθειαν Wil.   16
δικάσασθαι F2 Meib. διδασκάσασθαι rel. δικάζεν ἐπίστασθαι Wil.   17 δαμαγορέν Meib.   19 ἐγένετο P4.6 V2
ἐγίνετο rel. / πρᾶτον Tr.

περὶ πάντων ὀρθῶς καὶ πράσσεν; (3) ἔτι δὲ ὁ τὰς
τέχνας τῶν λόγων εἰδὼς ἐπιστασεῖται καὶ περὶ πάντων
ὀρθῶς λέγεν. (4) δεῖ γὰρ τὸν μέλλοντα ὀρθῶς λέγεν
περὶ ὧν ἐπίσταται περὶ τούτων λέγεν. <περὶ> πάντων
5 γ᾽ ἆρ᾽ ἐπιστασεῖται· (5) πάντων μὲν γὰρ τῶν λόγων τὰς
τέχνας ἐπίσταται, τοὶ δὲ λόγοι πάντες περὶ πάντων
τῶν ἐ<όντων ἐντί>. (6) δεῖ δὲ ἐπίστασθαι τὸν
μέλλοντα ὀρθῶς λέγεν περὶ ὅτων καὶ λέγοι[†]< >
καὶ τὰ μὲν ἀγαθὰ ὀρθῶς διδάσκεν τὴν πόλιν πράσσεν,
10 τὰ δὲ κακὰ τὼς κωλύειν. (7) εἰδὼς δέ γε ταῦτα
εἰδήσει καὶ τὰ ἄτερα τούτων· πάντα γὰρ ἐπιστασεῖται·
ἔστι γὰρ ταῦτα τῶν πάντων, τῆνα δὲ ποτὶ τωὔτόν τὰ
δέοντα παρέξεται, αἱ χρή. (8) κἂν μὴ ἐπιστᾶται
αὐλέν, αἱ δυνασεῖται αὐλέν, αἴ κα δέῃ τοῦτο πράσσεν.
15 (9) τὸν δὲ δικάζεσθαι ἐπιστάμενον δεῖ τὸ δίκαιον
ἐπίστασθαι ὀρθῶς· περὶ γὰρ τούτω ταὶ δίκαι. εἰδὼς

<u>1</u> ὀρθῶς <καὶ λέγεν> καὶ πράσσεν; Blass ὀρθῶς <δικάζεν>
καὶ πράσσεν; Heidel ὀρθῶς καὶ <τὰν πόλιν διδάσκεν>
πράσσεν; Diels / δὲ Diels δή O <u>3</u> λέγεν. (alt. ε in
ras.) R λέγειν. rel. λέγεν, Or., qui per error. subiung.
περὶ ὧν ἐπίσταται, περὶ τούτων λέγεν (ex 8.4) / λέγεν
Vl N. λέγειν rel. <u>4</u> <καὶ> περὶ τούτων Mull. / <περὶ>
πάντων Rohde πάντ᾽ ὧν Diels <u>5</u> γ᾽ ἆρ᾽ scripsi γὰρ O δὲ
Rohde [γὰρ] Diels <u>6</u> [πάντες] Wil. πάντως (in prima
edit.) Diels <u>7</u> τῶν ἐ<όντων ἐντί> Or. τῶν ἐ L P3 Z St
τῶν ε rel. (τῶν om. B) tum lac. pauc. litt. O <u>8</u> λέγεν
P3 St λέγειν rel. / ὅντων V2 / καὶ λέγει F1.2 δεῖ λέγεν
Mull. κα λέγῃ Blass / post λέγοι lac. 4-5 lin. O
(ἐλλιπὲς τὸ χωρίον ad mrg. P3) <τὰ πράγματα> Diels <u>9</u>
τὰ ἀγαθὰ μὲν P4.6 V2 <u>10</u> κακά πως susp. Or. κακὰ [τὼς]
Mull. κακὰ παντῶς Blass κακὰ [†]τὼς Weber κακὰ ὀρθῶς Tr.
κακά τως Diels / διακωλύεν Mull. / γε ταῦτα Blass γε
αὐτὰ O [γε] ταῦτα Diels <u>11</u> γὰρ O ἄρα Blass δὲ Weber
<u>12</u> ταυτά Diels / τῆνα P3 κεῖνα rel. ἐκεῖνα Mull. κῆνα
susp. Weber πάντα Tr. / δὲ [ποτί] Tr. <ὁ> δὲ ποτὶ Diels /
τωὔτόν P3 ταὐτόν rel. καττωὔτόν Tr. <u>13</u> παρέξεται, αἱ
χρη. scripsi παρασσεῖται. χρή vel πρασσεῖται. χρή O
παρεσσεῖται. χρή Blass πραξεῖται· χρή Tr. πράξει, αἱ χρή

of everything also be able to act rightly in regard to
everything? (3) Furthermore, the man acquainted with
the skills involved in argument will also know how to
speak correctly on every topic. (4) For the man who
intends to speak correctly must speak on the topics of
which he has knowledge; and he will, one must at any
rate suppose, have knowledge of everything. (5) For
he has knowledge of all argument-skills, and all arguments are about everything that is. (6) And the man
who intends to speak correctly on whatever matter he
speaks about must know <   > and <how to> give sound
advice to the city on the performance of good actions
and prevent them from performing evil ones. (7) In
knowing these things he will also know the things that
differ from them--since he will know everything. For
these <objects of knowledge> are part of all <objects
of knowledge>, and the exigency of the situation will,
if need be, provide him with those <other objects>, so
as to achieve the same end. (8) Even if he does not
know how to play the flute, he will always prove able
to play the flute should the situation ever call for
his doing this. (9) And the man who knows how to plead
his cause must have a correct understanding of what is
just; for that is what legal cases have to do with.

Diels (αἱ χρή antea Wil.) / <γάρ> κἄν Blass <γάρ> καὶ
αἱ Weber καὶ Diels καὶ H. Gomperz / μὴ O μὲν Diels μὰν
H. Gomperz / ἐπιστᾶται scripsi ἐπίσταται O 14 ἀἰ (=ἀεἰ)
Diels αἱ vel ἀἰ O οὗ Blass ᾇ Weber / ἀἰ δυνασεῖται αὐλὲν
om. Or. / comma post δυνασεῖται Blass post δέῃ Tr. /
Ἐκεῖνα δὲ πάντα πότε δεῖ πράσσεν ἐπιστασεῖται. Διὰ τοῦτο
χρὴ κἄν μὴ ἐπίστηται αὐλὲν, σκοπὲν αἶκα δέῃ τοῦτο
πράσσεν. Mull. 15 ἐπιμένον P4.6 V2 16 τούτω P3 τούτων
rel. τοῦτο Wil. / ταἰ δἰκαι Blass τὰ δἰκαια O τὰ
δικαστήρια Matth. de Varis τὸ δικάζεσθαι Meib.

δὲ τοῦτο εἰδήσει καὶ τὸ ὑπεναντίον αὐτῷ καὶ τὰ
<ἄλλα αὐτῶ? ἐ>τεροῖα. (10) δεῖ δὲ αὐτὸν καὶ τὼς
νόμως ἐπίστασθαι πάντας· αἱ τοίνυν τὰ πράγματα μὴ
ἐπιστασεῖται, οὐδὲ τὼς νόμως. (11) τὸν γὰρ ἐν
5 μωσικᾶ νόμον τίς ἐπίσταται; ὅσπερ καὶ μωσικάν· ὃς
δὲ μὴ μωσικάν, οὐδὲ τὸν νόμον. (12) ὃς γα <μάν>
τὰν ἀλάθειαν τῶν πραγμάτων ἐπίσταται, εὐπετὴς ὁ
λόγος ὅτι πάντα ἐπίσταται. (13) ὃς δὲ <κατὰ> βραχὺ
<διαλέγεσθαι δύναται>, δεῖ νιν ἐρωτώμενον ἀποκρίνασ-
10 θαι περὶ πάντων· οὐκῶν δεῖ νιν πάντ' ἐπίστασθαι.

9. (1) μέγιστον δὲ καὶ κάλλιστον ἐξεύρημα εὕρηται
ἐς τὸν βίον μνάμα καὶ ἐς πάντα χρήσιμον, ἐς φιλοσοφίαν τε καὶ σοφίαν. (2) ἔστι δὲ τοῦτο, ἐάν
προσέχῃς τὸν νοῦν· διὰ τούτω <γὰρ> ἐλθοῦσα ἁ γνώμα
15 μᾶλλον αἰσθησεῖται σύνολον ὃ ἔμαθες. (3) δεύτερον,
δεῖ μελετᾶν, αἴ κα ἀκούσῃς· τῷ γὰρ πολλάκις ταὐτά

---

1 καὶ vel καὶ τὰ O praeter καὶ τὼς νόμως P4.6 tum lac.
10 fere litt. O 2 <ἄλλα αὐτῶ? ἐ>τεροῖα scripsi ἐτεροῖα
Mull. τέρεια vel τερεία O <πάντα τὰ> ἄτερα Wil. ἄτερα
Tr. †τέρεια Weber <τούτων> ἄτερα Diels / δὲ καὶ αὐτὸν
καὶ P4.6 5 τίς Y2 St [τίς] Wil. ὡυτὸς Diels / ἐπίσταται; ὅσπερ scripsi ἐπίσταται, ὅσπερ O praeter ἐπίσταται,
ὥσπερ E Yl.2 6 ὃς γα <μάν> Wil. ὃς γὰρ L Fabr. ὃς κα
Meib. ὃς <δέ> γα Blass 7 εὐπετὴς Matth. de Varis ἀπετὴς
O praeter εὐπατὴς (ex ἀπατὴς, ut vid.) Y2 εὐπετὴς
<τούτῳ> Mull. 8 ἐπίστασθαι L Z ἐπιστάσθαι N. Fabr. / ὃς
δὲ <κατὰ> Blass ποδδὲ Wil. ὡς δὲ <καὶ κατὰ> Diels /
βραχὺ <διαλέγεσθαι δύναται,> δεῖ Blass βραχὺ <διαλέγεσ-
θαι δύναται, αἴ κα> δέη Diels / pro ὃς δὲ βραχὺ coni.
ὡς δ' ἐν βραχεῖ εἰπέν Mull. 10 οὐκῶν scripsi οὐκοῦν Y2
Or. οὔκουν rel. praeter οὔκων (ω ex ου) P3 11 δὴ P4.6
V2 12 χρήσιμον <τὰ τ' ἄλλα καὶ> ἐς φιλοσοφίαν Blass
13 <ἐς> σοφίαν Or. / εὕρηται μνάμα καὶ ἐς πάντα χρήσιμον,
ἐς τὰν φιλοσοφίαν τε καὶ ἐς τὸν βίον Wil., item praeter
σοφίαν pro φιλοσοφίαν Diels / τοιοῦτο Mull. τοῦτο
<πρῶτον vel πρᾶτον> susp. Sch., lac. etiam maior. post

And in knowing this he will know both that which is the
contrary of it, and the <other things?> different in
kind <from it?>. (10) He must also know all the laws.
If, however, he is going to have no knowledge of the
facts, he will have no knowledge of the laws either.
(11) For who is it knows the rules (laws) of music?
The man acquainted with music. Whereas the man unac-
quanted with music is also unacquainted with the rules
that govern it. (12) At any rate, if a man knows the
truth of things, the argument follows without difficulty
that he knows everything. (13) As for the man who is
able to converse in brief questions and answers, he must
under questioning give answers on every subject. So he
must have knowledge of every subject.

    9. (1) A very great and most attractive discovery
that has been made for the way we live is <the power of>
memory; it is useful for all purposes, for both general
education and practical wisdom. (2) This is true, <as
you will see> if you concentrate your attention <upon
the matter>. For by following this course your mind
will come to perceive more 'as a whole' that which you
have learned. (3) Second, you must, whenever you hear
anything, go over it carefully. For by frequent

τοῦτο susp. Wil. τοῦτο <πρᾶτον> Diels / αἲ κα Blass ἆν
Tr. 14 διὰ τούτω Or. διὰ τούτων Ο δι᾿ ὦ πρῶτον Mull.
<τὰ> διὰ τούτω Diels / <γὰρ> ἐλθοῦσα Blass παρελθοῦσα Ο
παρελθόντα Wil. / <ἁ> γνώμα Or. 15 σύνολον ὃ ἔμαθες
transp. post παρεγένετο (9.3) Diels <τὸ> σύνολον Mull. /
δεύτερον Ν. δευτέραν Ο 16 δεῖ scripsi δὲ Ο / μελετᾶν Ν.
μελετᾶν Ο <διὰ τῶ> μελετᾶν Mull. / ἆ κα Blass (antea
ἆκε vel ἆκα Matth. de Varis) / τῷ γὰρ Sch. τὸ γὰρ Ο /
ταὐτά Ρ3 Υ2 (ex ταῦτα) Meib. ταῦτα rel.

142

ἀκοῦσαι καὶ εἶπαι ἐς μνάμαν παρεγένετο. (4) τρίτον
αἴ κα ἀκούσῃς, ἐπὶ τὰ οἶδας καταθέσθαι, οἷον τόδε·
δεῖ μεμνᾶσθαι Χρύσιππον; κατθέμεν ἐπὶ τὸν χρυσὸν
καὶ τὸν ἵππον. (5) ἄλλο, Πυριλάμπη· κατθέμεν ἐπὶ
5 <τὸ> πῦρ καὶ τὸ λάμπειν. τάδε μὲν περὶ τῶν ὀνυμάτων. (6) τὰ δὲ πράγματα οὕτως· περὶ ἀνδρείας ἐπὶ
τὸν Ἄρη καὶ τὸν Ἀχιλλῆα, περὶ χαλκείας δὲ ἐπὶ τὸν
Ἥφαιστον, περὶ δειλίας ἐπὶ τὸν Ἐπειόν. . . .

2 ἄ κα Blass (antea ἄκε vel ἄκα Matth. de Varis) αἱ
<ἄ> κα Sch. / ἐπὶ τὰ Matth. de Varis ἔπειτα O / οἶδας
O δ' εἰδῇς Mull. 4 Πυριλάμπη nomen propr. Blass
πυριλάμπη O πυρίλαμπιν Or. πυριλάμπην Mull. 5 <τὸ>
Blass / λάμπεν Meib. / ὀνυμάτων Tr. ὠνυμάτων P3 ὀνομάτων rel. 6 οὕτως περὶ St / ἀνδρείας St ἀνδρίας O /
om. ἐπὶ (bis) P3 Ad fin. Σῆ: ἐλλιπὲς οὕτω καὶ τὸ
ἀντίγραφον, ὡς ὁρᾶτε P3 Σῆ ὅτι τὸ ἐπίλοιπον οὐχ εὑρέθη
rel. om. St

repetition of what you hear you commit it to memory.
(4) Third, you must, whenever you hear anything, connect it to what you know, as in the following example:
you need to remember the name Chrysippus? Then you
ought to connect it with χρυσός (gold) and ἵππος
(horse). (5) Another example, the name Pyrilampes:
you should connect it with πῦρ (fire) and λάμπειν (to
gleam). These examples have to do with names. (6) In
the case of things you must act as follows: if you need
to remember 'courage' you should connect it with Ares
and Achilles; you should likewise connect 'metal-
working' with Hephaestus, and 'cowardice' with Epeius.

. . .

COMMENTARY

COMMENTARY

1. On Good and Bad

(1) δισσοί] -- 'double', 'twofold', with overtones
of contrast. See, e.g., A. Ag. 122, λήμασι δισσούς,
Eur. Hipp. 385-387.

λόγοι] -- for λόγος in the sense of 'account' or
'definition' see LSJ[9] s.v. More generally, it can be
taken as an 'opinion' (see North's translation, 'senten-
tia'), but in the present context it seems more precisely translatable as 'argument'. Cf. Pl. Lgg. 663d5
(κατά γε τὸν νῦν λόγον), Protag. 320c3-4 (μῦθον λέγων
. . . ἢ λόγῳ κτλ). For the phrase δισσοί λόγοι see
Eurip. Antiope
        ἐκ παντὸς ἄν τις πράγματος δισσῶν
        λόγων ἀγῶνα θεῖτ᾽ ἄν, εἰ λέγειν εἴη σοφός;
                                (Fr. 189 Nauck[2])
According to Diogenes Laertius (9.51), it was Protagoras
who πρῶτος ἔφη δυὸ λόγους εἶναι περὶ παντὸς πράγματος
ἀντικειμένους (cf. Isoc. Helena 1, δύο λόγω περὶ τῶν
αὐτῶν πραγμάτων).

φιλοσοφούντων] -- is the reference to a new class
of 'professional' devotees of φιλοσοφία (e.g., Socrates
and the sophists), or to 'thinking people' in general,
or to both groups? The verb φιλοσοφεῖν is of sufficiently wide extension to cover certainly the latter
two possibilities, if not the first (cf. Thuc. 2.40,
φιλοσοφοῦμεν ἄνευ μαλακίας, and Isocrates' equation of
φιλοσοφία with παιδεία [Burkert (I) A3, n.4]; on the
whole question of the origin of the word see Burkert
147

[II] 159-177) and has perhaps been deliberately chosen
by the author for that very reason. A discussion of
problems that elicit responses from all 'thinking
people' (including would-be 'professional' φιλόσοφοι)
may draw criticism, but is unlikely to be written off
as an intrinsically barren or worthless exercise; a
discussion of problems eliciting responses from 'professional' φιλόσοφοι alone could very likely be, and
frequently is.

It is, however, uncertain whether φιλοσοφεῖν and
φιλοσοφία had become technical terms for 'philosophiz-
ing' and 'philosophy' at so early a date; see Burkert,
art. cit. If the word φιλοσοφούντων at Δ. Λ. 1 is now
being used wholly or in part in a 'professional' sense,
it is clearly of some significance in the word's historical development, but the matter is a doubtful one.
As in Δ. Λ. 9.1, it is probably 'generally educated
people' (including, rather than in contradistinction
to, would-be 'professional' φιλόσοφοι) that are in question. The Δ. Λ. at various junctures undoubtedly sets
forth views known to be held by various sophists, and
perhaps even by Socrates (see Introd., #4), but the
presence of similar views in, e.g., Herodotus and
Euripides is a caveat in favour of understanding the
class of φιλοσοφοῦντες in its broadest sense. For a
use of the term φιλοσοφία in what appears to be an
equally broad sense see Δ. Λ. 9.1 (fin.), with n.

τοὶ μὲν γὰρ κτλ] -- if, as I think is the case (see
above, 41), the document dates from ca 400 B. C., Socrates will no doubt be included in this group.

τοὶ δὲ ὡς τὸ αὐτό ἐστι] -- the obvious known philosophical candidate here is Heraclitus. See Heraclitus

B 57, 59, 60, 67, 88 DK[6]. But in these gnomic assertions he does not seem to be committed to any identity-
thesis proper; see Kirk and Raven 189-191. The same
would appear to be true for Anaxagoras (ibid. B 8).
All that Anaxagoras does is to equate apparent opposites when they are viewed within a particular frame
of reference. As for the specific identity of τὸ
ἀγαθόν and τὸ κακόν, Heraclitus nowhere equates the two,
though Diels-Kranz (ad B 58) might for a moment give
the opposite impression. As the context in Hippolytus
makes clear, the opening words in this fragment are not
(pace Levi [I] 304, n.59) those of Heraclitus himself,
but of his commentator (see Philosophoumena, ed. P. F. M.
Cruice [Paris 1860] ad loc.). The identity-statement
is not, apparently, to be attributed to Protagoras
either. What Plato (in the Theaetetus; cf. Crat. 385e
ff.), arguing from the ἄνθρωπος μέτρον doctrine, claims
as a natural consequence is relativism rather, and this
is the drift of Δ. Λ. 1.1 fin. (καὶ τοῖς μὲν ἀγαθόν
κτλ). See next note, and compare Ar. Metaph. 1062b15
(cf. 1063a26-27), where the predicative statement (τὸ
αὐτὸ . . . κακὸν καὶ ἀγαθόν)--propounding a doctrine
of relativism--is once more taken as a natural consequence of the ἄνθρωπος μέτρον doctrine. Neither Plato
nor Aristotle attributes ethical nihilism to Protagoras
(see above, 58).

    τοὶ δὲ ὡς -- τότε δὲ κακόν] -- a sentence exemplify-
ing ambiguities which run through a large part of the
Δ. Λ. The phrase τοὶ δὲ ὡς τὸ αὐτὸ is (from the evidence of the preceding sentence) most naturally unpacked
as τοὶ δὲ λέγουσιν ὅτι <τὸ ἀγαθὸν καὶ τὸ κακὸν> τὸ
αὐτὸ ἐστιν--i.e., as an unqualified identity-statement.

150

The phrase καὶ τοῖς μὲν ἀγαθόν κτλ, however, is most
naturally unpacked as καὶ ὡς <τὸ αὐτό> τοῖς μὲν ἀγαθόν
εἴη, τοῖς δὲ κακόν κτλ--i.e., as a (very innocuous, and
apparently trivially true) predicative statment, the
subject being τὸ αὐτό. If 1.2-10 fairly represents
their arguments, the supposed 'identity-theorists'
adhere to the predicative statement only, and are
simply common or garden contextualists (see, e.g., Pl.
Protag. 334a ff.). If they ever expressed themselves
at all in the form τὸ αὐτό ἐστι τὸ ἀγαθόν καὶ τὸ κακόν
they were presumably doing so for its arrestingly paradoxical effect; what they were philosophically committed
to was something much less startling, and much more
easily defensible: i.e., a utilitarian interpretation
of the terms ἀγαθός and κακός.

If this is true, the counter-thesis (1.11 ff.)
attacks a straw man, and draws any apparent strength it
has from a witting or unwitting failure to distinguish
an identity-statement which does not appear to be meant
seriously from a predicative statement which does. See
nn. on 1.16 (αἵπερ τωὔτόν κτλ) and 2.1 (τωὔτό) and compare the way in which the author, in arguing the
counter-thesis, switches from an identity-statement
(1.12, fin.) to a predicative statement (1.14, fin.;
1.15) to combined identity- and predicative statements
in a single section (1.16) to a final predicative
statement, with a covert identity-statement (1.17). In
similar fashion, in Δ. Λ. 2, we have disconcerting
moves, during the discussion of the counter-thesis,
from a predicative statement (2.20) to an identity-
statement (2.21) to a predicative statement (2.22, 24),
as though there were no difference between the two

classes of statement. This could be simply philosophical naiveté on the author's part, but a respectable
propaedeutic purpose (based, perhaps, on a feeling for
problems rather than a knowledge of their solution)
cannot in my estimation be discounted (see Introd., 76).

For all this, the tantalizing question remains: why
should anyone of sophistication (even if it was three
generations or so before Aristotle) have taken the
supposed dilemmas of Δ. Λ. 1-4 to be anything other
than purely verbal? The answer, if there is one, seems
to me to lie in the basic ambiguity in linguistic form
of what I have called the identity-statement. For the
linguistic form τὸ + neuter adjective (participle, etc.)
can be taken as a reference either to the particular or
to the universal, with dramatically different philosophical results. In a word, the sentence τὸ ἀγαθὸν
καὶ τὸ κακὸν τὸ αὐτό ἐστι can be understood either as

(a) "that which is good and that which is evil are
identical <i.e., in particular respects>, or

(b) "whatsoever is good and whatsoever is evil are
identical."
If the identity-theorists ever expressed themselves in
the way attributed to them by the author of the Δ. Λ.,
they were obviously frequently understood as uttering
proposition (b), though the defences put up in the Δ.
Λ. make it clear that what they were committed to was
proposition (a).

(2) ἐγὼ δὲ καὶ αὐτὸς κτλ] -- compare 4.2, init.
For the translation of ποτιτίθεμαι see LSJ[9] s.v. προσ-
τίθημι B[I], 2, 3; cf. Guthrie 3. 317 init. The apparently strong adherence to the identity-thesis must be

read in conjunction with statements of apparently
equally strong adherence to the counter-thesis (hereafter the 'difference' thesis) in other parts of the
treatise (e.g., at 1.11). On the possible methodological significance of the fact see Introd., 75 f.

ᾧ ἐπιμελὲς] -- for the translation see LSJ[9] s.v.
ἐπιμελής, II.

(3) πωλεῦντι] -- present participle active, dat.
masc. plural; see also 1.3, 1.16, ἀσθενεῦντι, and compare 1.2, ἀσθενοῦντι, dat. masc. singular. Schwyzer
(1.272 & 2.5) dubs the form "hyperdorisch", along with
the Messenian νομίζοντι (a form called by DK a stonemason's mistake; but see Thesleff 94, n.1); Høeg (107
ff.) takes it to be Coan. For further litt. see Thumb-
Kiekers #108 (fin.), and for further discussion, above,
52.

(7) καὶ τοὶ παλαισταί] -- the hanging nominative
is awkward, but should probably be left; see 1.17,
καδδὲ τόδε καὶ τἆλλα πάντα. The writer is no stylist,
and is much addicted to "etcetera"s: see 2.25, καὶ
τἆλλα οὕτως; 3.16, καὶ τἆλλα καττωύτό. Wilamowitz'
conjecture produces good sense, but has no MS. support, and cannot be said to be necessary.

ἄλλοι] -- 'as well'. See LSJ[9] s.v. ἄλλος, II, 8.

αὐτίκα ἁ κιθαρωδία] -- with the MSS. Wilamowitz'
conjecture again makes good sense, but is part of a
larger conjecture that has no MS. support, and seems
unnecessary; and the same can be said of the DK conjecture. Though the author's phraseology is again awkward, it seems likely that we are expected to see the

notion of νίκα contained in the phrase τῷ νικῶντι, which itself appears to operate as a protasis: "lyre-contests are good if you win them, bad if you lose them."

(8) ἔν τε τῷ πολέμῳ κτλ] -- a reference, it seems, to the end of the Peloponnesian War in 404 B. C. On the significance of the passage for the dating of the treatise (or what remains of it) see Introd., 38.

ἅ τε νίκα] -- probably a reference to the victory of Plataea and/or that of Mycalae in 479 B. C. See North ad loc.

(9) τὰ τῶν Θηβαίων -- Ἀργείων πάθη] -- North, followed by Orelli, remarks "respicit auctor in Thebanis infortunia, quae Oedipo et filiis contigerunt; in Argivis ea quae Agememnoni et Oresti, apud Tragicos declamatissima." But, if this interpretation is correct, one misses a contrast between ἀγαθόν and κακόν. Blass sees the difficulty, and conjectures that after πάθη something like τοῖς μὲν Θηβαίοις ἀγαθόν, τοῖς δ' Ἀργείοις κακόν has dropped out. But such a phrase seems readily understandable, without the further assumption that it once featured in the text. The πάθη in question are presumably the outcome, for Thebans and Argives respectively, of the expedition of the Seven against Thebes.

(10) καὶ ἁ τῶν Κενταύρων κτλ] -- i.e., at the marriage of Pirithous. For source-references see Rose 280, n.7. Dumont (ad loc.) suggests from the evidence of the phrase τοῖς δὲ Κενταύροις κακόν that the author's

source must have been Antimachus, since only in Antimachus' version do the centaurs die (having been
enticed to the island of the Sirens). But the testimonium for this account is of doubtful authenticity,
and is in fact rejected by Wyss (see Antimachi Colo-
phonii Reliquiae, ed. B. Wyss [Berlin 1936] fr. [165]).

μάχα καί νίκα] -- with the MSS. The style creaks,
as so often, but (pace Wilamowitz) it is easier to
explain an original phrase μάχα καί νίκα than to explain
how καί νίκα could ever have become inserted at a later
date.

καί ἁ τῶν θεῶν κτλ] -- for source-references see
Rose 57 ff., 73-74 (nn.74-86).

(11) τἀγαθόν εἴη] -- cf. 1.1, ἀγαθόν εἴη, 1.17,
τωὑτόν εἴη, and 4.8, ὅ τι κρίνοιντο. Indicatives might
have been expected, after the primary main verb, but
as has been pointed out by G. L. Cooper, III ("The
Ironic Force of the Pure Optative in ὅτι (ὡς) Constructions of the Primary Sequence" [TAPA 105 (1975)] 32),
the device is frequently used to express apparent non-
commitment on the part of the author, and this seems to
fit the atmosphere of the Δ. Λ. perfectly.

πρᾶγμα] -- 'reality', a word which subsequent discussion (both here and in the rest of the treatise)
makes clear covers events, actions, and states of
affairs. The word seems to have been used in the same
'general' sense by Protagoras (see n. on 1.1 [λόγοι]
above), and occurs frequently with the same wide extension in Plato; see, e.g., Pl. Euthyd. 283e9, 284d1,
286a5, 286a7, Protag. 349b3, 4, 349c1, 330c1 ff., and
cf. Ar. Top. passim.

On the ὄνυμα/πρᾶγμα distinction (here and at 3.13,
4.6) see Eurip. Phoen. 499-502, with Nestlé (II) 299,
439, n.52, and Ar. Met. 1006b22. Müller (186, n.1,
after Joël 2.138 ff.) feels that the argumentation
comes close to that of Antisthenes (see ibid. 183); and
he refers to the ὀρθοέπεια of Prodicus (see Prodicus A
13, B 4 DK[6]). But Protagoras, too, stressed ὀρθοέπεια
(Protagoras A 25-29 DK[6]), as did the sophists in general (Pl. Crat. 391b), and I see nothing in the 'argumentation' of Antisthenes frs. 20, 60, 38 Caizzi to
suggest a commitment to the ὄνυμα/πρᾶγμα distinction;
though fr. 38 and the title περὶ ὀνομάτων χρήσεως do
support a commitment to ὀρθοέπεια. More interesting,
it seems to me, is Anthisthenes fr. 45, with its contention that λόγος (=statement, definition) ἐστὶν ὁ
τὸ τί ἦν ἤ ἔστι δηλῶν, but even this is not really a
theory of natural affinity between ὄνομα and πρᾶγμα
(such as the one found at Pl. Crat. 429b ff.; cf. 383a);
see Field 168. (For a different view see Guthrie
3.215, and n.2, with litt.)

ἐγὼ δὲ καὶ αὐτός] -- see nn. on 1.2 (ἐγὼ δὲ καὶ
αὐτὸς κτλ) and 1.1 (τοὶ δὲ ὡς -- τότε δὲ κακόν).

διαιρεῦμαι] -- cf. Heraclitus B 1 DK[6] (διαιρέων),
Prodicus A 17 (fin.) DK[6] (διαιρεῖν).

τοῦτον τὸν τρόπον] -- i.e., in the manner described
in the preceding sentence. Cf. 1.12, ταῦτα ("the above-
mentioned things").

ποῖον ἀγαθὸν κτλ] -- i.e., ποῖον <ἂν εἴη> ἀγαθὸν
κτλ, if ποῖον -- εἴη is to be seen as a 'remote future'
conditional sentence. However, given the author's
(methodological?) propensity for the use of the optative in oratio obliqua, even after primary main verbs

(see n. on 1.11 [τἀγαθὸν εἴη]), ποῖον ἀγαθὸν may simply
be a shortened version of ποῖον <εἴη> ἀγαθὸν (=ποῖόν
<ἐστιν> ἀγαθόν), in which case we would be looking at
an 'open' condition. Either way, Blass's emendation
<κ> ἦμεν seems unnecessary.

ἑκάτερον εἴη] -- see n. immediately above. Given
the other indications of the author's apparent aim in
the use of optatives, Wilamowitz' conjecture seems
unnecessary.

(12) ταῦτα] -- i.e., that τὸ ἀγαθόν and τὸ κακόν
are identical. For Kranz (231-232; cf. Ramage 422-424)
Δ. Λ. 1.12 ff. is a small piece of dialogue that is
genuinely 'socratic', even if primitive and unelaborated.
This is it seems to me an over-statement. See Introd.,
72.

ἤδη το τὼς κτλ] -- the strength of Schulze's emendation lies in the sense of the sentence immediately following: that is, "You may as well return evil for good,
if evil and good are supposed to be identical". Unfortunately, it is backed by no MS. evidence, so I hesitantly print the manuscript version. The sense will
then be: "You have already performed acts of kindness
to your parents? Then you ought to perform a number
of acts of unkindness towards them--since good and evil
are identical". That is: it is illogical to confine
your actions towards your parents to actions of a particular nature (i.e., 'good' actions), since actions
of an antithetical nature (i.e., 'bad' actions) are
equally 'good'.

ἄρα] -- the 'ergo' of Euclid, and a particle frequently found at the conclusion of quasi-syllogistic

157   [1.12-15]

arguments throughout Plato's dialogues. In the Δ. Λ.
we appear to be looking at an early use of a word soon
to achieve importance in the fields of logic and mathe-
matics.

κακὰ καί] -- with the MSS. κακὰ [καί] Wil. Perhaps
<καί> κακὰ [καί] or <καί> κακὰ καί?

αἵπερ τωὐτὸν κτλ] -- see n. on 1.1 (τοὶ δὲ ὡς --
τότε δὲ κακόν).

(13) The mood changes from prescription (cf. 1.12,
ὀφείλεις) to description; the argument-form is again
that of reductio ad absurdum. The DK insertion "<καί
πολλὰ καὶ μεγάλα.>" seems unnecessary; some such answer
is readily understood from the context.

καὶ πολλὰ καὶ μέγιστα] -- again one can fairly
assume that some such phrase as "καὶ πολλὰ καὶ μέγιστα."
is to be understood as the tacit statement which prompts
the remark. On the whole interchange compare Antiphon
B 44 fr. B cols. 1-2 DK[6].

(14) ἔχοντι, πάλιν] -- a strong, but not impossible,
asyndeton. The argument is a would-be reductio ad
absurdum, as is that of 1.15 below. See Nestlé (II),
438.

αἵπερ τωὐτὸ κτλ] -- see n. on 1.1 (τοὶ δὲ ὡς --
τότε δὲ κακόν).

(15) τὸν βασιλῆ] -- i.e., the King of Persia.

αἴ γα] -- with DK. αἴκα (MSS.) is never found elsewhere except with the subjunctive; the emendation αἴ γα
seems the most economical and plausible. However, as
has been noted (above, 90), the author is no stylist,

and it is not impossible that the use of αἶκα with an indicative mood is one of his syntactical idiosyncrasies.

τωὐτόν κτλ] -- see n. on 1.1 (τοὶ δὲ ὡς -- τότε δὲ κακόν).

(16) καθ' ἕκαστον] -- the "individual cases" mentioned in 1.2-10. If we assume that a portion of the treatise has not been lost, the apparent promise by the author that he will refute in turn each of the points made at 1.2-10 is unfortunately not fulfilled. This is a pity, since it is hard to see how, if he had faced each one squarely, he could have failed either

(a) to accept that the evidence for 1.2-10 is empirically unimpeachable (in which case the genuine counter-thesis to it, τὸ αὐτὸ οὐκ ἐστιν ἀγαθὸν καὶ κακόν, is false); or,

(b) to continue maintaining the counter-thesis in its absolute form, i.e., as a thesis of non-identity (τὸ ἀγαθὸν καὶ τὸ κακὸν οὐκ ἐστι τὸ αὐτό), but to admit that it is not the utilitarian thesis of 1.2-10 (where "good" and "bad" are unpacked as "good for --", "bad for --") that is its contrary, but rather the identity-thesis τὸ ἀγαθὸν καὶ τὸ κακόν ἐστι τὸ αὐτό.

τωὐτὸ γὰρ κτλ] -- with Orelli. The minor emendation makes good sense, without need for more drastic measures. The stressed word is, of course, ἀγαθόν (the point being that most people assume the contrary; see 1.2). τωὐτὸ is adverbial: "in the same way (as has been mentioned above)" (cf. 7.4). Both arguments in the section are, as in the previous instances, would-be reductiones ad absurdum.

ποιέν] -- with F2 P1.2. ποιεῦν, like ἀξιόοντι
(3.15), seems a clear instance of intentional or accidental scribal 'levelling', due to the proximity of
ἀσθενεῦντι (and perhaps an awareness of the form
ποιεῦντι at 2.28).

αἵπερ τωὐτόν κτλ] -- for the significance of the
two phrases here see nn. on 1.1 (τοὶ δὲ ὡς -- τότε δὲ
κακόν) and 2.1 (τωὐτό). In the first instance we have
an (innocuous) predicative statement, in the second an
identity-statement. The second, as the examples of
1.2-10 make clear, was never in fact intended by the
proponents of the thesis; the first was intended, as
the same examples show, with the addition of the tacit
rider "depending on context". Without such a rider, as
Aristotle sees, we have συκοφαντία: ἐπὶ τῶν ἐριστικῶν
τὸ κατὰ τί καὶ πρὸς τί καὶ πῆ οὐ προστιθέμενα ποιεῖ τὴν
συκοφαντίαν (Rhet. 1402a14-15).

(17) καδδὲ τόδε] -- i.e., the principle underlying
the arguments of 1.2-10 is seen to be absurd as soon as
it is exposed to critical examination, as in 1.16. But
the supposedly critical examination does not touch upon
the arguments of 1.2-10; a supposed identity-thesis is
attacked, without reference to its clear explication as
a predicative thesis by its proponents.

If the author is himself aware of what is going on,
and has failed to see that a crucial ambiguity has
undermined the attempted criticism of the thesis, then
there appears to be a good prima facie case for dubbing
him, in Diels' phrase, "talentlos". If he is aware,
and still perseveres in the pseudo-rebuttal, we seem to
be offered the choice of dubbing him as either

(a) one of those ἐριστικοί for whom Socrates,
Plato, Isocrates (cf. Helena 1) and Aristotle evinced
such hearty contempt, or

(b) a man who, though convinced that on many philosophical topics supposedly antithetical views can
indeed be advanced, is not at all convinced that the
supposedly antithetical views are really antithetical,
and still less that supposedly antithetical views are
of equal truth-value; a man who, as a consequence,
expects his audience to participate in the intellectual
battle, and disentangle for themselves the valid and
the fallacious arguments, as a basic, and highly in-
structive, philosophical exercise.
If (b), rather than (a), is the more correct description, the author of the Δ. Λ. is pursuing in a blunt
and stylistically unadorned way a policy that many have
attributed to Plato, too, particularly in the so-called
"Socratic" dialogues (with one or several of which, as
it happens, the Δ. Λ. is very possibly contemporaneous).
On the whole question, see Introd., 69 ff.

καὶ οὐ λέγω κτλ] -- for Untersteiner (n. ad loc.;
cf. Dupréel 207-208) "l'autore rifiuta la definizione",
and a close similarity is seen between this phrase and
Pl. Hipp. Mai. 301b, with apparent corroboration of the
view that 1.11 ff. represents the views of Hippias.
But see above, 91, n.78.

For Kranz (230) the whole sentence is "eine echt
Sokratische Haltung". On this see Introd., 70.

κακὸν καὶ ἀγαθόν] -- with the MSS. Compare 2.1,
τωὐτὸ καλὸν καὶ αἰσχρόν. DK read εἴη as the identity-
sign, and import a τό and a τ' into their text without
signalling the fact that no MS. in fact reads them.

κακόν and ἀγαθόν are most naturally read predicatively
(see n. on 1.1, τοί δὲ ὡς -- τότε δὲ κακόν); τωὐτόν
("the same thing") is presumably, from the evidence of
1.11-16, to be unpacked as "the same action" and/or
"the same state of affairs". If this interpretation is
correct, the chapter has come full circle, with a repetition of the crucial ambiguity found in 1.1. For
ἑκάτερον is most naturally unpacked as "each of the two
identity-components τὸ ἀγαθόν and τὸ κακόν" (cf. 2.21),
while the immediately preceding phrase (ὡς οὐ -- ἀγαθόν)
is, of course, merely predicative. The supposed contradiction is no contradiction at all.

   ἀλλ' <ἄλλο> ἑκάτερον] -- i.e., ἀλλ' <ὡς ἄλλο> ἑκάτερον <εἴη>. If Blass's insertion <ἄλλο> is accepted, as
it seems to me it should (on grounds of probable haplography at some point in the textual transmission), we
have here a general conclusion to the counter-thesis
that the author has been expounding from 1.11 onwards.
If it is not, we must, it seems, credit the author with
self-contradiction, since the statement "but each of
the two (i.e., τὸ ἀγαθόν and τὸ κακόν) is bad-and-good"
would appear to be incompatible with the position
implied in 1.16 (fin.).

   2.   On Seemly (Noble/Beautiful) [καλόν] and
        Shameful (Base/Ugly) [αἰσχρόν]

   (1) οὕτω καὶ τὸ σῶμα] -- with the MSS. (see also
Kranz 224, Untersteiner ad loc.). πρᾶγμα, the emendation of St, is in line with 1.11 and 2.21, τὸ αὐτὸ
πρᾶγμα (cf. Pl. Tht. 177e), but the lectio difficilior
is to be preferred. Just as the term ὄνομα came to
pass from the meaning 'name' to that of 'noun' (or even

'word'), so too the term σῶμα could conceivably have passed from the meaning 'body' or 'person' (cf. Th. 1.85, περὶ πολλῶν σωμάτων καὶ χρημάτων βουλεύειν) to that of 'referent' for a particular ὄνομα. The one apparent problem is that in Δ. Λ. 2 the discussion centres upon actions, events, and states of affairs (especially upon actions)--not upon physical objects, the natural counterpart, it would seem, of ὀνόματα understood as nouns. If, however, one understands the two ὀνόματα discussed in the chapter--τὸ καλόν and τὸ αἰσχρόν--in terms of the noun-<u>phrases</u> into which they naturally expand, i.e., as <u>ἐκεῖνο</u> ὅ ἐστι καλόν/αἰσχρόν (or <u>πᾶν</u> ὅ ἂν κτλ; or ὅ τι ἂν κτλ) the apparent diffi-culty vanishes, since such phrases are indeed general enough, and of sufficiently wide extension, to cover physical objects, actions, events, and states of affairs.

For Untersteiner (tr. <u>ad loc</u>.; cf. n. <u>ad loc</u>.) σῶμα = "il manifestarsi naturale". But see above, 91, n.78.

τοὶ δὲ κτλ] -- τωὑτὸ subject, καλὸν καὶ αἰσχρόν predicate; cf. 1.17. As in Δ. Λ. 1, a great deal turns on the interpretation of the thesis. The supposed identity-theorists (like those of 1.2-10) are, from the evidence of 2.2-20, clearly 'contextualists': one and the same action/event/state of affairs will vary in moral colour according to context. The proponents of the supposed counter-thesis, like their counterparts at 1.11 ff., again appear to be shooting down straw men, since they are (wittingly or unwittingly) interpreting the proposition τωὑτόν <ἐστι> καλὸν καὶ αἰσχρόν as an identity-thesis when both the evidence of the sentence's own syntactical structure and that of the arguments of

2.2-20 make it clear that it is merely predicative.

It is of some interest that in this second λόγος the author has, even before discussion gets underway, (wittingly or unwittingly? see n. on 1.17, καδδὲ τόδε) framed the supposed antithesis of views in such a way that the perspicacious reader can see at once that it is in fact a pseudo-antithesis (in Δ. Λ. 1 it only became clear with the exposition of the counter-thesis). This is done by a shift from the identity-components τὸ καλόν and τὸ αἰσχρόν to the predication-components καλόν and αἰσχρόν. At 1.1 τὸ ἀγαθόν and τὸ κακόν appeared to be dubbed "identical" (τὸ αὐτό)--the definite article on either side of ἐστι being the flag signalling the identity-relationship; at 2.1 such a flag is not to be found, and καλόν and αἰσχρόν are most naturally read predicatively. A fair inference, even before arguments and counter-arguments are proffered, is that the supposed contrariety between the two assertions is in fact nothing of the sort.

(2) πειρασεῦμαι κτλ] -- for πειράομαι followed by a participle see LSJ[9] s.v. πειράω, B. The author will "attempt an exposition (sc. 'of the latter position first') along the following lines" (τόνδε τὸν τρόπον); i.e., he will illustrate first of all the thesis that one and the same action/event/state of affairs is both καλόν and αἰσχρόν (2.2-20); the counter-thesis he will illustrate from 2.21 onwards. The diffidence suggested by a word like πειρασεῦμαι is in marked contrast with the apparent self-assurance suggested by a word like ποτιτίθεμαι (1.2). On the question of the author's commitment to particular arguments in the Δ. Λ., see

Introd., 73 ff.

αὐτίκα γὰρ κτλ] -- compare Pl. Phdr. 230e ff. (the speech of Lysias) and 237a ff. (Socrates' rejoinder); and cf. Symp. 183d6-8.

ἐραστᾷ μὲν χρηστῷ κτλ] -- the reading of all MSS., except that (Pl.2 apart) they repeat μὲν after χρηστῷ. There seems to be no need to tamper with the sentence in substance (an instance of chiasmus), since χρηστῷ and καλῷ can without difficulty be understood as suppressed protasis and concessive adjective respectively; i.e., if the lover is χρηστός the action is καλόν; if, although the boy is handsome, the lover is not a genuine lover, the action is αἰσχρόν. The interpretation is strengthened if one reads <καί> καλῷ, attributing the loss of καί to haplography.

(4) With this section compare Hdt. 1.203; 3.101; Xen. An. 5.4.33; Pl. Hipp. Mai. 299a. For references to later literature see Schmid-Stählin 1.3.206, n.6.

(5) αἴσχιστον] -- superlative; cf. αἰσχρόν (only) of the man!

γε] -- emphatic. See Denniston, Greek Particles 118.

(6) τῷ μέν] -- with the MSS. In sections 4 and 5 immediately above the phrase τῷ ἀνδρί referred to the husband in a marriage; it is less clear that in section 6 ἀνήρ and γυνή are to be seen as husband and wife. If we could be sure that the author has in section 6 generalized his comments to cover 'man' and 'woman' as such, τᾷ (Weber) would undoubtedly be a better reading. How-

ever, the status of ἀνήρ and γυνή in section 6 is unclear, and the MS. reading is therefore tentatively
retained. I take sections 4, 5, and 6 as a single,
unified discussion of the marriage relationship, and
so translate τῷ ἀνδρί and τᾷ γυναικί (2.6) as "husband"
and "wife" respectively.

(7) ἀγωνιστάς] -- with the MSS. Orelli's emendation ἀνταγωνιστάς is unnecessary; see LSJ[9] s.v. ἀγωνισ-
τής.
For Dupréel (90) the doctrine of this section is Gorgian; for evidence he refers to Pl. Meno 71e. But the
notion that ἀρετή consists in doing good to friends and
harm to enemies was a very traditional one, and hardly
a distinguishing mark of Gorgias; see, e.g., Bluck,
Plato's Meno 218. (On the question of 'Gorgian' elements in the Δ. Λ. see Introd., 65-68.)

(9) εἶμι δ' <ἐφ> ἅ κτλ] -- with St; cf. 3.15. But
for a rare use of εἶμι in the sense of "go through" or
"go over" (followed by an accusative case) see Hdt.
2.25.1 (<ὁ ἥλιος> ἰὼν τὸ μέσον τοῦ οὐρανοῦ) and 2.26.2
(<ὁ ἥλιος> ἤιε ἂν τὰ ἄνω τῆς Εὐρώπης). The exact
sources for the author's ethnological lore cannot be
established with certainty. Some of the statements coincide with what can be found in Herodotus, but it
would be rash to assume that the author has copied
directly from him, since on a number of occasions he
offers detail not found in Herotodus; and a fair number
of the more general points he makes are not to be found
in Herodotus at all. A possible explanation of 2.9 ff.
is that the author is drawing upon earlier sources some

or all of which were also tapped by Herodotus (e.g.,
Hecataeus and Hellanicus; see Aly 120), and also perhaps a number of sources contemporaneous with Herodotus
(e.g., Gorgias? See Aly, ibid.), but independent of
him; see Mazzarino, 291-292. For Gomperz ([II] 163-164;
cf. Trieber 228, Kranz 225) the contents of Hdt. 3.38
and 7.152 suggest that they and Δ. Λ. 2.18, 2.26-27
have a common source, which he thinks might be Protagoras, but this view seems to be pure speculation, based
upon the Platonic rendering (in the Tht.) of the ἄνθρωπος μέτρον doctrine.

Kranz' statement (228) that Protagoras and his followers collected ethnographical material for the purpose of demonstrating the relativity of moral concepts
has, as far as I know, no firm foundation in any source
material; the only hint (if that is what it is) that I
can find is the statement in the Suda that Hecataeus
was an ἀκούστης Πρωταγόρου. And I cannot see (pace
Untersteiner [II] 113) how Hippias' book Ἐθνῶν ὀνομασίαι
need have been anything more than it purports to be--
i.e., a book on the nomenclature of tribes or races.

ταὶ πόλιές τε] -- with the MSS. The excision of τε
by Wilamowitz (τε would in polished Greek have followed
ταί) seems to be one more attempt to change the author
into the prose stylist that he fairly evidently is not.
For the doublet see Pl. Resp. 348d5, πόλεις τε καί
ἔθνη (Kranz 223, after Friedländer).

ἀχειριδώτως κτλ] -- compare (with Taylor 96) Eur.
Andr. 595-600; cf. Sext. Emp. Hypot. Pyrrhon. 1.145-146.

ἄγηνται] -- it should not be inferred from this that
what had been outlined at 2.2-8 were something other
than opinions. At 2.2-8 the author is viewing the

problem from within a particular culture--i.e., the
Greek culture, and is formulating positions which had
won general acceptance within that culture; from section 9 onwards he is comparing and contrasting different cultures as such. In each instance we are operat-
ing at the level of 'accepted belief' only.

(10) καὶ τὼς παῖδας] -- sc. "among the Spartans".
The additions of Wilamowitz and Diels seem unnecessary,
given the context in which the remark is made.

(11) Θεσσαλοῖσι] -- with the MSS. For the sentiment see (with Taylor, 96) Eur. Electra 815 ff. The
dative, if the MSS. have preserved the correct reading,
presumably has locative force, "among Thessalians". It
seems not impossible, however, that the proximity of
the adjective καλόν, and the repetition of καλόν and a
dative in preceding and subsequent sentences, led to
the omission of some such preposition as ἐν (Orelli)
or παρά (Mullach).

(12) The first sentence is perhaps distinguishing
pre-marital and extra-marital intercourse; the context,
particularly the clause ἐπεί -- γάμηται (where <ἀνδρί>
seems to mean <ἄλλῳ τινι ἀνδρί>) suggests that the
first ἀνδρί refers to a future husband, the second to
some unspecified pre-marital partner. 'Trial marriage'
(with one's future husband), however, is possibly the
meaning the author intended. If the first suggestion
is correct, the double use of ἀνδρί must be characterized as potentially misleading; if the second is correct, the repetition of ἀνδρί is stylistically awkward,

as Wilamowitz noticed.

ἔρασθαι] -- see Veitch, Greek Verbs (Oxford 1866)
s.v. ἔραμαι, the deponent synonym of ἐράω (227). ἐρᾶσθαι would mean "to be loved by".

ἄμφω] -- i.e., "both pre-marital intercourse (with
one's future husband) and extra-marital intercourse",
or "both pre-marital intercourse (with some unspecified
partner) and extra-marital intercourse". See n. on
2.12 (init.) above.

(13) στίζεσθαι] -- cf. Hdt. 5.6.2.

κατακανών] -- from κατακαίνω (=κατακτείνω).

κόμιον] -- the first appearance of the word in
Greek literature. Its form is that of a diminutive of
κόμη, but its linguistic function in the present text
seems indistinguishable from that of προκόμιον ("scalp").
In later Greek (Arr. Epictet. 2.24.24, 3.22.10) it is
used simply as a diminutive form of κόμη.

χρυσώσας καὶ ἀργυρώσας] -- with the MSS. Since καί
can itself serve as a weak disjunctive, the conjectures
of Wilamowitz and Diels seem unnecessary. For the cus-
tom see Hdt. 4.26, 65, 66 and (perhaps) Pl. Euthyd. 299e.

(14) Compare Hdt. 1.216.2; 3.38.3-4. For Untersteiner (n. ad loc.) the phrase ἐν τοῖς τέκνοις τεθάφ-
θαι is of Gorgian origin; his evidence is the phrase
Γῦπες ἔμψυχοι τάφοι attributed to Gorgias (Sofisti 4
[82] B 5a fin.). For Aly (120) the phrase is evidence
that the direct source of the ethnography of the Δ. Λ.
is Gorgias. But all this seems to me to be clutching
at straws. On the question of Gorgias and the Δ. Λ.
see Introd., 65-68.

κακά κ'] -- the adverbial use of the accusative
neuter plural (see Goodwin, Greek Grammar 367); κ' was
probably lost by haplography.

(15) For the sentiments compare Hdt. 3.31.68, 88;
Xen. Mem. 4.4.20, Inst. Cyr. 8.1.41; cf. Trieber 243
n.2, Nestlé (II) 272, and n.31. Xen. Mem. 4.4.20 seems
hardly (pace Untersteiner, n. ad loc.) to count as
evidence here, and the fact that in the passage in
question Hippias is portrayed as an interlocutor seems
a thin reason for suggesting, as do Zeller (II) (1.1334
n.) and Dümmler (251), that Δ. Λ. 2.15 probably goes
back beyond Herodotus to Hippias. On the question of
Hippias and the Δ. Λ. see Introd., 59-65.

(16) Compare Hdt. 1.93.4.
οὕτως] -- i.e., thanks to having acquired the necessary dowry by prostituting themselves. Untersteiner
interprets, "in queste condizioni" (i.e., "while living
as prostitutes"); cf. Hdt. 1.93.4, τοῦτο ποιέουσαι.

(17) Compare Hdt. 2.35; Soph. OC 337-341.
τῇδε] -- i.e., in Greece (including Magna Graecia);
see Introd., 52 ff.
ἐργάζεσθαι] -- with the MSS. For ἐργάζεσθαι in the
sense of "to perform (manual) labour" see LSJ[9] s.v., 1.

(18) Compare Hdt. 3.38; 7.152.2-3; cf. Dümmler 252,
Trieber 228-229. The argument is hardly (pace Taylor
104-105) a "fallacy of composition". There is no suggestion that what is αἰσχρόν to a Spartan ceases to be
so, simply because it is καλόν to a Macedonian or

Persian. The point is rather that what is αἰσχρόν to
X is καλόν to Y (and so taken away by Y as καλόν), and
that what is αἰσχρόν to Y is καλόν to X (and so taken
away by X as καλόν): no 'change of view' on the part of
X or Y is envisaged, though in fact both objects
brought as αἰσχρά have been removed as καλά. Taylor's
reference (ibid.) to Ar. Phys. 250a19 seems therefore
irrelevant to the argument.

ἄγηνται] -- perfect passive, ἡγέομαι.

λειφθῆμεν] -- aorist infinitive passive (doric form).

(19) The verses were taken by Meineke, Cobet, and
Valckenaer to be Euripidean, and are printed as adespota
by Nauck[2] (adesp. 26).

τὸν ἄλλον] -- with the MSS. Nauck's emendation
leaves the author uncommitted as to the number of νόμοι;
the text of the MSS. confines him to two (which is of
course very much in keeping with the drift of the first
two chapters of the Δ. Λ.). The one law is presumably
that which takes things to be absolutely and unequivocally (πάντη) καλόν or αἰσχρόν, i.e., καλόν or αἰσχρόν
simpliciter; the ἄλλος νόμος the law which takes them
to be only contextually so. If this reading is correct,
the two seem to square exactly with the antitheses set
forth in Δ. Λ. 1.1 and 2.1.

ὧδε -- διαιρῶν] -- i.e., by distinguishing what is
the case simpliciter from what is the case contextually
or secundum quid, as the propositions οὐδὲν ἦν -- καλά
make clear. For διαιρεῖν of logical division or distinction see LSJ[9] s.v., III 1, 3, IV. Valckenaer's
emendation is attractive, but unnecessary; διαιρεῖν is
not confined to treatises of logic, or even prose-works

(see LSJ[9] s.v., III, 1). For the importance of the
concept of τὸ διαιρεῖν in Heraclitus and Prodicus, see
n. ad 1.11 (διαιρεῦμαι). Cf. also Aristoph. Clouds 742.

   ἦν] -- for the tense see Smyth, Greek Grammar 1902.

   ὁ καιρός] -- for Rostagni (172-173, referred to by
Untersteiner ad loc.) the lines allude both to "il
comune concetto retorico del καιρός" and to "la ragione
filosofica di esso, incercata nella natura e nella cos-
tituzione dell' universo". The first statement is very
likely true, the second very doubtful, at least as far
as the poet is concerned. See Wilamowitz (IV) 178, n.1.

   On the whole question of Gorgias and a putative
"doctrine of καιρός" see Introd., 65 ff.

   (20) At [Pl.] περὶ δικαίου 375a2 ff. just actions
are said to be distinguishable from unjust by their
being performed ἐν τῷ δέοντι καὶ τῷ καιρῷ, and in his
Life of Protagoras (52) Diogenes Laertius mentions how
Protagoras πρῶτος . . . καιροῦ δύναμιν ἐξέθετο (though
the reference, given the general context in which it
is found, may simply be to a point of grammar, or eristic, or rhetoric in general). At Sext. Emp. Adv. Eth.
64-67 a similar--but not identical--Stoic theory
(ascribed by him [64] to Ariston of Chios) is expounded,
in which "precedence" (πρόκρισις) is said to depend on
"circumstance" (περίστασις). An analogy is drawn from
the different placing of letters in the spelling of
names (ibid. 67; cf. Δ. Λ. 5.12), which is said to
depend upon the force of οἱ καιροί (ibid. 67; cf. Δ. Λ.
2.20, καιρῷ). While it would no doubt be rash to infer
from this that Sextus is drawing directly upon the Δ.
Λ. for his analogy, the Δ. Λ. is nonetheless apparently

the earliest extant treatise in Greek which in fact draws the analogy. (For what seems a similar situation in regard to a much-repeated mathematical analogy, see n. on Δ. Λ. 5.14.)

(21) The counter-thesis is now asserted. As in the case of the counter-thesis at 1.11 ff., it draws any force it has from a (witting or unwitting) misunderstanding of the original thesis; see nn. on 1.17 (καδδὲ τόδε) and 2.1 (τοὶ δὲ κτλ). For a flat contradiction of the theses of Δ. Λ. 2 and 3, based on a correct interpretation of them, see the comments of Socrates at [Pl.] Minos 316ab (cf. 317b).

καὶ καλῶ] -- with the MSS. The author appears to treat καλόν and αἰσχρόν as a doublet; cf. 2.1, τῶ καλῶ καὶ αἰσχρῶ.

αἴ τις ἐρωτάσαι -- ὁμολογησοῦντι] -- for another example of the author's willingness to vary the degrees of remoteness between the protasis and apodosis of a conditional sentence, see 3.4.

ὁμολογησοῦντι] -- i.e., "they will (be forced to) agree".

αἴπερ τωὐτὸν κτλ] -- a lexically minute but crucial reformulation of the thesis under attack (2.1, fin.), converting it from a predicative statement to an identity-statement. See nn. on 2.1 (τοὶ δὲ κτλ), 1.1 (τοὶ δὲ ὡς -- τότε δὲ κακόν).

(22) τινά] -- the holders of the thesis, however, confined themselves to events/actions/states of affairs. At no stage in the argument was an object said to be simultaneously καλόν and αἰσχρόν. Compare 3.14, n. on

καὶ μέγαν κτλ.

αἵπερ τωὐτὸν κτλ] -- a reversal to the <u>original</u>
(and intelligible) formulation of the thesis (2.1,
<u>fin</u>.). Coming so soon after the reformulation of 2.21,
it suggests that the holders of the counter-thesis (at
any rate as reported by the author of the Δ. Λ.) have
simply failed to sense the crucial difference between
an identity-assertion and a predicative assertion.
Compare 2.24, τωὐτὸν αἰσχρὸν καὶ καλόν, and see n. on
1.1 (τοὶ δὲ ὡς -- τότε δὲ κακόν).

λευκόν, καὶ μέλανα κτλ] -- at Pl. <u>Euthyd</u>. 303d we
have the two sophists criticised by Socrates for saying
that μήτε καλὸν εἶναι μηδὲν μήτε ἀγαθὸν πρᾶγμα μήτε
λευκὸν μήδ' ἄλλο τῶν τοιούτων μηδέν. It is of interest
that neither the supposed identity-theorists of Δ. Λ.
2 (cf. Δ. Λ. 3.14) nor the sophists in the <u>Euthydemus</u>
go so far as to claim that black is white; in the
latter case Socrates simply attributes the belief to
them, and in the former it is groundlessly attributed
to them as a logical consequence of what are supposed
to be their beliefs. In view of the remarkable affinity
between the two statements, it seems very possible that,
on this point at any rate, there is a direct link
between the Δ. Λ. and Plato's dialogue. (Cf. Sext.
Emp. <u>Adv. Log</u>. 48.64, where Dionysodorus is associated
with Protagoras.)

(24) Answering to 2.6 specifically, and to all analogous situations (τἆλλα) generically.

(25) Answering to 2.9 specifically, and to all analogous situations (τἆλλα) generically.

(26) Answering to 2.18. The first sentence merely restates the contention, the second offers a weak statement of astonishment rather than a counter-argument. Dupréel (208) sees in the second sentence, coupled with 27 below, an allusion to the Hippias of the Hippias Maior (see also Dumont ad loc.), but it is hard to see why Hippias, rather than anyone else, should be singled out for the possession of so pervasive a common-sense notion.

οἷάπερ] -- for Untersteiner (n. ad loc.) another allusion to the putatively "Hippian" doctrine of "qualità" (see nn. on 1.11, οὕτω καὶ τὸ πρᾶγμα, and ποῖον ἀγαθὸν κτλ, with Introd., 60).

ἐσεῖται] -- a Doric, and specifically Megarian, future (see Bechtel 2.194, and Untersteiner, ad loc.). For its possible significance for the question of the prospective audience of the treatise, see Introd., 53.

(27) The situation seems hardly analogous to that outlined at 2.26 (answering to 2.18). The point there was that things considered by one group of people αἰσχρά could be seen by other people as καλά. But things themselves suffered no transmutation. Here, however, the possibility of transmutation is envisaged, only to be (rightly) rejected; but no part of the thesis has been destroyed, since its proponents never suggested the possibility of transmutation in the first place.

The force of the ἐπεί clause appears to be that, since homogeneous or near-homogeneous substances like metals used in money-transactions do not normally undergo spontaneous transmutation, this will be true a forti-

ori of much larger, heterogeneous substances like horses
and oxen. For the examples of gold and bronze the
author may be unconsciously drawing upon Iliad 6.234-
236.

The whole section carries on directly from 2.26.
One must understand it to run: αἱ . . . [sc. οἱ συνενη-
νοχότες] ἄγαγον . . . οὐκ ἄλλο τί κα [sc. οἱ ἀπενηνοχό-
τες] ἀπᾶγον· ἐπεὶ οὐδ' αἱ χρυσὸν ἤνεικαν [sc. οἱ συνενη-
νοχότες], χαλκόν [ἀπήνεικαν], οὐδ' αἱ ἀργύριον ἤνεικαν
[sc. οἱ συνενηνοχότες], μόλιβδόν κα ἀπέφερον [sc. οἱ
ἀπενηνοχότες].

(28) The author returns to the attack on the specific thesis of 2.18.

ἀντὶ δ' ἄρα κτλ] -- a rhetorical question drawing
what little force it has from the veiled suggestion
that, according to the thesis of 2.18, the same group
of persons is supposed to take away as καλά what they
had brought in as αἰσχρά. But the clear import of 2.18
is that it is different groups of persons who do this.
For another example, see the immediately subsequent
sentence, φέρε -- ἀπάγαγε; (though not too much stress
should perhaps be laid on it, in view of the doubtful-
ness of the text).

αἱ ἄρα τις κτλ] -- one of the hardest sentences in
the treatise. The minimum number of changes necessary
to make sense of the sentence appears to be as follows:
1. ἀπάγαγε (MSS.) should be read as ἄγαγε (the proxim-
    ity of ἀπαγαγόντι and ἀπάγαγε immediately preced-
    ing and following would plausibly account for the
    original error).
2. The sentence should, as Wilamowitz suggests, be

read as a question rather than as a statement.

3. The majority of the MSS. should be followed in omitting δ' before αὖ (αὖ being itself an apparently necessary correction of ἄν); a possible reason for the intrusion of δ' would perhaps be the inadvertent substitution at some stage of τόνδ' for τοῦτον.

4. καί should be read as κα (see 2.26, πάντα κα ἐν καλῷ).

αὖ κα] -- with Diels, to avoid the duplication of ἄν and κα. It will be noticed that ἄν is here excised on grounds other than the tacit agreement of many editors to excise all instances of the particle ἄν that are found in the MSS. For instances in which ἄν should, in my estimation, remain, see 3.2, 6.4. On the whole question of the dialect of the treatise, see Introd., 51 ff.

αἰσχρόν] -- while ambiguous as such, the adjective is unequivocally characterized as masculine by the subsequent τοῦτον. Diels' insertion <ἄνδρα> turns the author into a more fastidious stylist than the rest of the treatise suggests that he is.

καλὸν ἀπάγαγε] -- with the MSS. The emendation of Diels brings the syntax of the sentence into line with the syntax of 2.27 (and that of Wilamowitz into line with the preceding ἀπάγοντι--itself his emendation), but the moves seem unnecessary. The author is attempting to reply to 2.18 with one of his strongest reductio formulations--the 'past unfulfilled' condition, couched as a rhetorical question.

ἐπάγονται] -- compare 3.17 and 5.9, and see Taylor 112-113 (cf. 105) for the suggestion that we are here perhaps looking at a military metaphor ("bringing in

the 'reserves'--ἐπακτοί--to reinforce the front line").
Alternatively, it could simply mean "they cite as wit-
nesses" (see LSJ[9] s.v. ἐπάγω, II, 3, with Taylor 73).
Either way, the sense of the proposition is not affected.

ποτὶ ἀδονὰν κτλ] -- compare 3.17 (fin.). For similar sentiments see Hdt. 7.101.3, Thuc. 1.21.1, 1.22.4,
Gorgias B 11 #10 DK[6], Eratosthenes ap. Strab. 1.1.10.
The notion, it need hardly be pointed out, is central
to the thinking of Socrates and Plato; see, e.g., Pl.
Gorg. 501e, 502a, Resp. 607c; cf. Kranz 230, Levi (I)
302, n.52, Dupréel 381. As Müller points out, however
(148, n.2), Kranz and Levi go too far in taking the
sentiment to be specifically Socratic; cf. the other
sources cited at the beginning of this note.

οὐ ποτ᾽ ἀλάθειαν] -- an allusion perhaps (see Untersteiner ad loc.) to the doctrine (Δ. Λ. 3.10-12) that
art is a form of ἀπάτη (on which see Schmid-Stählin
3.159, n.8, 2.206, n.4). For further references see
Untersteiner ad loc., and for the most recent discussion de Romilly 160 f.

ποιεῦντι] -- with the MSS. Compare 3.17, ποιέοντι.
εο>ευ is of course common in Doric, and I assume that
we are looking at such a standard dialectal transforma-
tion here. The forms πωλεῦντι (1.3) and ἀσθενεῦντι
(1.3, 1.16) are of course another question; see Introd.,
52, and n. ad 1.3.

3. On Just and Unjust

(1) With this section one should compare 1.1 and
2.1. As in 2.1, the phrase τοὶ δὲ τωὐτὸ κτλ propounds
a 'contextualist' thesis, as the subsequent discussion
attests. It will also be noticed that, as in 2.1, the

formulation τοῖ δὲ τωὐτὸ κτλ is strictly predicative
in form; the potentially misleading formulation τοῖ
δε ὡς τὸ αὐτό ἐστι (1.1) does not occur. With the
whole chapter compare [Pl.] περὶ δικαίου and Xen. Inst.
Cyri 1.6.26 ff.--a passage that Untersteiner, ad loc.,
following Nestlé, argues stems from Gorgias.

τούτῳ] -- sc. τῷ λόγῳ (see Trieber, 214, n.1), "the
latter view"--i.e., that the same πρᾶγμα (see 1.11,
2.21, 3.13) is just and unjust. Is the author suggesting that in his estimation this argument is the weaker
of the two, and so needs a helping hand, or that it is
in fact the stronger one, and that he intends to give
it his support? τιμωρέν could tolerate either interpretation without difficulty. (The sentence can hardly
be interpreted simply as "I shall defend the latter
view first [and the former from 3.13 onwards]", since
that would appear to be the role of the subsequent
sentence, with its opening καὶ πρῶτον μὲν). I have
finally opted for the translation "bolster", on the
grounds that the verb πειρασοῦμαι suggests a mild
degree of diffidence (see also 2.2), but the point is
not an important one; as the whole of the Δ. Λ. makes
clear, the author is in each instance doing his best
to put forward the strongest case he knows for thesis
and counter-thesis alike.

(2) τὼς μὲν πολεμίως] -- cf. Pl. Resp. 382c7-10,
389b4-8, 459d1-2; [Pl.] περὶ δικαίου 374c3 ff.

ἄν ἐξείποιεν] -- with the MSS. (cf. the common
εἴποι ἄν τις). Sc. as subject "the holders of the dif-
ference-thesis", or something similar. On ἄν see n. on
2.28, αὖ κα, and Introd., 64. The author's style is

crabbed, as so often, but not so irretrievably obscure
as to warrant the emendations of Blass and DK. One
might paraphrase: "even if (per impossibile) they (i.e.,
"the holders of the 'difference' thesis") thought that
it was αἰσχρόν and πονηρόν to lie to and deceive one's
enemies, they would never deny that it is, in certain
circumstances, proper to lie to and deceive one's
φίλτατοι".

πιὲν καὶ φαγὲν] -- καὶ in its mildly disjunctive
sense, as so often. See below, ἐν τῷ ῥοφήματι καὶ ἐν
τῷ ποτῷ.

(3) For the relationship between this section (and
ff.) and Xenophon's account of a conversation between
Socrates and Euthydemus (Memorab. 4.2.14 ff.) see
Trieber 218-219, Maier 54, n.2, Taylor 106, Kranz 231,
Dupréel 310, Untersteiner n. ad loc., Müller 144 ff.
The structure of the two passages is remarkably similar, and verbal affinities (often the very same examples) abound (see Trieber 218). Trieber (ibid.), who
dates the Δ. Λ. some time between 404 and 401, concludes that the Δ. Λ. chapter is the original of the
Xenophon passage (see also Maier, ibid.), on the grounds
of its "ausführlichere Fassung". Other possibilities,
however, would surely be that both Xenophon and the
author of the Δ. Λ. had heard Socrates on the matter
(though Xenophon's acquaintance with Socrates seems to
have been at best impressionistic; see Chroust 10 ff.);
or that Xenophon had heard Socrates personally, while
the author of the Δ. Λ. had heard a fairly accurate
report (perhaps from some sophist teacher), or vice
versa. Untersteiner, n. ad loc., attributes both this

passage and that in the Memorabilia to a "fonte sofistica comune" (i.e., Hippias), as does Dupréel also
(310), though he does not go so far as to claim (as
does Dupréel, 208) that a detailed study of Xen. Mem.
4.2 and Mem. 4.4 would furnish fresh arguments in
favour of his thesis that all three are Hippian in
origin. (On the question of Hippian influence in the
Δ. Λ., see Introd., 59-65.)

For Kranz (231) both the Δ. Λ. passage and that in
the Memorabilia represent the views of Socrates; the
Δ. Λ. passage is simply the "älter und ausführlicher"
of the two. This is certainly partly true, and perhaps
wholly true (if, as seems probable, the Δ. Λ. slightly
antedates the Euthydemus). But nothing can be inferred
from it about the fons et origo of the discussion, who
could be either Socrates, the author of the Δ. Λ., or
some earlier thinker.

With the whole passage one should compare Pl. Resp.
331c.

ἤδη] -- i.e., all one needs (and what one now has)
is a single incontrovertible counter-example to shake
the foundations of a supposedly all-embracing contention (in this case the 'absolutist' contention [appar-
ently ascribed by the author to the holders of the
'difference' thesis] that τὸ ψεύδεσθαι is at all times
and under all possible circumstances πονηρόν).

καὶ κλέπτεν κτλ] -- the author is getting a little
ahead of himself; the evidence for his contention
emerges in 3.4. The particle μάν makes it clear that
he is aware that the assertion κλέπτεν -- φιλτάτως
has not yet been substantiated in the way that the
assertion ψεύδεσθαι -- γονέας has; so Diels' emendation

<δίκαιον> seems unnecessary. (For a similar stylistic
trait see 3.7, καὶ τὸ ἱεροσυλέν, and n.).

κλέπτεν] -- Dumont ad loc. refers to Gorgias B 11
#10 DK[6] (ἀπατήματα), but the situations do not seem to
be analogous. The Gorgias quotation appears, if anything, more relevant to Δ. Λ. 3.10 (ἐν γὰρ τραγωδοποιίᾳ
κτλ). His other reference, to Heraclitus C 1 #24 DK[6]
(= Hippoc. de victu 1.24), also seems more appropriate
to Δ. Λ. 3.11 (q.v.).

μάν] -- "for that matter", "doubtless".

(4) With the contents of this section compare Xen.
Mem. 4.2.18; with 3.2-4 generally compare Pl. Resp.
331c, 382d, [Pl.] περὶ δικαίου 374cd. Dupréel (353)
sees in the section an example of what he calls Gorgias'
"situation morality".

δίκαιόν ἐστι] -- for other examples of the author's
idiosyncratic usage when expressing himself condition-
ally see the relevant nn. on 2.14, 2.18, 2.21. In this
instance the author has combined within a single conditional sentence the most remote and the least remote
constructions possible. See also below, n. on 3.5, αἴ
τις κτλ.

(5) πῶς οὐ δίκαιον κτλ] -- here, as in the whole
section 3.2-12, the author confines himself to an elu-
cidation and defence of the thesis in terms of action
(by contrast with his practice in Δ. Λ. 1 and 2).
Stress is laid on the fact that the context makes certain actions just; the reader is simply left to infer
that the same actions are under different circumstances
unjust. The only time the point comes near being

spelled out is in 3.2 above, τὼς μὲν πολεμίως -- εξεί-
ποιεν;

αἴ τις κτλ] -- for the type of conditional sentence
see 3.4 above, with the n. ad loc. (δίκαιόν ἐστι) for
further examples. Diels' insertion <καί> seems unnecessary; the author is presumably discussing the morality
of "selling free men into slavery" (ἀνδραποδίξασθαι)
--a question which crops up forcibly when one has the
opportunity (δύναιτο) to "sell off" a complete enemy
city (πόλιν ὅλαν ἀποδόσθαι) after capturing it in war.

τῶν ἐχθρῶν] -- i.e., his political enemies.

(6) δίκαιά <κα> ποιῆσαι] -- with Matthaei. See
above, 2.26 (πάντα κα), 2.28 (αὖ κα) for similar instances of fairly easily recognisable corruption. It
should be pointed out, however, that there is some
evidence to support the view that Greek could tolerate
a rendering of a 'remote future' apodosis with the
optative alone. For a survey of the instances in Doric,
Lesbian, Homeric, Ionic, and Attic Greek see Slotty
183-185, 275, 279, 290, 312, 322, 340 ff.; cf. Hǿeg 109.
In the light of this (hereafter 'Slotty's Law'), I have
deemed it prudent to leave alone all MS. instances of
what appear to be such 'potential' optatives, unless
some clear 'scribal' reason for suspected textual corruption (as here, and at 2.26, 2.28) presents itself.

(7) ἐγὼ μὲν γὰρ κτλ] -- compare 1.2, ποτιτίθεμαι.
On the question of the author's own putative philosophical standpoint in the Δ. Λ. see Introd., 73 ff.

σῶσαι <ἂν τὰ> πατρῶϊα] -- the ease with which αἱ
and ἂν get confused in MSS. is notorious, and the same

holds true for the letters τ and π. However, if 'Slotty's Law' (above, n.6) is well-founded, ἄν may be
superfluous, and the reading would run simply: σῶσαι
<τὰ> πατρώϊα. For other instances of the particle ἄν
in the treatise see 3.2, 6.4, and perhaps 4.2.

καὶ τὸ ἱεροσυλέν] -- for the stylistic trait compare 3.3. The author enjoys attracting attention with
a rather startling 'ear-fixer', and then bringing forward evidence to support his contention. In the
present instance he undoubtedly misleads: συλᾶν and
λαβέν are hardly synonyms.
For the sentiments of the passage cf. Hdt. 5.36.

(8) τὰ μὲν ἴδια] -- i.e., temples of particular
πόλεις only, with no claim on the respect (or pocket)
of citizens outside of the πόλις in question.

μέλλοντος κτλ] -- the protasis of a general condition. While the author no doubt has in mind the period
of the Persian invasions of the early fifth century,
and perhaps the period after 412, when Persia had again
interfered in Greek affairs (see Trieber 217-218), the
form of the conditional sentence here suggests that he
is trying to universalize a moral point. With δίκαιον
sc. ἐστι.

λαβέν] -- cf. Hdt. 5.36, where the historian Hecataeus offers precisely such advice before the Ionian
revolt against the king of Persia. For similar advice
during a domestic conflict see Thuc. 1.21.3; 1.43.1
(cf. 2.13.4).

(9) Ὀρέστας] -- the son of Agamemnon and Clytemnes-
tra, who killed her and her lover Aegisthus in revenge

for the murder of Agamemnon.

Ἀλκμαίων] -- with the MSS. Son of Amphiareus and
Eriphyle, Alcmaeon killed his mother in requital for
her treachery to his father. See Ar. NE 1110a28,
Apoll. 3.6, Virg. Aen. 6.445-446.

ὁ θεός] -- i.e., the Delphic Apollo. See Eur.
Orest. 416.

(10) ὅστις -- ἐξαπατῇ] -- see below, 3.12, for the
use of a similar indicative mood to express the generically true. On the Doric ending ῇ (for Attic ᾷ) see
Ahrens 310, Thumb-Kiekers 1. #79, 3 (b). As an example
of the type of poetic ἀπάτη in question Dumont (ad loc.)
refers to Critias B 25 DK[6], but fails to convince.

ἐν γὰρ τραγῳδοποιίᾳ] -- for the sentiment see
Gorgias B 11 #10, B 23 DK[6]; cf. Madyda 56 ff., Dupréel
91, Untersteiner ad loc., de Romilly 160 f. For a sug-
gestion that it might be an echo of Simonides (ap.
Plut. Glor.Ath. 3.346 F) see Nestlé (II) 318 ff., 324;
Levi (I) 302 (with litt.); Untersteiner, ad loc.

ὅμοια κτλ] -- see, e.g., Od. 19.203, Hesiod Theog.
27, Theog. 713, Xenoph. B 35 DK[6]; on ποίησις as μίμησις
see, inter alia, Xen. Mem. 3.10.1 ff.; Pl. Resp. 377e,
595c, Prot. 312d, Crito 107b, Legg. 668b.

(11) Κλεοβουλίνης] -- on the (sixth-century) poet
of this name see P-W s.v. and Crusius 1.4. For litt.
on attempts to solve the riddle see Nestlé (I) 580-581,
Untersteiner ad loc. Bergk (according to Nestlé, loc.
cit.,; I have been unable to verify the reference)
refers to Ar. NE 1134a17 ff. (ἔστιν ἀδικοῦντα μήπω
ἄδικον εἶναν κτλ) and concludes that the solution to

the riddle is "the artist"; Wilamowitz (<u>Eurip. Hera-</u><u>kles</u>[2] [1895] 1.97, n.179) refers to [Hippocr.] περὶ διαίτης 1.24: παιδοτριβίη τοιόνδε· διδάσκουσι παρανομεῖν κατὰ νόμον, ἀδικεῖν δικαίως, ἐξαπατᾶν, κλέπτειν, ἁρπάζεσθαι. For κλέπτειν in the sense of "take by trickery" see Xen. <u>Anab.</u> 4.6.15, Pl. <u>Resp.</u> 333c-334a (a shift from <u>λαθεῖν</u> ἐμποιήσας [νόσον] to <u>κλέψαι</u> [τὰ τῶν πολεμίων]); the move to "winning a contest" or "winning points" by trickery is not a large one, and adds some strength to Wilamowitz' contention that the solution to the riddle must have been "the wrestler". His solution also has the advantage of accounting for the adverbs βιαίως and βίᾳ in a way that the Aristotle passage does not.

(12) The point that Aeschylus (fr. 601 f. Mette) appears to be making is that God (like man in 3.11) can on occasion justifiably deceive. Untersteiner, however (<u>ad loc.</u>), goes further, and sees the section as evidence that "egli (<u>sc.</u> the author of the Δ. Λ. or his source, "probabilmente Gorgia"; cf. Dupréel 91) dalla poesia tragica ha scoperto a un tempo la legge dell' arte e la legge del mondo". But this is to commit the author to too much; like many another Greek (including --notoriously--Plato) he could be "quoting scripture" to bolster the thesis he happens to be discussing, without commitment to the complete <u>Weltanschauung</u> that (perhaps) generated the original remarks.

ἦν πάλαι ταῦτα] -- with the MSS. For an analogous use of πάλαι and the existential εἶναι see Ar. <u>V.</u> 1060, πάλαι ποτ' ὄντες. Wilamowitz (III) 219, n.2 corrects to ἐν πάλᾳ (= ἐν πάλῃ) in line with his resolution of

Cleobuline's riddle by reference to [Hippocr.] περὶ
διαίτης 1.24 (see n. on 3.11 above). But, as Kranz
sees (223-224), this would solve the riddle for the
reader too early, leaving the Aeschylus quotations
unrelated to what has gone before.

ἀπάτης] -- cf. Gorgias B 23 DK[6]. But to base upon
this a "Gorgian" theory of "art as illusion" (see
Untersteiner, ad loc.) is, as Lucas rightly points
out, highly temerarious (270, and xviii, n.2, with
litt.).

καιρὸν] -- cf. 2.19-20, 5.9, with nn. Müller (147)
usefully adduces in comparison Eur. Hipp. 385-387 and
the [Hippocratic] treatise περὶ τόπων τῶν κατ' ἄνθρωπον
44 (VI.338 Littré).

τιμῇ] -- with the MSS. Aeschylus presumably wrote
τιμᾷ (which Nauck[2] prints): the author converts to the
Doric τιμῇ. See n. on 3.10 above, ὅστις -- ἐξαπατῇ.
The sense of each of the two lines makes it clear that
they stem from different sources, as North sees, and
do not form a single fragment. So Diels' <καί·> seems
superfluous.

(13) ff. The counter-λόγος: verbal distinctions
mirror distinctions in re.

By contrast with the way proponents of the counter-
thesis in Δ. Λ. 1 and 2 had compared identity-asser-
tions and predicative assertions on the part of their
supposed adversaries, in Δ. Λ. 3 proponents of the
counter-thesis (as reported, at any rate, by the author)
at least do their supposed adversaries the favour of
reporting them correctly (compare 3.1 with 3.13 [fin.],
3.15). But they still contrive to misunderstand them

completely. Having seen, apparently, that their supposed adversaries are making a predicative statement,
not an identity-statement, they proceed to take the
said statement to be a statement made simpliciter, when
all the evidence of 3.2-12 makes it clear that it was
meant to be taken secundum quid (see Joël 1.401, n.1).
Their attack, as a result (as in 2.21 ff.; cf. 1.11
ff.), is an attack on straw men.

    πρᾶγμα] -- see 1.11, with n. ad loc. (πρᾶγμα), 4.6.

    αἱ ἤδη] -- see 1.12, 13.

    (14) γινώσκει κτλ] -- the subject is presumably
τις, from the preceding section.

    μέγαν] -- of size. North mistranslates "magis (in-
justum)"; for this to be a possibility one would need
μέγα, as Orelli sees. As for the whole phrase καὶ
μέγαν κτλ, it is a gratuitous and ineffective debating
point. As all the examples of 3.2-12 make clear, the
'contextualist' thesis turns entirely on the contextual
propriety or impropriety of particular actions; it
makes no pretence of venturing beyond the bounds of the
sphere of ethics. See also 2.22, with n. (τινά).

    ἀποθανέτω κτλ] -- almost certainly corrupt. For
the many attempts to emend see the app. crit. The
argument I take to be an attempted reductio ad absurdum:
if justice and criminality are really to be equated,
the (supposed) identity-theorists ought logically to
condemn all just men to death. The phrase πολλὰ ἀδικήσας seems to function as a concealed protasis, and the
second ἀποθανέτω (found in C P6 V2) I tentatively re-
write as ἄτε θανάτω ἄξια, or some such phrase. πράτ-
τεσθαι in the sense of 'perform' (an action) seems

without parallel; διαπράττεσθαι (Blass) may well be
right, being normally used as it is of the "bringing
about" or "accomplishment" of states of affairs (see
LSJ[9] s.v.). However, it is still, strictly speaking,
the unjust actions that warrant death, rather than a
situation or state of affairs that has been brought
about by unjust actions.

(15) τούτων] -- i.e., the general considerations
preceding a more precise examination of the other side's
arguments. See 1.11-15, 2.21-23.

λέγοντες] -- cf. 1.16 (καθ' ἔκαστον) 2.23 (τὸν λόγον
-- λέγοντι). Sections 16 and 17, however, fail to ful-
fil this promise.

ἀξιοῦντι] -- the uncontracted form of ἀξιόω, found
in the MSS., is different from other curious forms in
the Δ. Λ. in that it has no parallel in any dialect of
West Greek (Bechtel). The regular form in such Greek
would be ἀξιοῦντι, which I read with Mullach. ἀξιώοντι
(Blass) is an uncontracted form of the variant ἀξιώω,
which is usually regarded as Aetolian in origin but
turns up in Aeolic, North West Greek, and island Doric.
ἀξιῶντι (Wilamowitz) is presumably the 'regular' third
person plural of ἀξιώω, but in West Greek, with the o-o
contraction, ἀξιοῦντι would more likely be found.
ἀξιόωντι (St) is a subjunctive form, and clearly out of
place.

The form ἀξιόοντι can, I think, be reasonably
accounted for in terms of the near-irresistible scribal
tendency to 'level' analogically. Just above, for
example (3.13), the text reads ὁμολογέοντι, and just
below (3.17) ποιέοντι.

(16) γάρ] -- the force of the conjunction seems to
be: "For make no mistake about it: <to demonstrate> the
fact that stealing the enemy's possessions is just is <u>eo</u>
<u>ipso</u> to demonstrate the truth of the antithetical posi-
tion as well, if their reasoning is sound." The unpacked version of the sentence would run: τὸ γὰρ κλέπτεν τὰ τῶν πολεμίων δίκαιον <εἶναι ἀποδεικνύεν> καὶ
ἄδικον <ἐστιν> ἀποδεικνύεν τοῦτ' αὐτὸ <εἶναι> κτλ. An
alternative interpretation would perhaps be: "For make
no mistake about it: the fact that stealing the enemy's
possessions is just is <u>eo ipso</u> a demonstration of the
truth of the antithetical position as well, if their
reasoning is sound." The unpacked version of the sentence, if this is a correct understanding of its meaning, would run: τὸ γὰρ κλέπτεν τὰ τῶν πολεμίων δίκαιον
<εἶναι> καὶ ἄδικον <ἐστιν> ἀποδεικνύεν τοῦτ' αὐτὸ
<εἶναι> κτλ. Either way the claim is a philosophically
interesting one, but again it seems to involve a mis-
statement of the views of the supposed identity-
theorists. For them any identity lay in action, not in
acceptance-of-fact and/or demonstration (see 3.2-12).
As in earlier instances, the erroneous interpretation
of the views of the supposed identity-theorists in this
matter stems from a mistaken assumption on the part of
their opponents that their assertions are to be taken
<u>simpliciter</u>, not <u>secundum quid</u>.

(17) ἐπάγονται] -- cf. n. on 2.28 (ἐπάγονται).
καὶ τοὶ ποιηταί] -- compare 2.28 (<u>fin.</u>). The suggestion seems to be that the products of ποιηταί are
fictitious, and calculated to induce feelings of pleasure only; in a word, the world of ποίησις is not the

'real' (ἀλαθής) world--and only actions in the 'real'
world can be in the strict sense of the word character-
izable as δίκαια and ἄδικα. See n. on 2.28, ποτί
ἀδονάν.

4. On Truth and Falsehood

With the whole chapter compare Pl. Euthyd. 283a ff.,
Ar. Soph. El. 178b24 ff., Cat. 4a23-b13. Pohlenz (60)
refers, less convincingly, to Pl. Hipp. Min., and
Dupréel (92; cf. 296-297), even less convincingly, to
the Gorgian Περί τοῦ μή ὄντος. On this see Introd., 68.

(Title) ψεύδεος] -- genitive of the noun ψεῦδος,
not of the adjective ψευδής. For examples of <τὸ>
ψεῦδος as opposed to <τὸ> ἀληθές see below, 4.5, and
Pl. Euthyd. 272a, Gorg. 505e, Resp. 382d, et alib.
ἀλάθεια seems to be a variant on τὸ ἀλαθές.

(1) καὶ τῶ ἀλαθέος] -- with DK. The MS. reading
τῶ suggests a neuter genitive; ἀλαθείας has probably
supplanted ἀλαθέος under the influence of the wording
of the title.

(2) τόνδε] -- sc. τὸν λόγον. As in the first
three chapters, the author will put forward the case
for the supposed identity-thesis first (4.2-5); for the
counter-thesis see 4.6 ff. If the punctuation of
editors earlier than Blass--τὸν αὐτόν. αὖ κἀγώ--is
accepted, the author would seem to commit himself
fairly strongly to the thesis, as apparently in 1.2
(ποτιτίθεμαι); αὖ in such a position, however, would
constitute a ἅπαξ in the language. According to the

reading I have accepted, the phrase κἀγὼ τόνδε λέγω
still suggests a wholehearted commitment to the attempt
to put the best possible case at any rate for the thesis; so much so that he is prepared to talk in propria
persona in marshalling the arguments for it. (On the
whole question of the author's own putative philosophical position in the Δ. Λ., see Introd., 73 ff.).

For τόνδε = "the latter" (rather than "the following") see 1.2, τοῖσδε.

λέγονται] -- sc. both the true statement and the
false statement.

ὡς <ἂν?> λέγηται] -- after the phrase ἂν μὲν (found
in all MSS. except P3) the introduction of another ἂν
(the particle) looks harsh, and the temptation to excise
it was probably strong, particularly if the scribe
thought that the subjunctive λέγηται could be adequately
accounted for in terms of its apparent parallelism with
γένηται (ὡς . . . οὕτω).

(3) κατηγορεῖ] -- sc. "a statement" (λόγος τις).

ὣς γε] -- if one prescinds from verse, ὣς for οὕτως
is a characteristic of Ionic Greek (see, e.g., Hdt.
3.13). On ionicisms in the treatise and their possible
significance see Introd., 51 ff.

καὶ τά γε δικαστήρια κτλ] -- cf. Pl. Tht. 201b7-c7,
Dupréel 296. In context, the statement is clearly
meant to be taken in a qualified sense, not absolutely.
See, however, 4.7-8 for a (predictable) attempt by the
proponent of the counter-thesis to make a case for himself by reading it au pied de la lettre.

(4) ἐπεί τοι καί] -- with the MSS. After ἐπεί sc.

perhaps "in the eyes of a court of law" (cf. above, τά
γε δικαστήρια), or some such phrase. καί . . . αἰ:
"even if"; but the separation of the words makes for a
harsh phrase.

αἱ λέγοιμεν] -- sc. "in unison".

μύστας εἰμι] -- see Introd., 41 ff. Rostagni suggests, interestingly (175), that the picture of an
initiate to the Mysteries speaking to non-initiates is
meant to conjure up the image of "un maestro di scuola
davanti ai suoi discepoli."

ἀλαθής] -- (of people) "honest", "truth-telling",
"truth-bearing". See LSJ[9] s.v., and below, 4.6.

(5) For the sentiment compare Ar. Cat. 4a23-4b13
(cf. Top. 178b25), Pl. Sympos. 207de. Dupréel (210)
refers to Pl. Hipp. Mai. 287c, but the objectivism
there ascribed to Hippias would only extend to the concepts of τὸ ἀληθές and τὸ ψεῦδος if Hippias also held
that all general terms in language refer. This is not
corroborated in any source, however.

παρῇ] -- compare, with Taylor (109, n.1) Pl. Phd.
100d5, 105c3, and cf. Euthyd. 301a, with R. K. Sprague,
"Parmenides' Sail and Dionysodorus' Ox", Phronesis 12
(1967) 91-98. The concept of παρουσία is a cardinal
one in Platonic metaphysics, serving as one of a number
that Plato uses in an attempt to link the world of
Forms and the world of sense-perception. Its use here
is evidence that the proponent of the views of this
section of the Δ. Λ. (like the proponent of the views
of Δ. Λ. 8--see n. ad 8.9 [τὸ δίκαιον]) is in an 'essentialist' tradition and, like Socrates/Plato, feels the
need to use different metaphors to express what he feels

to be the puzzling relationship between universal and
particular (cf. below, 4.9, ἀναμέμεικται). It is also
evidence, it seems, that the metaphor is not uniquely
Socratic/Platonic, and it could well be that Socrates/
Plato has drawn on some precursor for the metaphor--
perhaps even on the author of the Δ. Λ. himself. It
should be pointed out, however, that the 'universal'
under discussion is the property of 'truth' that inheres in all true propositions or of 'falsity' that
inheres in all false propositions; Socrates/Plato, when
using the metaphor of παρουσία, is more involved in the
question of the universal features of objects/events/
states of affairs. And of course the possibility
remains that it was <u>Socrates</u> who first used the metaphor, and that the author of the Δ. Λ. adopted it
directly from him. As so often in the case of the Δ.
Λ., no sure means of adjudicating the possibilities is
readily available.

(6) <ὥσπερ καὶ τὸ πρᾶγμα>] -- cf. 1.11 (with n.
[πρᾶγμα]), 3.13.

αἰ γὰρ τις κτλ] -- a shrewd statement, incorporat-
ing a number of elements of the so-called 'Liar Paradox'
(see Dümmler 209). According to Theophrastus (<u>ap</u>. D. L.
2.108) the Paradox in its fully articulated form was
first enunciated by Eubulides, disciple of Euclides of
Megara (who was himself a contemporary of the author of
the Δ. Λ.; see <u>P.-W</u>. <u>s.v</u>. Euklides [5]). For an analogous either/or paradox, used as a criticism of Protagoras' 'man the measure' doctrine (as Plato conceived
it) see Pl. <u>Tht</u>. 170e ff. (an argument perhaps adumbrated at <u>Euthyd</u>. 286e ff.; see Kranz 231--and for a

disclaimer Levi [I] 306).

Whether there is a linear relationship (in either direction) between Eubulides and the author of the Δ. Λ. does not seem to be open to demonstration. Whatever the case, either or both of them could well be indebted for the core of the argument to Democritus (cf. Democritus A 114 DK[6] = Sext. Emp. Adv. Math. 7.389); see Gomperz (II) 150, n.318, Kranz 231, Levi (I) 297-298, Untersteiner ad loc.

δύο εἴη] -- with the MSS. Sc. as subject ἐκεῖνος ὁ λόγος, "the sentence they are now uttering". For another example of the use of an optative in oratio obliqua after a primary main verb see this same section, ad init., λέγεται . . . ὡς εἴη κτλ. δύο--"two" in the sense of "different from one another".

παρῇ κτλ] -- compare 4.9 below.

ἀποκρίναιτο] -- for another disconcerting example of a change from plural to singular see below, 6.7 (ἃ καὶ αὐτός). That the change has been made seems to be confirmed by the subsequent verbs εἶπεν, ἐξεμαρτύρησε, and οἶδε.

ὁ αὐτὸς οὗτος] -- sc. λόγος, the point being that the original thesis is false because it made out the true and the false to be identical. As in the first three chapters, the proponent of the counter-thesis makes his would-be rebuttals by taking the identity-thesis absolutely, when the evidence of 4.2-5 makes it clear that it was understood contextually.

καὶ <αἱ>] -- with Blass. καί (Diels) is found elsewhere only in Theocritus (29.16), and appears to be a piece of crasis tailored specifically to the needs of verse.

καί ψευδῆ ἄρα] -- sc. εἶπεν ἢ ἐξεμαρτύρησε. See
immediately below, ψεύσταν τὸν αὐτόν, where οἶδε is to
be understood from the preceding clause.

ἀλαθῆ] -- "honest", "truth-telling". See above, n.
on 4.4 (ἀλαθής).

(7) (8) Many editors have suspected textual corruption here (see app. crit.), and perhaps even a sizeable
lacuna. However, it seems not impossible that the
author has simply conflated two ways of expressing an
indirect statement (see Smyth, Greek Grammar 2628).
Following normal usage, he begins with λέγειν and a ὅτι
construction, and then switches without warning to the
accusative and infinitive construction. This is disconcerting, like the change from plural to singular at
4.6 and 6.7, but hardly creates ambiguity. That the
author can combine λέγειν with an accusative and infinitive construction is clear from 5.6, q.v. In 4.8 a
verb of interrogation seems to have dropped out, and I
tentatively supply <ἐρέσθαι>.

ἐκ δὲ τῶ λόγω] -- see LSJ[9] s.v. λόγος, III, 7.
Spelled out in full, the meaning seems to be: "given
their argument, and compelled to put forward evidence
in support of it, they state . . ." etc.

οὐκῶν διαφέρει] -- the (false) assumption being
that identity-theorists claim that law-courts judge a
proposition to be simultaneously and in the same respect true and false (cf. 4.3, καί τά γε -- κρίνοντι)--
with the result that jury-decisions are misleading, if
not valueless. As so often, the proponents of the
counter-thesis take as their point of departure a
general (and--taken by itself--admittedly misleading)

statement of the identity-thesis, without reference to
the mound of contextual evidence that qualifies and
clarifies it. The result is a statement (οὐκῶν --
πράγμασιν) which, far from demolishing the case of the
identity-theorists, is in fact something with which
they would readily agree.

αὖθις] -- "in their turn"; see Pl. Charm. 153d,
αὖθις ἐγώ αὐτοὺς ἀνηρώτων (cf. LSJ[9] s.v., II[2], III;
Ast s.v.). The defendant has, one must assume, given
his version of what happened; the jury must then in
their turn offer their judgment (κρίνοιντο) on his
veracity or otherwise (cf. Pl. Tht. 201bc). The point
presumably being made is that in a court of law claims
and counter-claims are tested by reference to something
tacitly accepted by defendant, prosecutor, and jury
alike--i.e., a 'correspondence' theory of truth.

Dupréel (296-297), stressing the importance of discussion in court-cases, and by-passing, it seems to me,
the implications of the phrase τοῖς πράγμασιν, sees the
Gorgian doctrine of the "power of λόγος" as the basis
of Δ. Λ. 4.8-9, rather than a 'correspondence' theory
of truth--a theory he denies that the author of the
περί τοῦ μή ὄντος could ever have held. On the latter
point he could well be right--if the author of the
περί τοῦ μή ὄντος is taken to be propounding doctrine,
and not merely engaging in dialectical argument (as
seems more likely). But this does not seem to be relevant to the discussion at Δ. Λ. 4.8-9, where judgment
by reference to oral evidence is in question, and this
surely depends directly on a 'correspondence' theory of
truth. Whether the proponents of the counter-thesis
adhered to a further, 'Gorgian', belief in the power of

λόγος cannot be known from the present context; and it would not, in any case, be in itself incompatible with a 'correspondence' theory of truth.

κρίνοιντο] -- middle voice. Tr. "what their judgment is" (i.e., as to whether the supposed event took place or not). For the mood after a primary main verb see above, 1.1, 4.6.

οὐ γὰρ πάρεντι] -- compare (with Taylor 110-111, Dupréel 296-297) Pl. Tht. 201b ff. (For a disclaimer see Levi [I] 306.)

(9) καὶ αὐτοί] -- "even they themselves" (i.e., the proponents of the identity-thesis). The reference is presumably to 4.5, but the paraphrase is wholly unacceptable, suggesting as it does that the phrases ᾧ μὲν and ᾧ δὲ refer to two different statements, when the statement of 4.5 refers explicitly to ὁ αὐτὸς λόγος.

τὸ ψεῦδος κτλ] -- see n. on 4.5 above (παρῇ κτλ).

τοῦτο δὲ ὅλον διαφέρει] -- i.e., "but this view is totally different from their original one" (i.e., from the [unqualified] identity-thesis of 4.1 [fin.]). The confusion, however, seems to be in the minds of the proponents of the counter-thesis again; see n. on καὶ αὐτοί above.

διαφέρει] -- there is perhaps a small lacuna after this word, as North, Wilamowitz, and DK suggest (cf. Taylor 108, Schmid-Stählin 3.204). If this assumption is correct, its opening words (cf. n. on 5.1 ["ταὐτά κτλ] for the possible concluding ones) were perhaps either a brief statement why ὅλον διαφέρει or simply a phrase like τῷ πρώτῳ λόγῳ ἐκείνων, with the reason why-- being too obvious to mention--left unspoken.

Gomperz ([II] 145, n.210], Kranz (226), and Untersteiner (ad loc.) feel that there is no reason to suspect a lacuna.

5. [Untitled]

In this chapter the familiar introductory phrase
δισσοί λόγοι is missing, and at section (6) a blunt
οὐκ ὀρθῶς λέγοντι is found in place of the expected
ἄλλος δὲ λόγος ἐστιν, or the like. But the basic structure of the treatise as seen so far is retained: a conglomerate thesis is propounded (1-5), and a refutation
is offered (6-15). The conglomerate thesis consists of
two parts:

(a) people possessed of contrary properties may in
fact act and speak identically (1-2)

(b) the same person/thing is himself/itself possessed of contrary properties (3-5).
As in Δ. Λ. 1-4, the conglomerate thesis is predicative,
as the examples in its defence make clear. But it seems
not impossible that, as in all earlier instances, the
proponents of the thesis summed up their views in a way
that could be misunderstood; e.g., in some such phrase
as τὸ μαίνεσθαι καὶ τὸ σωφρονεῖν ἐστι τὸ αὐτό. That
the proponents of the counter-thesis believed their
opponents to hold such an identity-thesis as well as
the innocuous predicative thesis seems clear from 5.8
(οὔκων . . . τοὶ σοφοὶ μαίνονται κτλ).

"ταὐτὰ κτλ] -- I follow Diels in reading 5.1-5 as
oratio recta. It seems possible, however, that a brief
introductory statement of the form δισσοί λόγοι λέγονται
or the like has dropped out, and that the lacuna covers
a few words from the end of chapter four as well (see

n. on 4.9, τοῦτο δὲ ὅλον διαφέρει). Kranz (226; cf.
227, n.1) sees no reason to suspect a lacuna, consider-
ing the oratio recta merely a variation on the oratio
obliqua of Δ. Λ. 1-4.

τοὶ μαινόμενοι κτλ] -- on the interest displayed
by Socrates in the difference between τὸ σωφρονεῖν and
τὸ μαίνεσθαι see Schmid-Stählin 3.206, n.5.

(2) καὶ τἆλλα] --sc. ποιέοντι. For a germane sentiment in Gorgias Untersteiner (ad loc.) refers to Untersteiner Sofisti 4 [82] B 3 bis, 6.24 (cf. 4 [82] B 11a
26).

(3) οὕτω] --i.e., if we focus our attention on relational properties.
πάντα] -- sc. τὰ πράγματα. The discussion at this
stage appears to be confined to physical objects.

(4) A specific exemplification of 5.3 above. As
the point of 5.1 and 5.2 was, it seems, that apparently
different types of person are in fact the same type,
the point of 5.3 and 5.4 seems to be that apparently
antithetical relational properties can be possessed by
the same physical object (πρᾶγμα). Cf. Pl. Hipp. Mai.
289b, Phd. 102b ff., Tht. 154c ff.

(5) The discussion broadens at this point to the
question of whether substances can exist and not-exist,
or whether states of affairs can be the case and not
the case. Notoriously, the verb εἶναι can in different
contexts serve as the identity-sign, the existential
sign, and the sign of veridication (see C. H. Kahn,

Foundations of Language I [1966] 245-265). In the
present context the most natural translations are in
terms of existence and veridication. Compare Pl.
Euthyd. 283c-e, where a fallacy turns on the exploitation of the existential and predicative senses of εἶναι.

καὶ ταὐτά -- οὐκ ἐντί] -- for Dupréel (92) these
phrases, and indeed the whole chapter, are evidence
that Gorgias' περὶ τοῦ μὴ ὄντος has influenced the
author in the writing of his identity-theses. But it
is far from obvious that we have here a "théorie de
l'identité des contraires" or a denial of "la valeur
absolue des choses objectives". As the context makes
clear, the phrase ταὐτά ἔστι καὶ οὐκ ἔστι is meant to
be taken secundum quid, not simpliciter (cf. Ar. Soph.
El. 167a1-10); any similarity with Gorgias' paradoxical
claim that nothing at all ἔστι (if it is meant as a
serious claim, and not simply a dialectical gambit)
seems to be purely verbal.

καὶ ζώει -- καὶ οὐ ζώει] -- in Greek, as in English, it is possible to say "I live; you just exist."
See, e.g., Soph. Ant. 1165-1167, Pl. Resp. 329a8.

τῇδε] -- hardly "in Europe" (Trieber 219, DK,
Untersteiner ad loc.), from most of which the Greeks
considered themselves as far removed as from Africa
and Asia--if not further. Perhaps (with Kranz 224) "in
the Greek-speaking world" (if εἶναι is understood exis-
tentially), or "in the case of the Greek-speaking world"
(if εἶναι is understood veridically); cf. 6.12, where
τῇδε is contrasted with Πέρσαι. But Cyprus, too, was
Greek-speaking; so it seems possible that τῇδε means
simply either "here (in/in the case of Greece)" or
"here (in/in the case of this Greek-speaking city)".

Λιβύᾳ] -- "Africa" in general. See LSJ s.v. For
Wilamowitz ([V] 2.432) the reference to Λιβύα suggests
that the author was perhaps of Cyrenian origin, on the
grounds that the name "Libya" would be the first name
to spring to the lips of such a person living in Athens
if he were asked to name some other part of the world.
But if Λιβύα means "Africa" in general this argument
loses most of what little force it ever had.

ἐν Κύπρῳ] -- hardly a reference, as some have
thought (Bergk [II] 131 f., Nestlé [II] 437), to the
place in which the document was written. As Taylor
sees (94,n.1), the argument gains rather by the suppo-
sition that three places (not just two) are under con-
sideration: "here", "Africa", and Cyprus. In this way
the author is able to offer two illustrations of his
view, rather than simply one.
I see no reason for thinking (pace Untersteiner ad loc.)
that the term "Cyprus" stands for "Asia".

καὶ ἐντὶ κτλ] -- for the sentiment, or one aspect
of it, see Heraclitus B 49A DK[6], εἶμέν τε καὶ οὐκ
εἶμεν.

τὰ πράγματα] -- objects, or states of affairs, or
both (see trans.). From the evidence of 5.15 (init.)
objects appear to be in the author's mind, but it seems
at least possible that that phrase, being purely existential, answers to ζώει καὶ οὐ ζώει instead (5.5
init.), thus leaving the question of the denotation of
πράγματα an open one. See Dupréel 211.

(6) οὐκ ὀρθῶς λέγοντι] -- on the question of author-
commitment see Introd., 73-77.

(7) σοφίη ἀμαθίης] -- on the possible significance
of Ionic forms in the treatise see Introd., 51 ff.   DK
print σοφία, without signalling the reading of P3; presumably they see it (and the other instances at 6.1,
6.7) as an example of that "halbgelehrte Konjektur"
that in their estimation underlies P3's attempts at
"Dialektberichtigungen" (see also Mutschmann, Sext. 1.
vi). Yet they happily print the adjacent Ionic form
ἀμαθίης (5.7), found in all MSS., and the specifically
dialectal Doric forms πειρασεῦμαι (2.2) and ποιεῦντι
(2.28)--the latter two being found exclusively in P3.
They also accept the Doric readings τώυτόν (for ταύτόν
vel sim., rel.) at 3.14 and μέσαν (for μέσην) at 6.13--
both readings again being found exclusively in P3.   In
view of this, it seems strange that the reading σοφίη
(tris) should be singled out as inept, when the treatise is in fact interlaced with Ionic forms (for a
partial list, see above, 89, n.63). (Which is not, of
course, to say that P3 is wholly and unequivocally
reliable; see, e.g., 4.2, where ἂν is twice by the com-
monest of slips accidentally converted to αἱ.) As for
P3's "conjectures", I suspect they are confined to the
occasional and innocuous τούς>τώς and ἐστί>ἐντί.

(8) καὶ ἐξ ὧν κτλ] -- in the sense, presumably,
that the manner of performance of an action will rapidly
indicate whether we are dealing with a sane person or a
demented. Or perhaps the author is suggesting that not
all of the words and deeds of sane people and demented
are coincident; the identity-thesis is respectable as
an I proposition, but false as an A proposition.

ἑκάτεροι] -- 'each group', i.e., σοφοί and ἀμαθεῖς,

μανικοί and σώφρονες (5.7).

ὁμολογησοῦντι] -- i.e., will agree that it is the case that μανία differs from σωφροσύνη and σοφίη from ἀμαθίη. The subject of δᾶλοι is τοί τῆνα λέγοντες (i.e., the putative identity-theorists).

καί αἱ ταὐτά πράσσοντι] -- sc. ἑκάτεροι (i.e., the wise and the foolish). That some actions are structurally the same can be conceded to the proponents of the (supposed) identity-thesis; where they differ is in the manner of their performance. Or perhaps: some actions are identical, it may be conceded, both in structure and performance, but not all. See n. on καί ἐξ ὧν κτλ above.

σοφοί] -- a certain looseness of language is evident here. At 5.7 (cf. 5.1) the antonym of μανία was σωφροσύνη (sanity) and of σοφίη ἀμαθίη. Now σοφίη seems to be serving as a synonym for σωφροσύνη (see also below, 5.9).

πάντα] -- i.e., all accepted beliefs.

(9) καί ἐπακτέος κτλ] -- compare 2.28, ἐπάγονται.

ἀλλά γάρ] -- <"I mention the point> because", etc. The identity-theorists, in a word, admit that there are other considerations than simple verbal identity when one is discussing the speech at any rate of sane people and demented.

ἐν τῷ δέοντι] -- cf. [Pl.] περί δικαίου 375a2 ff. (ἐν . . . τῷ δέοντι καί τῷ καιρῷ κτλ); see Gomperz (II) 154, and n.327a, Kranz 230, and n.4, Untersteiner n. ad loc. Whether have a reference to a "Gorgian doctrine of καιρός" here, however (Untersteiner, n. ad loc.; Dupréel 90), is uncertain. That Gorgias was con-

vinced of the importance of καιρός ("the apposite
moment") for the rhetorician seems clear enough (Gorgias B 13 DK[6]; cf. Pl. Phdr. 267a, Isoc. Panegyr. 8
ff., esp. 9 [ἐν καιρῷ]); whether this extended to a
"doctrine of καιρός" in ethics and epistemology as well
is in dispute. For protagonists of the notion see Süss
18 f., Rostagni 147 ff., Nestlé (II) 316-317, and n.54,
Untersteiner passim; see also n. on 2.19 (ὧδε . . .
διαιρῶν).

For Gomperz ([II] 154) the contention of 5.9 fin.
is Socratic in form; for Kranz (230, n.4) the evidence
of [Pl.] περὶ δικαίου 375a2 ff. would, if it genuinely
represents a Socratic discussion, suggest that it is
also Socratic in content. Pohlenz (77, n.1) sees an
echo of Hippias in the verb δεῖν (see Pl. Hipp. Min.
369a), but this seems far-fetched. On the question of
Socratic and/or sophistic influence on arguments in the
Δ. Λ. see Introd., #4.

(10) τὸ αὐτό] -- i.e., "the same <thing that
σωφρονοῦντες and μαινόμενοι are supposed to be doing
and saying>".

(11) ἐγὼ δὲ οὔ κτλ] -- the proponents of the counter-
thesis are clearly taking the qualifying phrases ᾇ δεῖ
and ᾇ μὴ δεῖ quite differently from the way in which the
identity-theorists had intended them. The latter were
claiming that contextual propriety would make manifest
whether a particular statement had been uttered by a
sane person or a demented; the former take them to be
saying that contextual propriety affects meaning.
ποτιτιθέντος] -- i.e., to the earlier, unqualified

statements of the identity-theorists.

τὰ πράγματα] -- "things", in the apparent sense of
"meanings"; cf. the subsequent discussion (5.11-14).
For Untersteiner, ad loc., τὰ πράγματα = φύσις, which
is only changed "qualitatively" (the doctrine, he
claims, of Hippias); for Gorgias, he affirms, change
is quantitative (hence τοσούτω). But this, even if it
accurately describes the views of Hippias and Gorgias
in the matter (which appears to me very doubtful),
seems completely out of keeping with the examples (all--
including, apparently, that of 5.14--involving change
of meaning) that the proponents of the counter-thesis
use to illustrate their point (5.11-14).

ἁρμονίας κτλ] -- for the meaning "accent" see Pl.
Hipp. Mai. 285d3 (cf. Pl. Hipp. Min. 368d), and Untersteiner ad loc., with litt. In (wittingly or unwittingly) misunderstanding the drift of the remarks of
the identity-theorists at 5.9 the author has now involved himself in a discussion of semantic variation.
This leaves him open to the obvious criticism of the
identity-theorists: "How does this help us to distinguish the sane person and the demented when/if they
utter propositions which are identical down to the
minutest accentual and morphological detail?"

For change of meaning brought about by the addition
or taking away of particular letters see Pl. Crat.
418a, 432a.

The specialized use of ἁρμονία is perhaps a hint
of the "Hippian" origin of 5.11 ff. (see Untersteiner,
ad loc.); but even if this is true, τὰ πράγματα can
hardly mean what Untersteiner takes it to mean, unless
the author is to be accused of complete incoherence

(see above, n. on τά πράγματα). (For ἀρμονία = "Ton-verhältniss" [rather than "accent"] see Kranz 229, n.1.)

A further possibility, touched on by Gomperz (II) 171-172 and backed by Maier 16-17, is that we have in this passage evidence of the influence of Prodicus; see Pl. Crat. 384b = Prodicus A 11 DK[6] (ὀνομάτων ὀρθό-τητος), Euthyd. 277e. This is no doubt a genuine possibility, but hardly more of a possibility than that the author is here influenced by Protagoras, who was also interested in linguistic precision (see Protag. A 27, 28, 29 DK[6]; Pl. Crat. 391c, Phdr. 267c; Gomperz [II] 171; Kranz 229; Classen 223-226). As Guthrie points out (3.205, n.1), Plato attributes an interest in "correctness of names" to the sophists in general (Crat. 391b), and it seems hazardous to single out one over the next, except perhaps in the case of the use (apparently) of the term ἀρμονία in a rare and special-ized sense, where Hippias has a special claim to mention.

(12) καί "σακός"] -- with Weber. The author is talking at this stage about words which differ in respect of the length given to a particular vowel when they are spoken (ῥηθέντα). The reading σάκκος adds a further distinguishing mark, and would only be relevant to 13 below (ποτιτιθεῖ τι ἢ ἀφαιρεῖ). The form σακός is Doric, as is κάρτος. νόος is Ionic in form, but it also occurs in a fifth-century Corinthian inscription (Bechtel 2.227); for other occurrences in Doric of the uncontracted o-o in nouns and adjectives see Bechtel 2.173, 2.227, 2.390.

γράμματα διαλλάξαντα] -- cf. Pl. Crat. 318a.

καὶ "κρατός"] -- with Wilamowitz. κράτος (MSS.)
would be identical in meaning to κάρτος, whereas the
whole point of the discussion is to demonstrate that
an accentual or quantitative or syllabic change can
alter meaning.

(13) ποτιτιθεῖ] -- an (Homeric and) Ionic form.
On the possible significance of such forms in the
thesis see Introd., 51 ff.

τι] -- minimally, a single letter in a word. See
n. on (12) above (καὶ "σακός").

(14) With this section compare Pl. Crat. 432a8-b1,
Ar. Soph. El. 178a29 ff., Sext. Emp. Pyrr. Hyp. 3.85,
Adv. Math. 4.23-24, Adv. Phys. 1.303-330, 2.308-309.
The argument turns on a particular use of the word
"ten". The form can be used collectively (τὰ δέκα--cf.
words like "score", "dozen" etc. in English) or dis-
tributively (δέκα), leaving open a possibility for the
author to argue (as he apparently does here) that to
(supposedly) take away from "the ten" (τὰ δέκα) that I
have is to leave me without my ten, and so apparently
without even one of them! I no longer have all ten, so
apparently I have lost all ten. (In the same way, one
might argue, one cannot take one away from a 'rugby
fifteen' and get a 'rugby one' plus a 'rugby fourteen';
one either has a rugby fifteen or one has not.) If, as
seems more than likely, the Δ. Λ. ante-dates the Cratylus, it is the first document in extant Greek to use
this particular argument; cf. Δ. Λ. 2.20, n. And the
affinity of the argument with what is later found in
Sextus Empiricus could well be a reason why the Δ. Λ.

has in every instance survived as part of a larger MS. containing the works of Sextus: some early copyist understandably thought he was dealing with one and the same author. The impression was no doubt corroborated if he read chapters 1-4 as an expression of moral scepticism.

οὐκέτι] -- with the MSS. οὖ κ' ἔτι (Matthaei, DK) seems hardly possible, as Høeg sees (109, n.1), since οὐκέτι was felt to be a single word, as is evident from the existence of its congener μηκέτι.

ἂν εἴη] -- with L and Mullach. If 'Slotty's Law' (see above, n. ad 3.6) applies to the treatise, however, the reading εἴη alone could be correct.

(15) See above, 5.5, for the contention under attack. The reference to τὸν αὐτὸν ἄνθρωπον suggests that existence rather than predication is in question here (see 5.5: ζώει -- καὶ οὐ ζώει), and the simpliciter/secundum quid distinction used to counter the original argument has close affinities with one used by Aristotle at Soph. El. 166b37 ff., opening up the intriguing possibility that Aristotle may have scanned this particular sophistic document. (For Taylor, 113-114, the distinction is found also in Plato's Sophist, but this is doubtful; see Levi [I] 306.) The distinction, as Sprague remarks [I] 160-161), could have been usefully employed at Pl. Euthyd. 283b-e, but there seems to me no compelling evidence from its use at Δ. Λ. 5.15 to suggest that the author felt that the specific contention of 5.5 stemmed from an existence/predication fallacy. The ambiguity, if any, in the phrase ἔστι καὶ οὐκ ἔστι at 5.5 is an ambiguity between

existence and veridication (see n. ad loc.)

τί ἢ τὰ πάντα] -- the clear suggestion here is that
the identity-thesis is acceptable if understood secundum quid, but not acceptable if understood simpliciter
(see Taylor 113-114). But this is in fact precisely
the way the identity-thesis is taken by its proponents,
as all the evidence of chapters 1-4 makes clear.

ψεύδεται κτλ] -- for the use see Soph. Philoct.
1342, ἢ τάδε ψευσθῇ λέγων.

ταῦτα πάντα] -- i.e., physical substances, such as
ἄνθρωπός τις.

ὧν] -- "consequently", "in conclusion". For Sprague
([I] 160) it is the equivalent of γάρ, but this would
be, as far as I know, without parallel in Greek prose.
What we have in 5.15 is apparently the imprecisely
formulated contents of the following philosophically
interesting, though invalid and unsound syllogism:
All physical substances (e.g., ἄνθρωπός τις) exist
either τὰ πάντα or τί (πῃ). But no physical substance
exists τὰ πάντα. Ergo all physical substances exist
τί (πῃ).
The author has equated, it seems, the adverbs πῃ and
τί, though the one (πῃ) would appear to have a considerably wider extension than the other.

πῃ ἔστι] -- 'exist in some way <but not in other
ways; and certainly not simpliciter>' (cf. Ar. Soph. El.
166b37, 169b10, where πῃ is opposed to ἁπλῶς, and Met.
1011b22).

6. On Whether Wisdom and Moral Excellence Are Teachable

As Kranz points out (226), the much-discussed question of the teachability or otherwise of ἀρετή (see,
e.g., Pl. Meno 70a, with Bluck's commentary ad loc.;
cf. Klein 38-39, and n.18, and more generally Guthrie
3.250-260) follows naturally upon a discussion of the
distinction (if any) between σοφία and ἀμαθία, particularly in a climate of opinion in which one school of
thought at any rate, the Socratic, felt that ἀρετή and
σοφία were closely linked, if not identical. On the
question of the unity of the treatise, see Introd., 77-
81.

(1) οὔτ᾽ ἀλαθής κτλ] -- as in chapter 5, the phrase
δισσοί λόγοι is not used, but the structure of the
chapter is clearly one of λόγος (1-6) and counter-λόγος
(9.13). The phrase οὔτ᾽ ἀλαθής suggests a strong pro-
clivity on the author's part towards the counter-thesis
in this chapter as in previous chapters (cf. 6.7 ἐγὼ
δέ; 6.13 λέλεκταί μοι), but an important caveat is
inserted in the final sentence (see n. on 6.13 [οὐ λέγω
ὡς]. On the question of author-commitment in the Δ. Λ.
see Introd., 73-77.

καινός] -- with R. οὔτε κενός seems out of the
question (see Gomperz [II] 146, n.314), since the
author is going to argue in some detail that the λόγος
in question is κενός. The reason for the scribal error,
as so often, is that two different syllables (in this
case κε and και) were pronounced as near as makes no
matter identically in post-classical Greek. For the
phrase καινὸν . . . λόγον see Hippias B6 DK[6] (cf. Kranz

223, and Untersteiner ad loc., for whom it is "una
nuova conferma che lo spirito di Ippia ha determinato
i Dissoi Logoi"). But the phrase seems to me just as
likely Gorgian; see above, 92, n.85.

οὔτε διδακτὸν κτλ] -- at Pl. Prot. 349a Socrates
says to Protagoras:

σύ γ' ἀφανδὸν σεαυτὸν ὑποκηρυξάμενος εἰς πάντας τοὺς
Ἕλληνας σοφιστὴν ἐπονομάσας σεαυτὸν ἀπέφηνας παιδεύσεως
καὶ ἀρετῆς διδάσκαλον, πρῶτος τούτου μισθὸν ἀξιώσας
ἀρνυσθαι.

Compare Meno 95c:

Γοργίου μάλιστα . . . ταῦτα ἄγαμαι, ὅτι οὐκ ἄν ποτε
αὐτοῦ τοῦτο ἀκούσαις ὑπισχνουμένου [sc. διδάσκαλον εἶναι
ἀρετῆς].

Untersteiner (ad loc.; cf. Dupréel 93) takes Gorgias'
disclaimer at its face value, and understands the
thesis of Δ. Λ. 6 also, like the theses of 1-5, as
basically Gorgian, though the author "might" have used
other sources, such as Protagoras' Antilogies (for the
most recent defence of the "Gorgian" nature of the
thesis of Δ. Λ. 6 see Müller 226, n.2). The counter-
thesis (6.7 ff.) he reads as "Hippian", on grounds of
"methodological necessity", given the (supposed) structure of the first five chapters; the occasional Protagorean echoes in this or that argument are said to be
"co-incidental". But all this is to assume, not prove;
it does not follow from 1-5, even if Untersteiner's
general point is conceded for the sake of argument,
that all counter-theses in the treatise will reflect
the teachings of Hippias solely or even primarily.

(2) εἴη] -- for the possible significance of the

optative mood see n. on 1.11 (τάγαθὸν εἴη). However,
if 'Slotty's Law' applies to the treatise (see n. on
3.6), εἴη may be the equivalent of <ἄν> εἴη or <κ> εἴη.

παραδοίης κτλ] -- an allusion, claims Untersteiner
(ad loc.; cf. Dupréel 54, Müller 226, n.2) to the "Gorgian" doctrine of the incommunicability of knowledge,
in which it is argued that transmitted knowledge is
necessarily different in the recipient from what it is
in the purveyor (cf. Untersteiner, Sofisti 4 [82] B 3
bis, 6.23 [= De MXG 6.280b, 8-11]). But Δ. Λ. 6.2 is
surely talking about loss, not difference.

(3) διδάσκαλοί κα κτλ] -- see n. on 6.8 below (Πολύκλειτος) and Introd., 92, n.85; cf. Pl. Prot. 324d ff.

ἦν] -- third person plural, Doric (Buck 163.4).
This may also be the correct reading at 6.8 (with Blass,
for ἦεν O); I retain ἦεν hesitantly, on the grounds
that, among his many idiosyncrasies, the author does
apparently on occasion use forms from Epic verse.

τᾶς μωσικᾶς] -- "the fine arts" generally, rather
than the more restrictive "music". But cf. below, 8.11,
where it appears to mean specifically "music".

(4) τέκνα] -- see Pl. Prot. 319e-320b and n. on
6.8 below (Πολύκλειτος), and compare Pl. Prot. 324d
ff., Meno 93b-94e, Ar. NE 1181a. Untersteiner (ad loc.)
quotes Theophr. Car. proem 3 as evidence that Hippias
had posed the problem for himself, and answered it in
an original way (see also 6.11, n.). Untersteiner,
however, is to my knowledge unique in thinking that this
passage of Theophrastus reflects Hippian doctrine; for
his arguments see Mario Untersteiner, "Il proemio dei

Caratteri di Teofrasto e un probabile frammento di
Ippia", Riv. de filol. classica n.s. 26 (1948) 1-25.

(6) See Introd., 92, n.85 (fin.).

(7) What becomes clear as the counter-arguments
unfold is that the author would perhaps be willing to
accept a 'qualified' version of the thesis of 6.1-6
(see n. on 6.13 [οὐ λέγω ὡς]); in similar fashion, he
never actively attacks the 'qualified' version of the
identity-thesis in chapters 1-4 (and probably 5 also;
see 5.15, τί ἢ τὰ πάντα; the hypothetical statement αἰ
-- ταὐτά makes it clear that only the 'unqualified'
version of the identity-thesis is under attack). The
difference between chapters 1-5 and 6 is that in chapters 1-5 the identity-thesis was clearly understood by
its proponents in a qualified sense, whereas in chapter
6 the 'unteachability' thesis is (assuming the author's
exposition of the arguments to be an accurate one)
apparently understood by its proponents in an absolute
sense. As such, it invites demolition by the production
of counter-cases; and this is precisely what the author
does.

κάρτα] -- a word used by Protagoras, though from
what particular work is unknown (Protagoras B 9 fin.
DK⁶). On the possible significance of such ionicisms
in the treatise, see Introd., 51 ff.

διδάσκοντας] -- sc. <καὶ διατελῶντας διδάσκοντας>,
or some such phrase.

γράμματα] -- "letters", in the sense of "the rudi-
ments of literacy".

τυγχάνεν] -- the author has switched without warning

from the collective to the distributive. For a similar
unannounced change from plural to singular see 4.6.

τὸν σοφιστάν] -- see n. on 6.1 above (οὔτε διδακτὸν
κτλ), and compare Pl. Prot. 328a, Meno 91b ff.

διδάσκοντι] -- hardly an answer to 6.3, since it is
the acceptability of certain sophists' claims, rather
than the claims themselves, which is in question.

σοφίην] -- see n. on 5.7.

(8) Πολύκλειτος] -- compare Pl. Prot. 328c. For
the possible significance of the statement for the
dating of the treatise see Introd., 34 ff.

Ἀναξαγόρειοι καὶ Πυθαγόρειοι] -- see Pl. Crat. 409b,
Taylor 94 n.1, Untersteiner ad loc. The point, presumably, is that Ἀναξαγόρειοι and Πυθαγόρειοι (= "pupils
of Pythagoras and Anaxagoras", or "members of the
schools of . . ." etc.? See Burkert [I] 30, n.8, 215,
Guthrie [3. 18]) were clearly recognized teachers of
ἀρετή. Such references suggest that the author is
using the term σοφιστής in an extremely broad sense.

ἦεν] -- see n. on 6.3 (ἦν).

(9) The point seems to be: E and I propositions are
contradictory. If a single man is able to communicate
his σοφία to another, it is false that σοφία is incom-
municable.

μὴ διδάξῃ] -- in the sense of "does not succeed in
teaching".

ἔστι] -- i.e., ἔξεστι (sc. αὐτῷ). The ἔξεστι is
the ἔξεστι of possibility, rather than permissibility;
see LSJ[9] s.v.

δυνατόν] -- i.e., on the strength of the single

counter-case alone.

(10) τέταρτον κτλ] -- the expression is elliptical,
but makes good sense if seen in context as a reply to
6.5: "the fourth point <is valid only> if . . ." etc.
The reading σοφῶν should be retained, with the MSS.
(see Wilamowitz [II] 4.627, n.1). The author's point
seems to be that there are sophists and sophists: the
genuinely σοφοί among them can teach their ἀρετή, the
rest cannot necessarily do so. The σοφισταί mentioned
at 6.5 will presumably fall into the latter category.

καὶ γάρ] -- for the affirmative nuance see Denniston, Greek Particles 108-109.

τοι] -- North translates as though τοι = τινες (see
also the Untersteiner and Sprague translations), and DK
express their approval. But this putative ionicism has
no clear linguistic parallel in the language, and the
sentence is perfectly intelligible without it. (Untersteiner, n. ad loc., following Weber 83, cites [Hippocr.]
περὶ τῆς ἀρχ. ἰητρ. 6.24 [= 6.1, TMR], where τοῖσι, he
claims, = τισί. The reading, however, is rejected by
both Littré and Jones [its sole MS. support is that of
Parisinus A], and seems dubious as a piece of evidence.)

μαθόντες] -- i.e., from unskilled teachers.

(11) This section is (in some sense) a reply to the
fifth point, made at 6.6; but see the n. on 6.13 (οὐ
λέγω ὡς). The sentence is certainly corrupt in the
MSS., and emendation is more than usually speculative.
εὐφυὴς καὶ γενόμενος (by contrast with the concessive
καὶ εὐφυὴς γενόμενος) I take to be a concealed protasis;
for the idiosyncratic position of καί (= "also") see

also 8.2, καὶ πράσσεν, and the opening phrase of 6.11,
ἔστι δέ τις καὶ φύσις. Untersteiner, ad loc., refers
to Pl. Hipp. Mai. 301b and Theophr. Car. proem 3 as
evidence that 6.11 "rivela il pensiero di Ippia". For
the latter passage, however, see n. on 6.4 above; and
I fail to see how the passage of the Hippias Maior,
even if it be considered, for the sake of argument,
genuine Hippian doctrine, can be understood as suggesting that "tutte le qualità abbiano libero giuoco"
("qualità" being taken to include "human" qualities).
Kranz, more persuasively (228), compares sections 6.11
and 6.12 with Pl. Prot. 327b-328d (cf. Taylor, 116-117
and Müller 226, n.1) with regard to the adjective
εὐφυής and the verb ἐλλανίζειν, and one should also note
Prot. 327c3, ἱκανά. The evidence of Protagoras B 3
DK[6] is firm first-hand evidence of Protagoras' belief
in the need for a sound φύσις if education is to profit
a person, and also an early start; which suggests that
Protagoras himself is the source of the statements at
6.11-12 and Pl. Prot. 327b-328d, and perhaps of Δ. Λ.
6.8 and Pl. Prot. 326e as well (see Guthrie 3.318-319).

τις] -- "of importance". See LSJ[9] s.v., A II 5.

τὰ πολλά] -- sc. "of a subject", or perhaps, more
precisely, "of ἀρετή" (in its widest sense); cf. 6.6,
ἄξιοι λόγω. συνάρπαξαι (to "comprehend") seems to be
a synonym of συνιέναι, on which see Bruno Snell, JHS
93 (1973) 180; cf. Heraclitus B 51 DK[6].

ὀλίγα] -- sc. "of that subject", or "of ἀρετή".
See n. above. The sense seems to be restrictive: i.e.,
"<only> a few". If the printed text is correct, the
'reply' embodied in 6.11 turns out to be more of an
explanation of the point made at 6.6 than a denial of

it (see n. on 6.13 [οὐ λέγω ὡς]). On sections 8, 11,
and 12 in general compare Pl. Prot. 326e-328d, Isoc.
Contra Soph. 14; and see Introd., 55 ff.

(12) The clearest extant example of an 'innateness'
theory of this sort is to be found at Hdt. 2.2 (the
Psammetichus story); see Gomperz (II) 176, n.362,
Untersteiner ad loc.
    ὀνύματα] -- "words", in the sense, presumably, of
"the language we speak".
    Πέρσας] -- cf. Pl. Crat. 385e.
    οὐκ ἴσαμες] -- cf. [Pl.] Alc. I, 111.

(13) ἀρχὴν καὶ τέλος καὶ μέσαν] -- for Rohde (329,
and n.2) the words suggest that the treatise originally
ended at this point; his assumption being that the
'original' treatise was "sophistisch-dialektisch". But
on this see my introductory note to Δ. Λ. 7.
    οὐ λέγω ὡς] -- an interesting caveat, suggesting
that the author, in rejecting the λόγος of 6.1-6, is in
fact rejecting only the arguments currently used to
bolster it. The way is left open for better arguments.
The sentiment is, as Kranz points out (230), "eines
Sokrates würdig", but he goes too far, in my estimation,
when he uses it to paraphrase Socrates' attitude in the
Protagoras (see Levi [I] 302, n.51).
    What the author fails to mention is that the coun-
ter-arguments (6.7-12) are themselves of unequal worth.
While the first (6.7, γινώσκω -- κιθαρίζεν) is useful
for its purpose, the second (6.7-8, πρὸς δὲ -- ἦεν)
assumes the point to be proved (see n. on 6.7 [διδάσκον-
τι]). The third is again useful (6.8, τὸ δὲ τρίτον --

ποιεῖν), but the fourth, while bringing out a very
helpful distinction (6.10), fails to demonstrate that
the class of σοφοί σοφισταί is not in fact iself a
null class. The fifth argument (6.11), with its con-
cession that a young person needs to be εὐφυής γενόμενος if he is to be taught ἀρετή, has an undoubted
incidental value, in that it suggests a version of the
thesis which would in fact prove acceptable; and the
clear implication that an 'absolute' version of the
counter-thesis is as untenable as the 'absolute' version of the identity-thesis makes the <u>caveat</u> of 6.13--
provided it be understood, as it is apparently meant
to be, 'absolutely'--a perfectly natural conclusion to
the author's remarks. The sixth argument (6.12; see n.
<u>ad loc</u>.) is intrinsically interesting, but irrelevant
to the thesis under scrutiny.

ἀλλ' οὐκ] -- i.e., ἀλλ' <ὡς> οὐκ. Cf. οὐ λέγω ὡς
κτλ in the preceding phrase.

τῆναι] -- i.e., those of the thesis of 6.26. On
τῆνος and cognates see Weber (II) 82.

7. [<u>Untitled</u>]

As Kranz points out (226), chapters 7, 8, and 9 of
the Δ. Λ. are in no sense 'outsiders' to the treatise.
Any Greek interested in σοφία in public life would be
interested in the wisdom or otherwise of the lot-system
(chapter 7), the hallmarks of the best-equipped orator-
politician (chapter 8), and the importance of memory-
training as part of the latter's schooling (chapter 9).

In chapter seven a single λόγος is propounded and
criticized; no counter-λόγος is put forward. However,
it seems clear from 7.6 that the author could have, had

he so wished, defended the counter-λόγος "Offices in
public and military life should be elective".

(1) ἀπὸ κλάρω] -- for the system and its history
see Untersteiner ad loc., E. S. Stavely, Greek and
Roman Voting and Elections (London 1972) 61 ff., and
passim. For Socrates' apparent objection to the lot-
system see Xen. Mem. 1.2.9, Ar. Rhet. 1393b4-5. There
is no evidence, however (pace Chroust 58, and n.297,
Guthrie 3.411, n.3) to suggest that he got his objection from sophists such as the author of the Δ. Λ., or
that they got theirs from him. In all likelihood they
shared a common malaise on the matter, particularly as
the Peloponnesian War progressed.
For the relevance of chapter 7 to the question of the
author's citizenship, see Introd., 50.

(2) εἰ γὰρ -- ἐρωτῷη] -- if γὰρ is meant to be
explanatory, the sentence is an anacolouthon. An alternative move (adopted in the translation) is to treat
the whole phrase as an expression of exasperation: "If
only somebody would ask these people! . . ." (the point
being that the very question might make them see the
folly of their contention).
τὸν ταῦτα λέγοντα] -- the phrase appears to be a
clarificatory insertion by the author to explain the
sudden switch from the plural λέγοντι to the singular
αὐτόν. For the stylistic idiosyncrasy see also 4.6,
6.7.
ὅπως] -- of purpose.
τωὐτό] -- i.e., the principle of selection by lot
(λαγχάνειν).

(3) τὼς χαλκῆας κτλ] -- see Xen. Mem. 1.2.37, Pl. Gorg. 491a, [Ar.] Ath. Pol. 30.3, 50.2.

ἂν ἐπίσταται] -- a Socratic notion, as Kranz sees (230). Dupréel's further suggestion (213, n.1) that Socrates drew on Hippias for it is not substantiated with evidence. See below, n. on 7.4 (αὐλητὰς κτλ).

(4) τωὐτόν] -- adverbial (cf. 1.16).

διακλαρῶσαι] -- sc. (from 7.3) πῶς οὐκ ἠναγκάσαμεν, or ἔξεστιν ἡμῖν, or the like.

αὐλητὰς κτλ] -- cf. Xen. Mem. 1.2.9. Dupréel (213, n.1) also refers to Xen. Mem. 4.2.6 and [Pl.] Minos 317e, where the specific competence of musicians is again in question, but his further claim that here "l'influence d'Hippias est flagrante" is (as so often) not substantiated with evidence.

For a famous statement on the absurdity and ultimately undemocratic nature of lot-selection see Ar. Rhet. 1393b4-8 (a sentiment credited to Socrates).

(5) ἥκιστα -- δαμοτικόν] -- as so often in the treatise, a criticism is bolstered by the (witting or unwitting) exploitation of an ambiguity; in this instance, an ambiguity in the use of the adjective δαμοτικός. For the significance of the comments on democracy see Introd., 50.

On the assumption that for the author μισόδαμοι as a group are coextensive with or include οἱ ὀλιγαρχίας ἐπιθυμοῦντες, Isoc. Areop. 23 seems to be a relevant parallel passage (see Taylor 123-124, Levi [I] 305). Socrates, notoriously, found himself accused of μισοδημία; see Libanius, Apologia Socratis 54 init.

Foerster, Chroust 74 ff.

(6) στραταγέν, νομοφυλακέν] -- epexegetic. See Pl.
Ap. 28e1-2, οὒς ὑμεῖς εἵλεσθε ἄρχειν μου.

8. [Untitled]

In this chapter the last vestiges of discussion in
terms of λόγος and counter-λόγος have gone; what we
have in their place is what might be called an essay on
the characteristics of the paradigmatic sophist/orator/
politician. Its point of contact with most of the
earlier chapters is perhaps its defence of what could
be described as another identity-thesis (see 8.1, <τῷ
δ' αὐτῷ> ἀνδρὸς καὶ τᾶς αὐτᾶς τέχνας κτλ). With the
whole chapter compare Pl. Euthyd. 293-297 (where a
similar omniscience-thesis is professed by Euthydemus
and Dionysodorus); cf. Gorg. 458e [?] and Soph. 232b ff.
(where the said omniscience-thesis--among other things
--is criticized). In the Sophist in particular and Δ.
Λ. 8 (see Dupréel 311-312) a number of claims about
the sophist's τέχνη are couched in fairly similar
(though far from identical) terms: compare, e.g., Soph.
232d1-2, Δ. Λ. 8.6, 8.9, 8.10; Soph. 232c8-10, Δ. Λ.
8.1 (fin.); Soph. 232b11-12, d2, e3-4, Δ. Λ. 8.1 (init.),
8.3 (init.), 8.5 (init.), 8.13 (init.)--on the assumption
that Plato's references to ἀντιλογική, ἀμφισβήτησις,
etc., are references to what the sophist of the Δ. Λ.
calls τὸ κατὰ βραχὺ διαλέγεσθαι δύνασθαι, τὸ τὰς τῶν
λόγων τέχνας εἰδέναι, etc.; Soph. 234c4 (τῶν πραγμάτων
τῆς ἀληθείας), Δ. Λ. 8.1, 8.12; Soph. 232c4-5, Δ. Λ.
8.1 (περὶ φύσιος τῶν ἀπάντων), 8.2. In view of the

affinities, it seems a sound inference that Plato is
(consciously or unconsciously) drawing upon the Δ. Λ.
in writing this section of the Sophist; Dupréel (240)
makes the further suggestion, however, that Δ. Λ. 8 and
Δ. Λ. 7 (fin.), along with Pl. Polit. 305c-e, themselves have as a common sophistic source Hippias. But
Hippias, so far as is known, never laid claim to
omniscience (see n. ad 8.2 [περὶ πάντων]), and he can
hardly be singled out among Greek writers for the
belief that ἡ πολιτική was the supreme τέχνη.

Untersteiner (ad 8.13) sees in the 'ring-composi-
tion' of this chapter the influence of Hippias. But
this view turns on his belief that the Anonymus Iam-
blichi is also the work of Hippias (see Mario Untersteiner, Rend. Inst. Lomb. di Sc. e Lett. 77, f.2, 448-
449), and this is a view which as far as I know he is
unique in holding.
The chapter can be summarized as follows--
One and the same τέχνη gives a particular person
(a) the ability to discourse κατὰ βραχύ (see section 13)
(b) knowledge of "the truth of things" (see section 12)
(c) the ability to plead one's cause in court (see
     sections 9-11)
(d) the ability to speak in public (see sections 6-8)
(e) an understanding of argument-skills (see sections
     3-5)
(f) a knowledge of the nature of everything (see section
     2)

(1) <τῶ δ' αὐτῶ>] -- cf. Gorgias B 11 (2) DK[6].
Dupréel (197) refers to Pl. Hipp. Min. 367cd, with its
references to ὁ αὐτός, and sees further 'evidence' of

the influence of Hippias on the treatise. But in this
he seems to me mistaken. See Introd., 61-62.

κατὰ βραχύ] -- see Hippias B 6 DK[6], Pl. Prot. 329b3-
4, 334d ff., Gorg. 449b8 ff., Thuc. 1.64.2; cf. Pl.
Soph. 241e5, κατὰ σμικρόν. From the evidence of the
first three passages referred to, a natural translation
would be "briefly"; from the evidence of the latter
two, "little by little". Perhaps elements from both
are intended: the man under discussion can examine a
topic briefly, and also meticulously, going over each
and every aspect of the problem in patient and systema-
tic detail. If this was considered to be one of the
trademarks of σοφισταί, it becomes easier to understand
how Aristophanes could include a Socrates among their
number. For τὸ κατὰ βραχὺ διαλέγεσθαι is consonant
with, if not identical to, the procedures generally
adopted by Socrates himself in Plato's so-called 'Socratic' dialogues, and in some measure in later ones (see
Maier 203). For the apparent willingness of Hippias
to submit to interrogation on particular topics, see
n. below (διαλέγεσθαι) and n. on 8.2 (περὶ πάντων), and
for Protagoras' adequacy in κατὰ βραχὺ διαλέγεσθαι
(denied by Maier, 203) see Pl. Prot. 329b3-4.

διαλέγεσθαι] -- cf. Pl. Hipp. Min. 363d1-4, παρέχω
ἐμαυτὸν καὶ λέγοντα ὅτι ἄν τις βούληται ὧν ἄν μοι εἰς
ἐπίδειξιν παρεσκευασμένον ᾖ, καὶ ἀποκρινόμενον τῷ
βουλομένῳ ὅτι ἄν τις ἐρωτᾷ.

ἀλάθειαν] -- books on 'Truth' were written by Protagoras (B 1 DK[6]), and Antiphon (B 1 DK[6]). For the
phrase τῶν πραγμάτων τῆς ἀληθείας see Pl. Soph. 234c4
(cf. Phd. 99e6[?]), and compare 8.12 below.

δικάσασθαι] -- "to plead one's cause." See below,

8.9, δικάζεσθαι ἐπιστάμενον. The word refers to private
suits, as a rule, rather than to public prosecutions
(see LSJ[9], s.v. δικάζω, II 1).

ὀρθῶς] -- "correctly", "appropriately"; i.e., in a
way conducive to persuading the jury of the rightness
of one's cause. According to Plato (Crat. 391b) the
sophists as a group laid claim to ὀρθοέπεια; for more
specific testimony see Protagoras A 24, 26 DK[6]; Prodicus
A 11, 13, B4 ibid.; Hippias A 12 ibid.; Cratylus [A] 5
ibid.; and cf. C. J. Classen 223-226.

περὶ φύσιος κτλ] -- see Pl. Prot. 337d3-4 (Hippias
speaking), Soph. 232c, ὅσα φανερὰ γῆς τε καὶ οὐρανοῦ
κτλ; cf. Trieber 239, Pohlenz 76, Diels ad loc., Taylor
127, n.1, Levi (I) 300-301, and n.43, Untersteiner ad
loc. (with further litt.).

The phrase τῶν ἁπάντων suggests a reference to the
world 'as a whole', and the subsequent phrases would,
if this interpretation is correct, most naturally refer
to the origin and present state of such a world. Such
an interest in the world we can fairly guess that the
sophist Hippias professed and encouraged; see, e.g., Pl.
Hipp. Mai. 285, Pl. Hipp. Min. 367e, Levi 300-301.
But neither Δ. Λ. 8.1, 2 nor Pl. Prot. 337d3-4 appears
to justify the further contention of Levi ([I] 301, and
n.43; see also Kranz 230 f.) that Hippias anticipated the
Platonic conception of the philosopher-king. For even
if one were to concede that Δ. Λ. 8 is Hippian in
inspiration it would not follow that in Hippias' doc-
trines we are looking at an ethics based on "the nature
of the universe" (the shift from cosmology to ethics
seems to have been made by the author of the Δ. Λ. himself; see below on 8.2, περὶ πάντων), and even if we

were, Plato's philosopher-king makes no such claim.
His claim is to "knowledge" only of the Forms, with at
best true opinion concerning "Hinseits-πράγματα".
Hippias, as far as we know, does not appear to have
claimed omniscience at all; see n. on 8.2 below (περὶ
πάντων).

(2) περὶ πάντων] -- "in regard to everything" (in
the distributive sense; contrast the collective τῶν
ἁπάντων at 8.1, 8.2). For the use of περί see LSJ[9]
s.v., A II 5. The fallacy is, of course, the fallacy
of Division; collective and distributive propositions
are not such that the former always and necessarily
entail the latter. (The move is easily made in Greek,
where πᾶς can signify both "all" and "every".) Whether
Hippias ever claimed such omniscience in practical
matters seems to me in doubt (see below); and even if
he did, there is no particular reason for thinking that
he founded such a claim on the precise piece of fallacious reasoning that is found in this part of the Δ. Λ.
     For Untersteiner, ad loc., in this section "si
esprime la correlazione necessaria fra l'università di
physis, nelle sue molteplici qualità, e l' universalità
del conoscere, cioè la scienza enciclopedica". But
omniscience (here = "omnicompetence"; cf. πράσσεν) is
neither (pace Untersteiner) synonymous with encyclopedism nor even a logical corollary of it. So one must
search elsewhere than in Hippias' encyclopedism for
proof that Δ. Λ. 8.2 and 8.12-13 are Hippian in inspiration. One such source could be Pl. Hipp. Min. 363d1-4,
but even here it is not clear (assuming for the moment
--with Untersteiner [Sofisti 8 (86) A 8]--that we are

looking at a genuine testimonium) that the clause
ἀποκρινόμενον τῷ βουλομένῳ ὅτι ἄν τις ἐρωτᾷ is a claim
to omniscience; the καί . . . καί could be taken to
mean simply that Hippias is ready to read (or deliver
from memory?) his set pieces and answer any questions
concerning them that people might care to put--not any
questions on any (imaginable) topic.

For Dupréel (199) Socrates has Hippias' claim to
omniscience in mind when at Pl. Hipp. Min. 372b he
says, "I obviously know nothing" (φαίνομαι οὐδὲν
εἰδώς). But this again does not necessarily follow:
Socrates' remark is just as understandable if Hippias
proposed encyclopedism, or for that matter any degree
of knowledge.

ὀρθῶς] -- "rightly", in the sense of "correctly",
"fittingly", "appropriately". See n. on 8.1 (ὀρθῶς).
ὀρθῶς καί πράσσεν with the MSS. (see Gomperz [II] 148,
n.315); for the idiosyncratic position of the καί see
6.11 above, εὐφυὴς καί γενόμενος, and ibid., ἐστί δέ
τις καί φύσις. The textual change proposed by DK (in
the light of 8.6) seems unnecessary; the purely intel-
lectualist ethics that is apparently being proposed is
no more surprising than that which has frequently been
attributed to Socrates. However, the sequence know-
ledge-action is made without any attempt at explanation
of the basis for it. Perhaps the author is assuming
that knowledge 'how' (to act rightly) is one of τά
ἅπαντα that are known.

(3) τέχνας τῶν λόγων] -- "argument-skills" (?).
The phrase is a loose one, and could tolerate a number
of interpretations, like "linguistic skills", "logical

skills", "rhetorical skills", "reasoning skills", and
the like. Professor Sprague's "the art of rhetoric" is
perhaps a little too restricted, since there is no
evidence in 8.3-5 that it is <u>public</u> speaking that is
involved. Rather, 8.6-8 seems to deal with such public
speaking (δαμαγορεῖν), and 8.9-11 with the ability to
plead one's cause in court. So I tentatively opt for
a translation which underscores the sophist's dialectical ability in argument with his peers, be this in the
public glare of a πανηγυρίς or the semi-public forum of
a law-court or the privacy of a home.

ὀρθῶς λέγεν] -- given the ambiguities of the adverb
ὀρθῶς (see above, n. on 8.1 [ὀρθῶς]), the author is
able to make his case here because he has at his dis-
posal a word covering both "non-fallaciously" and
"soundly" and the combination of the two. All that his
argument in fact leads to is a claim that the sophist's
reasoning skills will enable him to produce <u>valid</u> arguments on every topic--though not necessarily <u>sound</u>
ones; but, given the ambiguity of ὀρθῶς, the argument
would perhaps appear to some to have proved that on
every topic a man knowing the τέχναι λόγων will produce
arguments that are both valid <u>and</u> sound (i.e., truth-
delivering)--and it is undoubtedly this latter effect
that the sophist is out to produce, as the subsequent
sections make clear.

(4) περὶ ὧν ἐπίσταται] -- a defence of the startling
phrase περὶ <u>πάντων</u> used in the preceding sentence.
Knowledge of the particular subject-matter involved is,
along with understanding of the τέχναι λόγων, in any
given instance a <u>sine qua non</u> of τὸ ὀρθῶς λέγεν. And

we know, says the author (see 8.2) that the σοφιστής in question has knowledge of everything (see n. on 8.2 [περὶ πάντων]). For a clarification of the latter claim see below, 8.7 (with n. on 8.7 [περὶ πάντων]), 8.8.

As Taylor sees (124), δεῖ -- λέγεν is unexceptionable <u>Socratic</u> doctrine; Dupréel (194) suggests that 8.4-5 is aimed at the rhetoric of Gorgias, with its stress on form at the expense of content, but this seems to be an aspect of the rhetorical art that is hardly uniquely Gorgian.

γ᾽ ἄρ] -- see Denniston, <u>Greek Particles</u> 43. The reference is back to the statement of 8.2 (<u>fin</u>.) "and he will, one must at any rate suppose (γ᾽ ἄρ) <as we have seen; see above, 8.2 (<u>fin</u>.) and see also 8.5> have knowledge of <u>everything</u>". But at 8.2 (<u>fin</u>.) all that was claimed was universal <u>practical</u> knowledge (εἰδὼς . . . περὶ πάντων . . . <u>πράσσεν</u>); there was no suggestion that omniscience was anything more than omnicompetence.

περὶ πάντων -- ἐπιστασεῖται] -- for a similar claim (based upon a series of arguments purporting to prove that a knowledge of anything implies a knowledge of everything) see Pl. <u>Euthyd</u>. 293b ff. Compare <u>Euthyd</u>. 295b ff. for the same claim, this time based on the argument that because we have a faculty (the ψυχή) with which we "know everything we know", therefore we know everything. At Pl. <u>Soph</u>. 233c it is suggested that sophists πάντα . . . σοφοὶ τοῖς μαθηταῖς φαίνονται because δοκοῦσι . . . πρὸς ταῦτα ἐπιστημόνως ἔχειν . . . <u>πρὸς ἅπερ ἀντιλέγουσιν</u> and δρῶσι . . . τοῦτο πρὸς <u>ἅπαντα</u> (cf. <u>Resp</u>. 598c7 ff.). Whether one can infer

from this, however, that any sophist ever made a _serious_
claim to such omniscience (now, apparently, from the
evidence of 8.5, understood in an all-embracing sense)
is doubtful; at best it might have been put forward as
a paradoxical debating point, or as a (pseudo-) synonym
for encyclopedism, on the safe assumption that intelli-
gent observers at any rate (not least other sophists)
would spot (or at least sense) the fallacies in the
reasoning. Plato, one must assume, had such a philosophically educational intention when writing the _Euthy-
demus_.

(5) This section is ostensibly a reason (γὰρ) for
the final claim of 8.4, <περὶ> πάντων -- ἐπιστασεῖται.
The first part is simply a repetition of earlier claims
(8.1, 8.3), except that the universality there implicit
is now made explicit; the second part is new. Liter-
ally, "All arguments are about everything that is", it
could _prima facie_ be interpreted in terms of argument-
form: i.e., there is no thing [=, one must assume, no
event, action, or state of affairs] that falls outside
of the purview of all argument-forms. A more likely
interpretation, however (if the section is to succeed
in its ostensible purpose of explaining the final claim
of 8.4, in which πάντων appears to be used distribu-
tively; cf. 8.2 _fin._), is in terms of argument-_content_:
i.e., the sum total of argument-content (actual and
possible?) covers the sum total of what is (actually
and potentially?) real/the case. On the first interpretation the sense of πᾶς is clearly distributive
("every argument"), on the second it is collective ("all
arguments"). Either way, one is now far beyond the

omnicompetence claim of 8.2 (περὶ πάντων . . . πράσσεν).

(6) δέ] -- the topic now under discussion would appear to be, following the general inverse-sequence of the chapter, δαμαγορεῖν (8.1, fin.), and the reference to διδάσκεν τὴν πόλιν seems to confirm this.

καὶ λέγοι⁺] -- with the MSS. It is not clear, given that the MSS. indicate a lacuna here of some four or five lines (DK mistakenly say "Lücke von 4-5 Buchstaben"), whether λέγοι is a complete word, and the end of a completed phrase, or part of a phrase such as λέγοι<εν οἱ πολῖται>. Either way, we appear to be presented with one more instance of the author's unwillingness to be bound by the so-called Sequence of Tenses (ἄν/κα + subjunctive would have been expected). See n. on 1.1 (εἴη) and passim.

Given the lacuna (as many as 40-50 words, if the MSS. do not mislead), it is impossible to tell whether ὀρθῶς λέγεν (for the phrase see Pl. Euthyd. 297b1) is to be taken as an already completed phrase or one completed by the words περὶ ὅτων κτλ. If the former is the case, περὶ ὅτων κτλ may either have been an indirect question, depending on ἐπίστασθαι (= "know"), or an indirect question; if the latter, the lacuna will certainly have included inter alia an infinitive of some sort, directly dependent on ἐπίστασθαι (= "know how to . . ."), if the subsequent καὶ . . . διδάσκεν is to make sense.

τὼς (accented)] -- the article (acc. plural, Doric) used as a demonstrative pronoun (see LSJ⁹ s.v. ὁ ἡ τό, init.). With the verse-nuance of the usage compare 4.3 (ὥς γε); τὼς = τοὺς πολίτας (cf. τὴν πόλιν in the pre-

ceding clause). With κωλύειν sc. πράσσεν from the preceding clause; Diels' correction τως (unaccented) (a
ἅπαξ in the language, if correct; cf. also his reading
of τοι at 6.16) seems unnecessary.

δεῖ -- κωλύειν] -- as in previous instances, any
prima facie plausibility the proposition has stems from
an exploitation of ambiguities: in this instance in the
use of δεῖ and ὀρθῶς. In the case of δεῖ, the natural
interpretation is in terms of duty: "the μέλλων ὀρθῶς
λέγεν has a duty to know . . .," etc.; the interpretation the author wishes the reader to place upon it,
however, is, "the μέλλων ὀρθῶς λέγεν cannot help knowing . . .," etc. For the same ambiguity (and the same
intent) see below, 8.9, 8.10. In the case of ὀρθῶς,
the first instance exploits the same ambiguities as
were found in its use at 8.3 and 8.4 (see nn. ad loc.);
the second is less problematic, and seems to mean
simply "sound", or something similar (compare 8.9
below, ἐπίστασθαι ὀρθῶς). For a similar stress on τὸ
ὀρθόν see [Pl.] Minos 317c.

(7) The sentence is one of the most difficult in
the treatise, and emendation and interpretation is more
than usually speculative. If my interpretation is correct, the author is suggesting that, should a δημηγορῶν
possess the knowledge requisite to giving the πόλις
sound advice, he can be sure that Necessity, the mother
of invention (see 8.8, δέῃ, and on the general topic
Guthrie 2.473), will provide him with all other (less
important?) knowledge. The possession of actual knowledge of what it takes to be a good δημηγορῶν is eo
ipso the possession of potential knowledge of everything

else (see 8.8, δυνασεῖται). In attempting to make these contentions plausible, the author appears to confine himself to instances of knowledge 'how'; at any rate no instances of other forms of knowledge are mentioned.

For alternative interpretations, see Untersteiner ad loc., with litt.

ταῦτα] -- i.e., the contents of 8.6 above.

ἐπιστασεῖται] -- sc. "at least potentially", as the rest of the section, and 8.8 below, make clear. The bald claim of 8.4 (fin.) has been clarified.

ἔστι γάρ κτλ] -- "are part of". See LSJ[9] s.v. εἰμί, C II.

τῶν πάντων] -- "all [objects of knowledge]" in the sense of "the totality of [objects of knowledge]" (see n. on 8.5 above, fin.).

τῆνα] -- i.e., τά ἕτερα above (like, e.g., knowledge of flute-playing; see 8.8 below).

τωὐτόν] -- i.e., the possession of knowledge of everything.

τά δέοντα] -- see Thuc. 1.22.1 et alib.; cf. Isocr. Ep. 3.25, οὐδέν τῶν δεόντων πράττοντες. Unique to the Δ. Λ., however, if my emendation παρέξεται is correct, is τά δέοντα in the subject-position.

παρέξεται] -- for παρέχεσθαι in much the same sense as παρέχειν see LSJ[9] s.v. παρέχω, παρέχομαι. Reading τά δέοντα πράξει Dupréel (194) sees another reference here to a doctrine of "situation-ethics" that he takes to be Gorgian.

(8) μή] -- with all the MSS. (from which DK unaccountably diverge without signalling the fact).

ἐπιστᾶται] -- Doric subjunctive. The author is,
of course, on the interpretation here suggested, discussing 'actual' knowledge only.

δέῃ] -- i.e., "whenever the situation calls for
his doing this"; see above, 8.7, τὰ δέοντα. For the
distinction between 'actual' and 'potential' knowledge
see n. on 8.7, and n. on 8.7 (ἐπιστασεῖται).

(9) δεῖ] -- see n. on 8.6 (δεῖ) above.

τὸ δίκαιον] -- simply, "that which is just". Taylor (126, n.2), recalling how Plato (Socrates) uses
the term αὐτὰ τὰ πράγματα at Phaedo 66e1-2 of the Forms,
takes τὸ δίκαιον here and τὰ πράγματα at 8.10 and 8.12
to refer to the Platonic (Socratic) "objective reality"
that is αὐτὸ ὃ ἔστι δικαιοσύνη. But τὰ πράγματα, as I
suggest below, is surely best taken as simply "the
facts", and as a hint that the proponent of the view of
Δ. Λ. 8 is in an essentialist (and in that sense, perhaps, even Socratic) tradition. That he should have
adhered to the further, Platonic doctrine of transcen-
dental essentialism seems most unlikely--though the
doctrine of the "presence" of τὸ ψεῦδος to a (false)
λόγος (Δ. Λ. 4.5) undoubtedly has a Platonic ring to it.

εἰδήσει καὶ τὸ ὑπεναντίον] -- i.e., τὸ ἄδικον.

τὰ <ἄλλα αὐτῶ? ἑ>τεροῖα] -- for a similar usage see
Vet. Med. 9, πολλὰ δὲ καὶ ἄλλα κακὰ ἑτεροῖα τῶν ἀπὸ
πληρώσιος. If this reconstruction is correct in
essence, the author is clearly acquainted with the
notion of concept-clusters; i.e., with the notion that
a concept of a particular sort (e.g., τὸ δίκαιον) can
only be said to be completely perspicuous in the context of a knowledge of its contrary (in this case, τὸ

234

ἄδικον; cf. Ar. De An. 411a5, 430b22-23) and of those related concepts which, in (actually or apparently) differing from it, shed light upon it (in the case of τό δίκαιον, such a related concept would perhaps be ἡ ἰσονομία).

ἐτεροῖα] -- with Mullach. The identity of pronunciation of the diphthongs οι and ει in post-classical Greek would plausibly account for the original corruption. See n. on 2.18 (κελεύῃ).

(10) δεῖ] -- see n. on 8.6 (δεῖ). The required sense here is "cannot help but".

αὐτόν] -- sc. τὸν δικάζεσθαι ἐπιστάμενον (8.9).

τὰ πράγματα] -- "the facts", "what goes on". See below, 8.12, τὰν ἀλάθειαν τῶν πραγμάτων. The term is much used by the author, and is of very large extension. See, e.g., 5.11, with n. (πράγματα). The sense of the section is, apparently, as follows:

The δικάζεσθαι ἐπιστάμενος cannot help but know all the νόμοι.

But knowledge of the laws is itself contingent upon knowledge of τὰ πράγματα.

Ergo the δικάζεσθαι ἐπιστάμενος has knowledge of τὰ πράγματα.

In an earlier argument, the author had glossed his own phrase "the skills involved in argument" (λόγων τέχνας, 8.3) as in fact a reference to the skills involved in all arguments [i.e., all forms of argument] (πάντων τῶν λόγων τὰς τέχνας, 8.5). In the present instance, too, one senses a similar desire to gloss τὰ πράγματα (i.e., all the facts relevant to law-making, law-implementation, etc.) as <πάντα> τὰ πράγματα (i.e., all

facts), so as to lead to the desired conclusion that
certain people can justifiably claim to know "everything" (8.12). But the cautious γα <μάν> of 8.12
indicates perhaps that he senses that the fallacy would
this time be too transparent, and the move is not in
fact made; an ambiguity in the phrase τὰν ἀλάθειαν τῶν
πραγμάτων (8.12) does the job instead.

For Taylor (126, n.2; cf. Levi [I] 301) τὰ πράγματα is the equivalent of the Platonic (for Taylor the
Socratic) αὐτὸ ὃ ἔστι δικαιοσύνη. But see nn. on 1.11
above (πρᾶγμα), 8.9 above (τὸ δίκαιον), and 8.11 below
(νόμον).

(11) νόμον] -- the author understandably assumes a
close analogy between law and the "rules" of μωσικά,
since a single Greek word, νόμος, covers both. But the
νόμοι of 8.10 relate to a body of facts (τὰ πράγματα),
while the νόμος of 8.11 relates to a τέχνη (ἀ μωσικά).
However, in context it seems possible that the term
μωσικά refers to the "field of music" as an object of
'acquaintance' knowledge, rather than to skill in play-
ing or composing μωσικά, thus lending the analogy some
measure of support. For a similar use of the term
μουσική see Pl. Tht. 206b (φθόγγοι are the στοιχεῖα
μουσικῆς--a piece of 'book' knowledge in no way contingent upon one's having mastered any instrument).

Taylor (126, n.2), interpreting the sentence as a
claim that the "laws of music" are unintelligible without knowledge of the "objective realities" that are the
mathematical ratios corresponding to the fundamentals
in the musical scale, takes πράγματα to be a word for
the "objective reality" that is αὐτὸ ὃ ἔστι δικαιοσύνη.

But this claim seems far fetched, despite <u>Phaedo</u> 66e1-2 (αὐτά τά πράγματα); see above, n. on 8.10 (<u>fin</u>.). Dupréel (214-216), apparently interpreting μωσικά as though it were ἀ τᾶς μωσικᾶς φύσις, sees a nexus between νόμος and φύσις here which he finds not immediately reconcilable with Pl. <u>Prot</u>. 337cd, in which Hippias makes a strong contrast between νόμος and φύσις. The difficulty, however, is self-made; the notion of φύσις is his own importation.

(12) γα <μάν>] -- an indication that in the author's eyes 8.10 and 8.11 have in themselves been insufficient to demonstrate the truth of the thesis of 8.4 (<u>fin</u>.).

τάν ἀλάθειαν τῶν πραγμάτων] -- see 8.10 (πράγματα) and n. on 8.1 (ἀλάθειαν). The author clearly feels that this is the proposition most likely to win general acceptance, and one sufficiently strong to prove the thesis of 8.4 (<u>fin</u>.), even if others are rejected. The reason for his assumption seems to be his confidence that the average reader will instinctively unpack the phrase τῶν πραγμάτων in a <u>general</u> sense--i.e., as <πάντων> τῶν πραγμάτων (see final n. on 8.10 above). Plato also uses the phrase (<u>Soph</u>. 234c)--a ἅπαξ in his writings--in what seems to be such an all-embracing sense, and given the context (a discussion of sophistic practices) a clear possibility emerges that τῶν πραγμάτων ἡ ἀλήθεια was a favourite sophistic catch-phrase (and perhaps even a specifically Protagorean one; see refs. in n. 1.1 [λόγοι] above), to which an allusion was in the context not inappropriate. For his more normal phrasing see <u>Phd</u>. 99e (τῶν ὄντων τήν ἀλήθειαν), <u>Meno</u> 86b.

(13) <κατὰ> βραχύ] -- given the apparently inverse
structure of the rest of the chapter, it seems natural
to expect at this point a reference back to 8.1; so I
follow Blass and DK in inserting <κατὰ>.

ἐρωτώμενον ἀποκρίνεσθαι] -- cf. Pl. Gorg. 449b8,
450cd, Prot. 329b3 ff., Phd. 73a7-8.

περὶ πάντων] -- see above, n. on 8.2 (περὶ πάντων),
8.4 (περὶ πάντων -- ἐπιστασεῖται), 8.5.

δεῖ . . . δεῖ] -- for the ambiguity see n. on 8.6
(δεῖ). The first instance involves duty (self-imposed
or otherwise), the second one hypothetical necessity.

9. [Untitled]

Though this chapter on memorization has the appearance of something 'tacked on' to what precedes, it is,
of course, of very great relevance to the whole question
of the marshalling and plausible deployment of λόγοι
which is the stock-in-trade of the sophist-rhetor.
According to Plato (Hipp. Min. 368d6-7), the sophist
Hippias had a μνημονικὸν τέχνημα which he taught to
others; and at Pl. Hipp. Mai. 285e Hippias claims that
he himself can remember fifty names after a single hearing. See also Philostr. V. Soph. 1.11.1 (= Hippias A2,
1 DK[6]), Xen. Symp. 4.62 and Ar. Soph. El. 183b37; cf.
Guthrie 2.283, and n.2, Untersteiner ad loc. (with
further litt.), Untersteiner, Sofisti 8 (96) A2, n. ad
τὸ μνημονικόν, Yates 44-45, Blum 58.

ἐξεύρημα -- μνάμα] -- for the translation "the
power of memory" see Simon. fr. 146 (Bergk), Ar. Rhet.
1362b24 (μνήμη a δύναμις). However, as 9.3 ff. makes
clear, the author is more interested in memorization
than in memory as such. Dupréel (199-200) suggests,

interestingly, that we may have here an echo of a claim
by Hippias that he himself was the "discoverer" of the
mnemonic method. See Pl. Hipp. Min. 372c, where Socrates, in what seems to be a mood of not-so-playful
criticism of his interlocutor Hippias, says οὐ γὰρ
πώποτε ἔξαρνος ἐγενόμην μαθών τι, ἐμαυτοῦ ποιούμενος τὸ
μάθημα εἶναι ὡς εὕρημα.

φιλοσοφίαν τε καὶ σοφίαν] -- for Kranz (230) a
clearly Socratic Sprachgebrauch. If φιλοσοφία here,
however, is being understood by Kranz in the sense of
"philosophy", its "Socratic" nature is doubtful, since
there is no clear evidence that φιλοσοφία was understood
in so technical a sense before the mid-fourth century.
See W. Burkert (I) 159 ff. (who seems to feel [173,
n.4] that φιλοσοφία and σοφία in this context are
merely synonyms). Against this, it could perhaps be
argued that the present passage is itself a piece of
evidence in favour of the view that the term φιλοσοφία
was becoming technical for "philosophy" among certain
sophists as early as the 390's; cf. also Δ. Λ. 1.1
(φιλοσοφούντων), with n. ad loc. But there is no
reason why μνήμη should be of particular value in
philosophy, rather than in "general education"; the
information and advice at 9.2 ff. offers no hint that
its would-be beneficiaries will be in any sense philosophical "specialists". So it seems to me prudent to
understand φιλοσοφία here (as φιλοσοφούντων was understood at 1.1) of "education" generally (where "professional" philosophy is no doubt included, but is not
considered to be co-extensive). σοφία I take to be the
"practical wisdom" of the sophist-rhetor.

(2) ἔστι] -- veridical: "this is true, <as you will see> if. . . ." The thought is slightly abbreviated, as so often, but the sense seems clear enough.

προσέχῃς τὸν νοῦν] -- sc. "upon the matter in question".

τούτῳ] -- "this course", "this path" (i.e., that of memorization, as the subsequent sections make clear).

διὰ -- ἐλθοῦσα] -- cf. LSJ[9] s.v. διά, A IV b, and Pl. Prot. 323a1-2, ἣν δεῖ διὰ δικαιοσύνης πᾶσαν ἰέναι καὶ σωφροσύνης.

ἀ γνώμα] -- cf. Demos. Phil. 1.44, δεῖ γὰρ ἐκείνῳ τοῦτ' ἐν τῇ γνώμῃ παραστῆναι, ὡς κτλ.

σύνολον ὃ ἔμαθες] -- the phrase should be retained in its original MS. position. One of the many functions of μνάμα (= "memorization"), suggests the author, is to help us view as a whole things learned only in a discrete series. Compare Pl. Resp. 537c7, ὁ . . . συνοπτικὸς διαλεκτικός.

(3) δεύτερον] -- the "first" obligation, to be inferred from 9.2, was presumably the mental scanning of what one had already learned (σύνολον ὃ ἔμαθες), with the aim of obtaining an overall, synoptic, view.

δεῖ] -- in keeping with the apparently preceptive nature of the context. But the infinitive can on occasion be used to convey precepts (Smyth, Greek Grammar 2013). If this is the case here, a δ' might have been expected after τρίτον (9.4 below).

μελετᾶν] -- "study carefully", "go over".

παρεγένετο] -- gnomic, and a mild anacolouthon. One might have expected σύ or ὑμεῖς as subject, if strict grammar had been observed; instead we have the (easily understood) subject ταὐτά, from the preceding clause.

(4) κατθέμεν] -- <u>sc</u>. δεῖ, from the preceding clause, unless the infinitive is itself meant to be taken preceptively. See also below, 9.5 (κατθέμεν).

(6) πράγματα] -- cf. the πρᾶγμα/ὄνυμα distinction found in earlier parts of the treatise (1.11, 2.1, 3.13, 4.6, 5.1, 5.6). The hint is a useful one in favour of the basic unity of the treatise (see Kranz 226, and Introd., 77 ff.).

Ἐπειόν] -- the conclusion to the treatise is missing, as the MSS. indicate. Pohlenz, however (73), finds 9.6 a "Zielpunkt", though no reason is offered for this view. It is also unclear why Epeius is in the author's eyes connected with cowardice; unless he felt that the use of the Wooden Horse (Epeius designed it) to capture Troy was the action of cowards.

PREVIOUS EDITIONS OF THE Δ. Λ.

1. H. Stephanus, <u>Diog. Laert. Opera</u> 1 (Paris 1570) 470-482.

2. John North, in Thomas Gale's <u>Opuscula Mythologica Physica et Ethica</u> (Cambridge 1671[1]) 47-76, (Amsterdam 1688[2]; some changes in Greek text and notes by M. Meibom) 704-731.

3. J. A. Fabricius, <u>Bibliotheca Graeca</u> 12 (Hamburg 1724) 617-635.

4. J. C. von Orelli, <u>Opuscula Graecorum Veterum Sententiosa et Moralia</u> 2 (Leipzig 1821) 210-233, 632-654.

5. F. W. Mullach, Fragmenta Philosophorum Graecorum
    1 (Paris 1875) 544-552.

6. E. Weber, Διϲϲοί Λόγοι: Eine Ausgabe der sogenann-
    ten Διαλέξειϲ, in Philol.-hist. Beitr. C. Wachs-
    muth überr. (Leipzig 1897) 33-51.

7. H. Diels, in Die Fragmente der Vorsokratiker[1-4]
    ad fin. (Berlin 1903, 1906, 1912, 1922).

8. H. Diels and W. Kranz, in Die Fragmente der Vor-
    sokratiker[5-6] ad fin. (Berlin 1934, 1951).
    (This text is the one adopted by Untersteiner and
    Dumont.)

9. M. Untersteiner, Sofisti: Testimonianze e Frammenti
    3 (Florence 1954) 148-191.

10. J.-P. Dumont, Les Sophistes (Paris 1969) 232-246.

PREVIOUS TRANSLATIONS OF THE Δ. Λ.

1. (Latin) John North (see [2] above). Adopted with
    minor changes by Fabricius and Orelli, and with
    major changes by Mullach.

2. (German) G. Teichmüller, Litterarische Fehden im
    vierten Jahrhundert vor Chr. 2 (Breslau 1884)
    205-224.

3. (Italian) M. Timpanaro Cardini, I Sofisti[2] (Bari
    1954) 213-227.

4. (Italian) M. Untersteiner (see [9] above).

5. (English) R. K. Sprague, Mind 77 (1968) 155-167
    (reprinted in The Older Sophists, ed. R. K.
    Sprague, University of South Carolina Press,
    1972, 279-293).

6. (French) J.-P. Dumont (see [10] above).

242

BIBLIOGRAPHY

Ahrens, H. L. De Dialecto Dorica. Göttingen 1843.

Aly, W. "Barbarika Nomina," Philologus 85 (1930) 42 ff.

Bechtel, F. Die griechischen Dialekte. Berlin 1921-24.

Bergk, Theodor. (I) Griechische Literaturgeschichte.
    Berlin 1872.

--------. (II) Fünf Abhandlungen zur Geschichte der
    griechischen Philosophie und Astronomie. Leipzig
    1883.

Blass, Friedrich. "Eine Schrift des Simmias von
    Theben?" Jahrbücher für Classische Philologie
    (1881) 739-740.

Blum, H. Die Antike Mnemotechnik. Spudasmata 15 (1969).

Buck, C. D. The Greek Dialects[2]. Chicago 1955.

Burkert, Walter. (I) "Platon oder Pythagoras?" Hermes
    88 (1960) 159-177.

--------. (II) Lore and Science in Ancient Pythagorean-
    ism. Tr. Edwin L. Minar, Jr. Harvard U. P., 1972.

Caizzi, F. Decleva. (I) Antistene. Studi Urbinati 38
    (1964).

--------. (II) Antisthenis Fragmenta. Milan 1966.

Capizzi, A. Protagora. Florence 1955.

Christ, Wilhelm von. Geschichte der griechischen Lit-
    eratur[6] 1. Munich 1912.

Chroust, A.-H. Socrates, the Man and the Myth. London
    1957.

Classen, C. J. "The Study of Language amongst Socrates'

Contemporaries." In Sophistik. Darmstadt 1976. 223-226.

Cobet, C. G. Collectanea Critica. Leyden 1878.

Croiset, A. Histoire de la littérature grecque 4. Paris 1900².

Crusius, O. "Litterargeschichtliche Parerga III: Kleobuline, Kleobulos und Aisopos," Philologus 15 (1896) 1-4.

Dal Pra, Mario. La Storiografia Filosofica Antica. Milan 1950. 43-45.

De Romilly, J. "Gorgias et le pouvoir de la poésie," Journal of Hellenic Studies 93 (1973) 155-162.

Diels, H. "Ein gefälschtes Pythagorasbuch," Archiv für Geschichte der Philosophie 3 (1890) 450-472.

Dümmler, F. Akademica. Giessen 1889.

Dupréel, E. Les Sophistes. Neuchâtel 1948.

Field, G. C. Plato and His Contemporaries. London 1930.

Fischer, J. L. The Case of Socrates. Prague 1969.

Freeman, K. (I) The Presocratic Philosophers. Oxford 1946.

--------. (II) Ancilla to the Pre-socratic Philosophers. Oxford 1948.

Giannantoni, Gabriele. La Filosofia Prearistotelica. Rome 1963.

Gaiser, K. Protreptik und Paränese bei Platon. Stuttgart 1959.

Gigon, Olof A. Sokrates. Sein Bild in Dichtung und Geschichte. Berne 1947.

Gomperz, H. (I) "Beiträge zur Kritik und Erklärung griechischer Schriftsteller," Wiener Sitz.-Ber., phil.-hist. Cl., 122 (1890) 4. 5-6.

--------. (II) Sophistik und Rhetorik. Leipzig and Berlin 1912.

Gruppe, O. F. Fragmente des Archytas. Berlin 1840.

Gulley, Norman. The Philosophy of Socrates. London 1968.

Gunning, C. P. De Sophistis Graeciae Praeceptoribus. Amsterdam 1915.

Guthrie, W. K. C. A History of Greek Philosophy 1-3. Cambridge 1962-1969.

Heiberg, J. L. "Über den Dialekt des Archimedes," Jahrbücher für Class. Philol. von Fleckeisen Suppl. 13 (1884) 543-566.

Heinimann, F. "Eine vorplatonische Theorie der Τέχνη," Museum Helveticum 18 (1961) 105 ff.

Heringa, A. Observationum Criticarum Liber Singularis. Leovardiae 1749.

Hermann, G. Aeschyli Tragoediae 1. Leipzig 1852.

Høeg, C. "Le Dialecte des Dialexeis," Mémoire de la Société Linguistique de Paris 22 (1922) 107-112.

Jacoby, Edgar. De Antiphontis Sophistae ΠΕΡΙ ΟΜΟΝΟΙΑΣ Libro. Berlin 1908.

Joël, K. Der echte und der Xenophontische Sokrates 1. Berlin 1893. 2 Berlin 1901.

Kirk, G. S. and J. E. Raven. The Presocratic Philosophers. Cambridge 1957.

Klein, Jacob. A Commentary on Plato's Meno. Chapel Hill, N. C. 1965.

Kneale, W. and M. The Development of Logic. Oxford 1962.

Koch, H.-A. "Protagoras bei Platon, Aristoteles und Sextus Empiricus," Hermes 99 (1971) 278-282.

Kochalsky, Arthurus. De Sexti Empirici Adversus

Logicos Libris Quaestiones Criticae. Marburg 1911.

Koen, G. Gregorius Corinthi . . . de dialectis. Ed.
G. H. Schäfer. Leipzig 1811².

Kranz, W. "Vorsokratisches IV: Die Sogenannten Δισσοὶ
Λόγοι," Hermes 72 (1937) 223-232.

Lana, I. Protagora. Turin 1950.

Levi, A. J. (I) "On Twofold Statements," American
Journal of Philology 61 (1940) 292-306.

--------. (II) Storia della Sofistica. Naples 1966.

Lucas, D. W. Aristotle: Poetics. Oxford 1968.

Luria, S. (I) "Bermerkungen zur Geschichte der antiken
Traumdeutung," Comptes Rendus de l'Académie des
Sciences de l'URSS, 1928 B, N.8, 173-179.

--------. (II) Anfänge des griechischen Denkens.
Berlin 1963.

Madyda, W. De Arte Poetica. Krakow 1948.

Maier, H. Sokrates. Sein Werk und seine geschichtliche
Stellung. Tübingen 1913.

Martano, G. Contrarietà e dialettica nel pensiero
antico 1. Naples 1972. 283-293. (= Studi Storici
in onore di G. Pepe. Bari 1969. 95-102.)

Matthaei, A. De Dialecto Pythagoreorum. Göttingen 1878.

Mazzarino, S. Il Pensiero Storico Classico. Bari 1966.

Meineke, J. A. F. A., ed. Menandri et Philemonis Reliquiae. Berlin 1823.

Minar, Edwin L. Jr. Early Pythagorean Politics in Practice and Theory. Baltimore 1942.

Müller, C. W. Die Kurzdialoge der Appendix Platonica.
Munich 1975.

Mutschmann, H. "Die Überlieferung der Schriften des
Sextus Empiricus," Rheinisches Museum 64 (1909)
244-283.

Nauck, August. Tragicorum Graecorum Fragmenta[2]. Leipzig 1889.

Nestlé, W. (I) "Bemerkungen zu den Vorsokratiker und Sophisten," Philologus 67 (1908) 579-581.

--------. (II) Vom Mythos zum Logos. Stuttgart 1940.

O'Brien, M. J. The Socratic Paradoxes and the Greek Mind. Chapel Hill, N.C. 1967.

Pedersen, H. "Das auf einen t-Laut zurückgehende σ und σσ im Griechischen." In Ἀντίδωρον. Festschrift Jacob Wackernagel zur Vollendung des 70. Lebensjahres. Göttingen 1923. 110-116.

Pohlenz, M. Aus Platos Werdezeit. Berlin 1913.

Porson, R. R. Porsoni Adversaria. Edd. J. H. Monk, C. J. Blomfield. Cambridge 1812.

Ramage, E. S. "An Early Trace of Socratic Dialogue," American Journal of Philology 82 (1961) 418-424.

Reinhardt, K. Parmenides und die Geschichte der griechischen Philosophie. Bonn 1916.

Renehan, R. Studies in Greek Texts. Göttingen 1976. [Hypomnemata 45.]

Rittelmeyer, Friedrich. Thukydides und die Sophistik. Borna-Leipzig 1915.

Robinson, Thomas M. (I) "Matthew de Varis and the Δισσοὶ Λόγοι," CQ 22.1 (1972) 195-198.

--------. (II) "A Sophist on Omniscience, Polymathy, and Omnicompetence: Δ. Λ. 8.1-13," Illinois Classical Studies 2 (1977) 125-135.

Rohde, E. Kleine Schriften 1. Tübingen and Leipzig 1901. 309 ff. (= Review of Bergk's "Über die Echtheit der Dialexeis," Göttingische gelehrte Anzeigen [1884] 24-30.)

Rose, H. J. A Handbook of Greek Mythology[6]. London 1958.

Rostagni, A. "Un nuovo capitolo della retorica e della sofistica," Studi Italiani di Filologia Classica, N.S. 2 (Florence 1922) 148-201.

Rüstow, Alexander. Der Lügner. Leipzig 1910.

Sartori, Franco. Problemi di Storia Costituzionale Italiota. Rome 1953.

Schanz, M. "Zu den sogenannten Dialexeis," Hermes 19 (1884) 369-384.

Schmid, W. and O. Stählin. Geschichte der griechischen Literatur 1.3. Munich 1940.

Schwyzer, Eduard. Griechische Grammatik^3. Munich 1966.

Shorey, Paul. "Varia," Classical Philology 3 (1908) 198-199.

Slotty, F. Der Gebrauch des Konjunctivs und Optativs in den griechischen Dialekten 1. Göttingen 1915.

Sprague, R. Kent. (I) "A Platonic Parallel in the Dissoi Logoi," Journal of the History of Philosophy 6 (1968) 160-161.

--------. (II) "Socrates' Safest Answer: Phaedo 100D," Hermes 96 (1968) 633-635.

Süss, W. Ethos: Studien zur älteren griechischen Rhetorik. Leipzig 1910.

Tarrant, Dorothy. Plato. The Hippias Maior. Cambridge 1928.

Taylor, A. E. Varia Socratica 1. St. Andrews University Publications. Oxford 1911. 92-128.

Teichmüller, G. Litterarische Fehden im vierten Jahrhundert vor Chr. 2. Breslau 1884.

Thesleff, H. An Introduction to the Pythagorean Writings of the Hellenistic Period. Abo 1961.

Thumb, A., E. Kieckers, A. Scherer. Handbuch der griechischen Dialekte^2. Heidelberg 1959.

Trieber, C. "Die Διαλέξεις," Hermes 27 (1892) 210-248.

Untersteiner, Mario. (I) Sofisti: Testimonianze e Frammenti 3. Florence 1954.

--------. (II) I Sofisti² 2. Milan 1967.

Versényi, L. Socratic Humanism. Yale U. P., 1963.

Vitali, R. Gorgia. Urbino 1971.

Weber, E. (I) "De Dione Chrysostomo Cynicorum Sectatore," Leipziger Studien zur Classischen Philologie 10 (1887) 79-268.

--------. (II) "Über den Dialect der sogenannten Dialexeis und die Handschriften des Sextus Empiricus," Philologus 57 (1898) 64-102.

Wilamowitz-Moellendorff, U. von. (I) "Memoriae Oblitteratae," Hermes 11 (1876) 291-304.

--------. (II) Kleine Schriften 4. Berlin 1962. 619-659. (= Commentariolum Grammaticum 3. Göttingen 1889.)

--------. (III) "Lesefrüchte," Hermes 24 (1899) 219.

--------. (IV) Sappho und Simonides. Berlin 1913.

--------. (V) Platon² 2. Berlin 1920.

Wuilleumier, Pierre. Tarente. Paris 1968.

Yates, Frances A. The Art of Memory. Harmondsworth [Peregrine Books] 1969.

Zeller, E. (I) "Platos Mittheilungen über frühere und gleichzeitige Philosophen," Kleine Schriften 2. Berlin 1910. 1-19. (= Archiv für Geschichte der Philosophie 5. 1892. 177 ff.)

--------. (II) Die Philosophie der Griechen in ihrer geschichtlichen Entwicklung. Ed. W. Nestlé. Leipzig 1920-1923.

Zeppi, Stelio. Protagora e la filosofia del suo tempo. Florence 1961.

INDEXES

1. INDEX OF PASSAGES QUOTED OR REFERRED TO

Presocratic philosophers are quoted in accordance with the DK⁶ edition, unless otherwise stated. All other authors are quoted in accordance with the most recent Oxford edition, unless otherwise stated (in which case the editor's name appears at the end of the first citation only, unless editorship varies from volume to volume).

2. GENERAL INDEX

GREEK TEXTS AND COMMENTARIES
An Arno Press Collection